Descriptive Inquiry
in Teacher Practice

Descriptive Inquiry in Teacher Practice

Cultivating Practical Wisdom to Create Democratic Schools

Cara E. Furman
Cecelia E. Traugh

TEACHERS COLLEGE PRESS

TEACHERS COLLEGE | COLUMBIA UNIVERSITY
NEW YORK AND LONDON

Published by Teachers College Press,® 1234 Amsterdam Avenue, New York, NY 10027

Copyright © 2021 by Teachers College, Columbia University

Library of Congress Cataloging-in-Publication Data

Names: Furman, Cara E., author. | Traugh, Cecelia, author.
Title: Descriptive inquiry in teacher practice : cultivating practical wisdom to create
    democratic schools / Cara E. Furman, Cecelia E. Traugh.
Description: New York : Teachers College Press, [2021] | Includes bibliographical
    references and index.
Identifiers: LCCN 2020039769 (print) | LCCN 2020039770 (ebook) | ISBN
    9780807764862 (Paperback : acid-free paper) | ISBN 9780807764879
    (Hardcover : acid-free paper) | ISBN 9780807779323 (eBook)
Subjects: LCSH: Public schools—United States—Case studies. | Democracy and
    education—United States. | Teacher participation in administration—United
    States—Case studies. | Educational equalization—United States—Case studies.
Classification: LCC LA217.2 .F868 2021 (print) | LCC LA217.2 (ebook) | DDC
    371.1/06—dc23
LC record available at https://lccn.loc.gov/2020039769
LC ebook record available at https://lccn.loc.gov/2020039770

ISBN 978-0-8077-6486-2 (paper)
ISBN 978-0-8077-6487-9 (hardcover)
ISBN 978-0-8077-7932-3 (ebook)

Printed on acid-free paper
Manufactured in the United States of America

Dedication:

To Marie and Joseph and Ethan and Max. I write for the world you fought for and the world you deserve. —CEF

I dedicate the book to my husband, Andy Doan, who every day shows me the power of recognizing strengths I have a hard time seeing, and to the teachers, like Andy, and school leaders who work every day to make schools humane and genuinely educative places. —CET

Contents

PART III: SEEING AND ACTING WITH OTHERS: HOW DESCRIPTIVE INQUIRY SUPPORTS PRACTICAL WISDOM

**PART IV: WHAT DOES IT MEAN
TO LEAD SCHOOLS FOR HUMAN DIGNITY?**

Acknowledgments

Cara: I begin with gratitude to my coauthor, Cecelia. Without her vision, efforts, and long-term commitment to these schools, there would be no story to tell. Thank you for inviting me into *Descriptive Inquiry*. Thank you to David Hansen and Megan Laverty for helping me to refine my philosophical thinking and for your ongoing faith that writing for teachers philosophically is a worthy endeavor. Thank you to my colleagues in philosophy of education and teacher education; your collegiality has pushed me to grow and refine my work.

Thank you to the principals who have joined us in interviews and authorship—I am grateful for the chance to hear your stories and the work that went into composing them. My resounding gratitude to my students and colleagues at the Earth School; you have helped me grow at every step of my teaching life. Thank you to my current students at University of Maine at Farmington. Finally, thank you to fellow attendees of the Summer Institute on Descriptive Inquiry for sharing your practice and brilliance with me all these years. You deserve schools that honor who you are and help you to grow.

Daniel, Mom, Dad: You make everything possible. Ethan and Max: You make everything matter.

Cecelia: Writing this book with Cara has drawn on so much of what I've learned through my life's experiences and work. The trail of my acknowledgments begins with my working with Vito Perrone and the opportunity he gave me and my friend and colleague, Sara Hanhan, to attend the first of over 30 years of Prospect's Summer Institute, now the Institute on Descriptive Inquiry. There as two teacher educators we sat in a circle of teachers who taught us so much about children and all that teachers know. Key to that circle was Patricia Carini, who saw my strengths in new ways and opened up a world of idea and process. The teachers at Friends Select Middle School and Penny Colgan-Davis, the head of the Lower School there, helped me turn those ideas and processes into practice and learn how to use them to lead and re-create practice. Finally, I acknowledge the educators with whom I've worked in New York City—in the schools, at the Institute for Literacy Studies, at Long Island University, and at Bank Street.

They have all deepened my understandings and given me the courage to work against the grain of conventional thinking. I name particularly Jane Andrias, Laurie Engle, Judith Foster, Abbe Futterman, Michelle Harring, Alison Hazut, Kathy McCullagh, and Rachel Seher.

Introduction

Cara E. Furman and Cecelia E. Traugh

We cannot rely on people doing the right thing in spite of the institutional structures in which they work. What we want is institutions that encourage the skill and the will to do the right thing. Such institutions are within our grasp, and there are people working to create them. These system changers are building institutions that encourage practitioners to develop practical wisdom instead of draining it from them. (Schwartz & Sharpe, 2010, p. 234)

"I have some little boys who really need space to move in the classroom and this leads to some wild behavior." So begins Meredith,[1] a new teacher at an inquiry group co-run[2] by Cara, one of the authors of this book. Meredith continues,

> When this happens they are removed by my assistant, but I worry about this. I don't like these boys out of the room all the time. I want them to feel like the classroom is for them. But I want it to be ours too, and the behavior is hard to be around. I also don't want to hurt my assistant's feelings. She's trying to help. I really don't know what to do.

Meredith's quandary, her desire to make the classroom belong to everyone, including her colleague, and her need for help in doing so is at the heart of this book.

Specifically, we ask: How can we help teachers teach in a manner that promotes "human dignity" (Carini & Himley, 2010, p. 9)? Or put differently: How can we help teachers create classrooms that "belong," in the words of Meredith, to everyone—both children and adults? In response to this question, we do not have an answer but an approach: Descriptive Inquiry.

Meredith's question in fact emerged after engaging in one of the processes of Descriptive Inquiry—the Anecdotal Recollection. After each person shared a personal story in response to a prompt about a time when an adult helped her work through a challenge, Cara summarized themes that emerged. Group members were then asked to share a conflict they needed to "re-story"—consider from a different perspective. Meredith commented that finding a way to make the classroom belong to these little boys had come forward for her after we had all shared our personal stories. In other words, by engaging in a Descriptive Process, an issue of human dignity came to the forefront for Meredith.

Yet, a commitment to Descriptive Inquiry is not the full story we seek to tell. Hearing her former student share this question, Cara felt both pride and unease. She was proud of the teacher Meredith was becoming, the teacher who asked such important questions, but also nervous for her. She knew that Meredith would return alone to her school the following week. She would have to find a way to bring back what she was thinking through in the inquiry group, and this was no small task. How, for example, might she broach her concerns with her assistant in a manner that honored her colleague and protected the children? How would she explain some of her students' full-bodied, loud play to colleagues and administrators who might want to see children sitting still and mastering letter sounds?

In taking on this question, we share another story about a new teacher challenged by children to act differently:

I (Cara) am a 1st-year teacher. Antonia, a student new to both my class and the country, is driving me crazy. She makes animal noises during meetings, gets in frequent conflict with her classmates, and rarely follows directions. She seems lost, lonely, and often confused in my classroom. Everything from the language to the social cues to the rules are foreign. In my teaching journal I am sympathetic, concerned, and aware of her very real struggles. This journal also attests to the fact that I am often angry at Antonia. Despite knowing better, I tend to read and respond to her behavior as defiance. At some point, I share my frustration with the principal, Michelle Harring, who suggests, to my befuddlement, that I get a map for the classroom and study it with Antonia. I say, "I've got a map" and point to a small placemat map I've tacked to the wall well above a child's eye level. Michelle patiently says, "No, a map big enough that she can find her homeland." I internally roll my eyes wondering how finding Antonia's homeland will stop chicken noises on the rug. I know Michelle loves maps, and I am tempted to dismiss her suggestion as an eccentricity. Michelle promises to visit my class to help out.

Though the event happened years ago, I can still picture Michelle's visit. First Michelle gently takes Antonia's hand. Though I felt citywide cautions against hugging children were absurd, the stigma against touch in schools had influenced me, and it had never occurred to me to do this simple and humane act. Michelle then unpins the placemat from the wall, brings it close to Antonia, and examines it with her, speaking in a low voice. Michelle traces her fingers across the map. She is gentle, and Antonia, so wild with me, is gentle with her. After a few minutes, Michelle leaves the room without a word to me. I anticipate a follow-up conversation—perhaps she will even check to see if I buy a better map—but neither comes.

Nevertheless, my world has shifted. I saw Antonia treated with kindness and that she responded in turn. The bar for both of our behavior has been raised. I saw that gentleness and physical affection can and should occur in school. I had worried about discussing with Antonia that she was from elsewhere, afraid she might not want to talk about that place or have her difference acknowledged. I have seen this is not the case. A week later, I find a book about Antonia's homeland in a used bookstore. When I shared the book with Antonia, she lit up and eagerly shared the book with her classmates. I devote a significant amount of my school-allotted funds to buying a large world map and display it prominently on the wall where the children can see it. I also retrieve a globe and place it within the children's reach. We use the map and the globe on a weekly basis and make it central to curricular studies the following year when I taught many of the same children.

Recently, over lunch with Michelle I recounted my response to this child. "I was so frustrated and so wrong," I laugh. She smiles. "But you didn't ever correct me," I note. "No," she responds and smiles. Again, there is no follow-up. She leaves it at that.

I have circled back to these moments and this child countless times. There are many stories to tell. There is the story of how Antonia and I came to work well together. It did not occur in an instant but was a year's worth of trial and error and patience on both sides (see Furman, 2016b, 2019b). Antonia's story is another one: how she came to navigate her way in a foreign country and a new school. This book focuses on the story of a principal and a teacher—specifically, how a principal was able to gently guide a teacher to do better by a child. In my years working with teachers, I have seen many educators become frustrated with children. All of them, like Meredith, like me, have desired to do right by the children in their care. Many, though, have struggled to realize that goal. As we will argue throughout this book, I did not "have the magic," as a consultant once said, in my capacity to deescalate conflict and engage children. Instead, I had a series of supports that helped me to move through my challenges in the classroom.

From these many years in schools, I can also attest that what Michelle did in that moment was no small feat. She saw the needs of a child many found confusing and met them. She also saw the needs of a frustrated new teacher and met those too. Both acts are extremely challenging on their own. Michelle could attend to both the young child and the child's young teacher at the same time. She did this constantly with me and others, and this ability to support two people with different needs conjointly is impressive.

What allowed both of us to find a way forward with Antonia and many other children? What allowed Michelle and me to find a way forward with each other? This book tells that story. Specifically, it focuses on seven public school principals, Michelle being one of them, to investigate how principals can support schools committed to honoring human dignity.

WHAT IS HUMAN DIGNITY?

What does it mean to make the classroom a home for every child? The school a home for every child and teacher? To ensure everyone, as Meredith hoped, feels like they belong? At the core of this commitment is honoring human dignity. Fundamentally, teaching is human, and hopefully humane, work. In teaching for human dignity, we call for an education that attends to who the child is and helps the child realize their capacity (broadly defined). For us, this means preparing children to succeed in the world as it is while also helping them add their voices into a process for changing it (Delpit, 2006). Although these are lofty-sounding claims, we are committed to their realization in daily occurrences (such as Meredith's need to change her classroom so that all children move their bodies safely and feel more at ease).

Additionally, protecting human dignity means speaking in positive ways about children. It means recognizing a child's many strengths in what we say about them and how we assess. It means making sure that Meredith's young charges have room to move their bodies in school. It means having a broad range of materials available for exploration in primary classes and choices for secondary students. It means providing opportunities for children to be part of the community that initially eluded Antonia with her peers and adults. Commitment to human dignity involves honoring the student in front of us as well as preparing the student for the days to come. Finally, as Meredith notes in her concern for her colleague, and Michelle exemplifies in her care with me, the commitment to human dignity must encompass the treatment of all people in schools. Although children are more vulnerable, adults too deserve to be spoken of with respect, have their needs looked out for, and have opportunities to showcase their strengths.

WHAT IS TEACHING?

What does it mean to *teach* for human dignity? What is teaching within this framework? How do we grow as teachers? The range of responses to these questions is vast, and each has different implications for how one learns to do the work.

First, a clarification. We use the word *educator* throughout this book broadly to include teachers, principals, and support staff, believing that all of these titles incorporate teaching. When we use specific terms such as *teacher* or *leader*, we are referring to people's official job title. *Teaching* as a verb is used more broadly. A principal, in their work with children or adults, is still often teaching.

Teaching is relationships. Teaching is learning. Teaching is an art. Teaching is following a set of rules. Teaching is performance. Teaching is dealing with the unpredictable. Teaching is a way of life. Each of these definitions implies an approach to the ongoing growth of the teacher. For example, if teaching is largely about following a set of rules, then teachers who want to grow are charged with practicing what is needed to enact those rules. If teaching is learning, then teachers grow by seeing themselves as learners and putting themselves in the way of increasing knowledge. If teaching is relationships, then teachers grow by attending largely to the socioemotional aspects of the classroom and to knowing students well. All these approaches are in some ways true. But, when thinking about the ongoing health and growth of educators in schools, they are each also unidimensional and so incomplete.

When we talk about teaching, what we envision poses both a practical and an ethical challenge. By *practical* we refer to a teacher's ability to convey content, skills, ideas, and experiences. On this front, teaching well involves many factors, including but not limited to having a host of methods at one's disposal as well as the ability to perceive student nuance and classroom dynamics. Meredith may need help setting up the physical space in her classroom so that the children can move without breaking anything. She may need to learn activities that expose the children to language and song as they move. She may want to get her students outside more—to explore a range of content in an environment better suited to their busy bodies. Cara needed ideas and resources to better sustain her student's identity as an immigrant and practices to engage with her more affectionately.

By *ethical*, we mean a set of values that guides our daily conduct. Meredith has stated a value: that every child and adult feels the room belongs to them. Far from mutually exclusive, the ability to teach practically well is intimately connected to doing ethically well. Meredith's stated commitment to making the classroom feel like home required her to take actions that reinforce everyone's sense of belonging. Cara's desire to welcome Antonia, as expressed in her journals, required her to change the ways she engaged with Antonia on a daily basis. Michelle needed (and had) practices that allowed her to gently steer her teachers and protect the children in her school. By modeling a different approach, she found a way to challenge what Cara was doing without putting her on the defensive.

To best elucidate the kind of teacher- and leader-knowing that is in the service of protecting children's dignity, throughout this book we draw on the ancient Greek concept of *practical wisdom*. Though described in depth in Chapter 1, here we summarize that practical wisdom is knowing how to act in the right way according to the right values in context. To act with practical wisdom requires clarity about what one's values are, a way of determining the context, and methods to draw on—three areas that we have found Descriptive Inquiry is especially well suited to support (Furman, 2018).

When considering our ethical commitment to human dignity alongside practice, we seek pedagogy and institutions that treat people as ends in themselves and not means. We are unequivocal about this. As Cara often says in her methods courses, no skill acquisition or content knowledge is worth doing harm to a child. If the teaching practice is interfering with attending to the humanity of a child, stop doing it. For example, though it is important for Meredith's students to learn to read, and it is valuable to endure some struggle and frustration in learning to read, it is not okay to sacrifice their physical wellbeing to teach them to read.

DEMOCRACY AND TEACHER DEVELOPMENT

Why focus on work in K–12 schools? We, the authors, are committed advocates of schools of education and see them as providing a necessary foundation. Yet, though Meredith and Cara were considered promising new teachers from well-regarded teacher education programs, both faced challenges that stressed their preparation. Facing unforeseen challenges is inevitable. Nevertheless, much of the literature on teacher cultivation focuses on preservice teacher development. Yet teachers' success is heavily dependent on what they learn after they graduate and continue to learn over the course of a career.

Because teachers' primary learning will be on the job, the conditions of the school in which they practice will also determine much of the education they receive upon graduation (Santoro, 2018). This attention to learning in schools speaks to our respect for teacher-time and commitment to the educative nature of democratic communities. Teachers are extremely busy. Those we know tend to stay at work long past children's departures. They plan in the evenings, the weekends, and the summer. Though some like ourselves will benefit from inquiry groups, they are a select few. Adding more to most teachers' plates is neither realistic nor helpful (Cochran-Smith & Lytle, 1993). Some will simply not add more. Others do squeeze in more but feel in danger of being spread too thin. Meredith, for example, expressed great interest in the inquiry group and gratitude that it existed, but she was not able to attend most sessions.

Additionally, as Barry Schwartz and Kenneth Sharpe (2010) note at the beginning of this chapter, we operate in and are shaped by community, and therefore, "what we want is institutions that encourage the skill and the will to do the right thing" (p. 234). How we operate therefore is influenced by how the community functions. We worry that teacher cultivation often misses the importance of context. The lone wolf, teacher of the year, and individual teacher fighting against all odds is extolled in our popular culture and educational lore. In contrast, Schwartz and Sharpe's claims resonate as applied to teaching, namely that the individual teacher is constantly interacting with and being shaped by their surroundings (e.g., institutional demands, other teachers, leadership, professional development activities, families, community). Put simply, teachers are shaped by the quotidian elements of their job, as well as experiences external to their work life. This means that what happens in their school environments matters a lot (Cole, 1997). Schools therefore have tremendous power for influencing how teachers enact their practice (Drago-Severson, 2004; Lawrence-Lightfoot, 1983). All of this is true of leaders as well. A critical aspect of the ongoing development of individual teachers and leaders is the continued use of a means of developing a body of thought and practice in the school itself (i.e., a practical wisdom shared by the group).

Though many factors go into a healthy school and, for that matter, a healthy democracy, one key factor is leadership. As Doris Santoro (2018) artfully showcases, a principal can be instrumental in promoting teacher cultivation and flourishing, as well as what she refers to as demoralization. Specifically, drawing on the original meaning of the word *principal* as principal teacher, the principal has significant authority over the kind of cultivation that teachers experience (Drago-Severson, 2004; Lawrence-Lightfoot, 1983; Santoro, 2018). In returning to Cara and Michelle, it was both the principal and the environment she helped foster that helped Cara to ultimately welcome Antonia.

With this in mind, though the question is perennially asked, a series of in-depth explorations have highlighted factors that make for successful schools (Bensman, 2000; Drago-Severson, 2004; Edwards, Gandini, & Forman, 1993; Lawrence-Lightfoot, 1983; Little & Ellison, 2015). Though many factors are highlighted, here are a few common themes we would like to emphasize: (a) a shared and coherent vision, (b) the ability for both the institution and individuals to grow and change with support, an attention to context, and concern, and (c) support in choosing methods for instruction. In essence, strong schools are places where practical wisdom is cultivated.

SOURCES AND METHODS

Though we describe many methods over the course of this book, we don't offer a methodology. There is no formula to be mixed to produce the practically wise. As we will argue throughout, teaching is highly situational, so we speak in philosophy and narrative, not in precepts, directives, or even suggestions. In providing a thick description (Geertz, 1973) of the cultivation of practical wisdom in four schools, we hope to expand the conversations about practical wisdom and Descriptive Inquiry, as well as teacher and school development.

As such, our story is about how Descriptive Inquiry was used as a significant part of professional development (PD) in three small elementary schools and one high school in New York City under the leadership of Jane Andrias, Central Park East 1; Michelle Harring, Alison Hazut, and Abbe Futterman, the Earth School; Judith Foster, the Neighborhood School; and Rachel Seher and Alan Cheng, City-as-School, the high school. We have chosen to look exclusively at public schools that serve an urban population. While the demographics vary slightly, the student body of each school has a significant percentage of low-income students and students of color.

This fact is especially important because rule-driven school reform has been aimed at these populations. Therefore, we hope to emphasize that the methods we propose are ideal for teachers in all kinds of environments, including those that are economically and racially diverse.

That our text takes place in New York City also matters. First, in writing from this context we highlight practices that served a diverse population of children and teachers. In a culture where the dignity of Black and Latinx children is rarely protected in schools (Love, 2019), we showcase schools committed to caring for children of color in a humanistic manner. As New York City is often at the forefront of educational reform (Ravitch, 2016), we also show how the schools we feature both used and resisted reform efforts to better serve their students.

The content of this book results from several different sources. One is interviews we did of principals who had used Descriptive Inquiry as one of the core methods to develop both individual teachers and the shared intellectual and pedagogical understandings of the school community as a whole. We chose three principals who were retired and four in mid-career. One, Alison, had taken a few years hiatus during the time of our interviews but has since returned to work at a different school.

We chose principals Cecelia had worked with closely, some of whom Cara had taught with. Because of our relationships with the principals, conversation quickly became intimate and honest, and we were able to ask more informed follow-up questions (Ben-Peretz, 1995; Elbaz, 1983; Florio-Ruane, 1991, 2001; Oyler, 1996). In choosing principals we knew quite well, we sought to undercut traditional hierarchies between researcher and practitioner (Florio-Ruane, 1991; Shagoury & Power, 2003). To this end, we shared the transcripts and subsequent writing with each principal for any follow-up feedback. Another source of content is narratives about the role of Descriptive Inquiry in these schools. Following in the tradition of other texts on teacher inquiry (Carini & Himley, 2010; Cochran-Smith & Lytle, 1993; Himley & Carini, 2000; Kroll & Meier, 2018; Meier & Henderson, 2007; Traugh et al., 1986), we have chosen to share authorship. As indicated at the beginning of chapters, a few were jointly written. Some were solely authored with small assists by one or the other of us. Others seemed best written by the principals themselves.

We live in a culture that rewards single authorship and at times even punishes collaboration. Teacher movies often showcase teachers perceived as acting alone without supportive school communities. This depiction is both largely inaccurate and damning to the profession. As educators, as our book demonstrates, we rely on one another for ideas, discussion, lessons, and simple commiseration. As Santoro (2018) argues, as educators we must rely on one another for professional survival. Therefore, we have chosen to write a multi-voiced text to acknowledge the multi-voiced nature of teacher development and success. Further, Descriptive Inquiry is at its core a democratic process rooted in community. We mimic this form in bringing in multiple authors throughout.

In the spirit of authorship, we also gave each principal in our study the option of using their name or a pseudonym. Ultimately, each chose to use their name. With this came additional responsibility. Principals have reviewed any references to their work prior to publication. They have had the option of removing information as well as tweaking word choice from the interviews to better reflect their ideas. Thus, each principal has played a role in authoring their own words. A third source of data comes from our personal histories and studies. Cara's background as an educational philosopher grounds much of our philosophical underpinnings. Cecelia brings decades of experience as a school leader using Descriptive Inquiry as a means of institutional development in a school, in higher education and as a professional developer/coach in urban schools. She also brings over 30 years of experience with Descriptive Inquiry. She entered the work in its early days and influenced both the theory and the practice in its development. She worked alongside the principals and featured as a colleague, friend, and mentor. Cara joined the story years later and has been practicing Descriptive Inquiry for nearly 15 years, most recently as Co-Director of the Summer Institute on Descriptive Inquiry. She learned from Cecelia and many of the principals in the book. They mentored her into both Descriptive Inquiry and progressive practices. Bridging their entry points, a fourth source of data is an interview between Cara and Cecelia about Cecelia's work in schools.

OVERVIEW OF THE TEXT

This book moves between philosophy and practice to explore what it means to develop practical wisdom in schools to teach for human dignity. We also move between looking at the schools and principals individually and bringing them into conversation with each other. To foster collaboration, welcome the reader's voice, and encourage experiential learning, we include prompts that utilize the Descriptive Processes to go deeper into the content of the chapter. In the spirit of democratic inquiry, we encourage you, the reader, to find a colleague, or better yet a group of colleagues, to explore each prompt. We have constructed prompts of the type we develop when acting as chairs and presenters in Descriptive Inquiry. They include the kinds of questions we encourage teachers and school leaders to consider when we work with them in person.

Part I: Philosophical Framings

Practical wisdom is a way of thinking about practice in which values and actions are symbiotically interrelated. Mirroring this commitment, we dually address a commitment to human dignity and methods that help to realize that commitment. We also seek to illustrate that, without accompanying methods, the philosophy itself loses meaning (Dewey, 1916/1944; Meier, 2002). In explaining philosophical concepts with classroom examples, we first set up the concepts as they apply to this book. Second, having found practical wisdom and care of the self to resonate with teaching professionals at the Summer Institutes and those with whom we work, we describe these concepts in enough depth that readers unfamiliar with the philosophy can draw on them to describe their work. Finally, philosophers of education frequently struggle to convince practitioners of the relevance of their philosophical frames. We therefore intend these chapters to help philosophers consider the practical implications of philosophical work.

In Chapter 1, we use the framework of practical wisdom to describe professional knowledge that couples ethics with effective methods and is responsive to context. We draw on a school-based situation that challenged Cara's commitment to human dignity in order to articulate why practical wisdom offers a useful frame for a teacher concerned with both values and methods. We then use Cara's example to provide an overview of the ancient Greek concept of practical wisdom and how contemporary scholars have applied it to teaching. Chapter 2 addresses how Cara learned to respond in the way that she did and how a school leader might support a teacher in being able to do so. We draw on Michel Foucault's work on the care of the self in which he describes how thoughtful exercises can help the individual develop their ethical self with intentionality. In Chapter 3, we argue that regular practice of Descriptive Inquiry serves as an exercise, in Foucault's sense of the word, through which practical wisdom can be cultivated. We provide an introduction of Descriptive Inquiry for those unfamiliar with the practice and the philosophy. We then showcase the ways in which Descriptive Inquiry is particularly suited to fostering practical wisdom because it encourages the practitioner to cultivate one's values, consider context, and learn new methods. Finally, we begin to look at how Descriptive Inquiry helps leaders in particular in their work with teachers in schools.

Part II: How Descriptive Inquiry Lived in the Schools: Promoting Human Dignity With Children and Teachers

What does Descriptive Inquiry look like when it becomes a school-based practice? What does teaching come to look like in such schools? How do the processes lead to communities that help teachers develop practical wisdom? The chapters in this section zoom in on the particulars. In Chapter 4 we showcase how a principal and Cecelia brought Descriptive Inquiry to the school and, in doing so, changed the way the community worked together. In Chapter 5 we illustrate how Descriptive Inquiry supported teachers and principals in creating curriculum that dually honored the needs of individuals and fostered community. Chapter 6 focuses on how Descriptive Inquiry fostered democratic collaboration and conversation over many years with an eye toward how it facilitated difficult conversations and change.

Part III: Seeing and Acting With Others:
How Descriptive Inquiry Supports Practical Wisdom

John Dewey (2007) argues that our conduct develops through our daily environment. Community is a key part of our environment. In these chapters we describe how a variety of environmental factors in conjunction with Descriptive Inquiry led to collaborative communities that supported teachers' development of practical wisdom. Having explored what Descriptive Inquiry looks like in schools in some depth, in Chapter 7 we take a more strictly philosophical stance to describe how Descriptive Inquiry helps practitioners change how they perceive, and in doing so, teach for human dignity. In Chapter 8 we then focus on how teachers change practices alongside the changes in perception, namely how daily structures in a school are influenced by and reinforce the work of Descriptive Inquiry. In Chapter 9 we look at one more important component of implementing Descriptive Inquiry: the role of the chair as confidante who helps people frame and reframe situations. In doing so, we provide a portrait of Cecelia's role in schools and put forth an alternative schema for engaging in professional development.

Part IV: What Does It Mean to Lead Schools for Human Dignity?

Where we began this book asking about the qualities of a teacher, we close by pulling together some implications for school leaders and schools. In Chapter 10, we investigate how Descriptive Inquiry helps principals have authority and lead in democratic schools to promote human dignity through honoring voice. Finally, in Chapter 11, we close with a discussion of schools as human works and what it takes for a school to enact a commitment to human dignity.

ADDING TO THE CONVERSATION

What does it mean to hold humanizing commitments in contexts where human dignity is often secondary, in a society where racial and cultural differences are often viewed as deficits? Where skills are frequently taught with little regard to children's interests, where children and teachers are spoken of pejoratively, where families and home culture are disregarded and where children and teachers have few opportunities to showcase their individual strengths? We have found that placing the person at the forefront is possible even in this context. Yet, to do so requires that the school constantly commit and recommit to this goal. To teach for dignity requires that this stance be practiced and strengthened regularly. Specifically, as we will illustrate, regular practice of Descriptive Inquiry serves as an exercise that helps both principals and teachers not only affirm their commitment to human dignity but also find strategies to support this commitment in work with students.

In a national teaching context where teachers are often asked "what works" and schools are constantly in search of the most "effective method," we must interrogate the ethics of any given practice and ask: works for what? Therefore, though this book addresses both effectiveness and ethics, we place ethics at the center of our text as, at core, our ethical commitments ought to drive instruction.

In doing so, we write from a place of optimism and experience. Cecelia has worked alongside the schools featured now for nearly 30 years. Cara taught at one of the schools. Both of us continue to practice Descriptive Inquiry in our respective communities. From this perspective, we have seen that protecting human dignity is extremely hard work and requires constant vigilance. We also know that it can be done because we have seen it happen in the schools we describe.

In joining the conversation, we begin by picking up where another on Descriptive Inquiry ends. Margaret Himley (Himley & Carini, 2000) closes *From Another Angle: Children's Strengths and School Standards,* with a powerful call, writing:

> Sometimes we *do* just have to get together with others and do this kind of collective work. We need the richness and the surprise of sustained intellectual conversation. We need the pleasure of each other's company. We need the sense of solidarity that comes from respectful face-to-face interaction and that emerges not from homogeneity but from collective aims within a recognition of difference. We need new ideas and new words and new images and new visions to sustain us in our daily teaching lives. In the face of dehumanizing economic forces and depressing institutional realities, we need comrades. (p. 2011)

We agree wholeheartedly and add that we need institutions, schools specifically, that support people in coming together to grow. The four schools we describe have done just that. And so we begin their story.

NOTES

1. We include the stories of a number of teachers, school leaders, and children. Where we use someone's real name, we've signaled this by using their full name. In these cases, they've given permission and had editorial power over what we wrote. In all other instances we've used a pseudonym and, at times, changed identifying details as well.

2. Much gratitude to Kathryn Will for co-leading this group with me.

Part I

PHILOSOPHICAL FRAMINGS

CHAPTER 1

The Need for Practical Wisdom
What It Is and How It's Developed

Cara E. Furman

We began this book by introducing you to two teachers, Meredith and Cara, grappling with how to do right by the people in their care. I now ask you to engage in one of the processes of Descriptive Inquiry, the Anecdotal Recollection. Think of a time when you were faced with a complex dilemma about how to act and ultimately resolved the situation in a manner that you found satisfying. By complex, I mean there was no obvious route forward, no clear-cut response. Choose a situation that felt ethically loaded. In other words, you felt that some actions would support your values and others would not. You therefore needed to resolve the dilemma in a manner that fit with your values. Think about what you needed to know and the specific skills you might have brought to the situation to be able to respond as you did. Consider how the context affected the way you acted.

Now, how would you tell this as a story? Seek out colleagues and share. What themes emerge? Specifically, focus on what you knew going into this situation that positively informed your response. As you read this chapter, keep your Recollection in mind as you work to understand how people can learn to make complex ethical decisions in situations that require action.

We open this book with the questions: What is teaching? How do we grow as teachers? We now add an additional question into the mix: What does it mean to prepare teachers and contribute to their ongoing growth? Policy makers, administrators, and teacher educators ask this perennial question, as do teachers themselves. As we discuss in the introduction, this question is dependent on what you believe a teacher is and how you think teachers grow. Our vision, for example, of a teacher is grounded in our ethical commitment to human capacity.

As noted in the introduction, to describe the kind of teacher we have in mind, we use the phrase "practically wise," one who can act in ways that are right, for children, for oneself, for larger educational purposes. In this chapter we explore the idea of practical wisdom as the basis of right action.

We believe that the preparation of teachers and the support of their ongoing growth as they work with children in schools should take into account the elements that support their becoming ever more practically wise.

PRACTICAL WISDOM IN A COMPLEX TEACHING SITUATION: MY RECOLLECTION

We have chosen the concept of practical wisdom first and foremost because it encompasses both values and an attention to how those values are enacted. To illustrate this, I share my own Recollection of a complex ethical challenge and then pull ideas from this story to elucidate practical wisdom.

Years ago, I worked as a support teacher at the Earth School (a position described in depth in Chapter 8). I spent a lot of time with children other teachers found frustrating. As someone children were sent to when the teacher was fed up, I felt tremendous pressure to be patient, positive, and effective.

One morning I came across 8-year-old Thomas in the hallway. He was sitting outside the school office where he had been sent for disciplinary reasons. He had been released back to his room, but as he shared with me, he was not going. Instead, his plan was to stay where he was, sprawled on the floor. I was concerned. If another adult found him unwilling to move, he might be sent back to the office. Thomas tended to anger quickly. He regularly refused to follow directions. Sometimes he simply stopped speaking and would completely ignore those around him. Other times he threw things when agitated and pushed people. He was on thin ice with many adults in the school because of this behavior, behavior I too found trying.

I wanted Thomas back in class so that he would rejoin his classmates and teacher and avoid further punishment. On the other hand, initially I had no idea how to get him to class. I didn't want a fight with him. We got along well typically. Thomas came to my room sometimes when he was angry at others, but he had also stormed out of my room in anger. I didn't want to estrange myself from this child who felt he had few allies. I also didn't want to be seen by my colleagues or other students trying to move Thomas and failing. This was about my ego. I was known for being effective with students. It would be embarrassing to fail so publicly in the hallway in front of the office.

Luckily, I had spent considerable time studying Thomas in his classroom and at recess and had noticed that Thomas liked to be on the floor or pressed against a wall. I had also recently done a Descriptive Review on Thomas in an inquiry group with Cecelia after school. Taking my previous observations and thinking into account, I decided that trying to order or physically move him off the floor where he was splayed would be counterproductive and wrong.

Aware that Thomas was quick to anger normally and likely predisposed toward anger that morning given he had already been sent from his room to the principal, I also sought a way to keep Thomas in control and lighten the mood. As an experienced teacher, I had a lot of methods for inspiring young children at my disposal. I knew that many children responded well to humor, challenges, and tasks that seemed out of the ordinary.

An idea came to mind that would allow Thomas the safety of the floor and might be entertaining for him. "Thomas, do you think you could roll all the way to your class?" I asked. Thomas had been mostly ignoring me, but now he looked up. A slight look of intrigue flashed across his face. Gaining a bit of confidence I pushed him further, "I don't think you can," I said with a grin, "It's too far."

"I can," Thomas said and began to roll. Fearing a colleague would step in and, in horror, discipline Thomas or challenge me, I announced, "Let's see how many rolls it takes," and began to count rolls loudly. In this way, we went down the entire length of the school (two city blocks). To keep the game moving, I teased, "I don't know if you can do it," and Thomas insisted, increasingly out of breath but now smiling, "I can. I can do it." Finally, we arrived at his room. "Okay, last step, roll into your room," I said with enthusiasm and a bit of fear. Again, I spoke loudly to signal to the teacher that the rolling was under an adult's control. Thomas rolled through the door, stood up, and joined his class.

PRACTICAL WISDOM: NAMING AND DESCRIBING TEACHER KNOWING

My challenge, both ethical and practical, was how I could effectively reach my goal of getting Thomas to class in a manner that supported my value of honoring his needs. To do so, I needed to focus on Thomas himself. What was going to help this child in this moment get to his class? Further, how was I, as a particular teacher with a particular relationship with Thomas, going to support his achieving the goal?

It is this very situational dependency and the accompanying uncertainty that teachers, teacher educators, policy makers, and administrators often find so maddening (Phelan, 2005). That teachers must respond to particulars is widely noted. There are countless theories on professional effectiveness that highlight the need to respond to the particular context with actions. Cecelia and I find practical wisdom to be the most helpful as it highlights the ability to act both effectively and ethically within a specific and unpredictable context.

Patricia Carini (1975) argues that philosophy describes and names conditions we discover through experience. When Cecelia first read about practical wisdom, she was thrilled. Finally she had found a name for what she had been seeing teachers able to do when they practiced Descriptive Inquiry.

When Cecelia as director brought the concept to the Summer Institute by having us read *Practical Wisdom: The Right Way to Do the Right Thing* (Schwartz & Sharpe, 2010), I was just as excited. Now I too had a phrase to describe a kind of knowing possessed by the teachers I admired. This enthusiasm launched me into a thorough study of practical wisdom in contemporary and ancient philosophy and served as the conceptual framework for my dissertation. In other words, the philosophical vistas provided by practical wisdom spoke to us as teachers.

Some discoveries unearth something previously unseen. Others just feel that way. In the case of practical wisdom, Cecelia and I are not the first teachers and teacher educators to discover in practical wisdom a useful frame. In fact, we happily found ourselves in very good company. Inspired by Aristotle's concept, *phronesis*, a number of contemporary thinkers have written about the kind of wisdom-in-action that professionals require.[1] This writing has taken a variety of directions and names such as métis (Scott, 2008; Traugh, 2009), tact (van Manen, 1991), practical wisdom (Nussbaum, 1992; Schwartz & Sharpe, 2010), practical judgment (Smith, 1999), personal practical knowledge (Clandinin, 1985), phronetic method (Levinson, 2015), and practical knowledge (Elbaz, 1983). These concepts differ slightly in emphasis and focus but share a common commitment to actions determined by values and responsive to context. Instead of burrowing into the rabbit hole of following all these permutations to explain practical wisdom, I first turn cursorily to Aristotle and then provide the definition we are using. To do so, I will expand upon the definition offered in the introduction of effective and ethical and then explain features of practical wisdom. Throughout, I will draw on my Anecdotal Recollection to elucidate the concepts. I encourage the reader to draw on their own Recollection as well to make sense of practical wisdom and determine whether the concept accurately describes the kind of knowing that informs successful action.

TEACHING: TO BE EFFECTIVE AND ETHICAL

I would be hard-pressed to find someone who wouldn't agree that teaching relies on being able to act effectively. What is subject to much debate is how that effectiveness is achieved. Much of the contemporary policy on cultivating masterful teachers has rested on establishing formulas and techniques that define action (Green, 2015; Lemov, 2010). If I had followed in this tradition with Thomas I might have turned to a management book for a technique. Though I take issue with some techniques presented as best practice, most I've found in popular books are relatively typical practice and do work with some children. For example, most teachers and manuals would agree that it is ineffective to talk over students and beneficial to wait until they are quiet before offering directions.

Unfortunately, none of these manuals describe what to do when faced with the unpredictable, volatile, and mysterious Thomas who was angry in that moment in the hallway. For example, I could have drawn on one of the most common strategies suggested, reward, and tried to bribe or praise Thomas. I'm not big on bribes, but I praise students all the time with comments like "I really like how you cleaned up so quickly." I could have drawn on another popular, though less openly endorsed, strategy, punishment, and threatened or demeaned Thomas as well. I think this is wrong. I could have brought in the security officer to lift him up and carry him. I believe there are rare times when a child might need to be safely moved by a trusted and trained adult, but I am opposed to enlisting law enforcement to do so. Further, a child should only be moved when they or someone else is in danger and as a last resort. I could have negotiated or reasoned. Many children I've worked with would have responded to a comment like "The floor doesn't look comfortable and your classmates miss you. Let's walk together." I could have barked a command at him: "Get up now!" I could have pleaded gently, "Could you please walk to class? It makes me sad to see you alone in the hallway." I've read all of these strategies described in books, used most of them, and seen most work with at least some children. That said, in considering these options, I determined, based on my knowledge of Thomas, that none were likely to bring him to class and all in fact would probably keep him in the hall longer.

My choice of response was further tempered by ethics. Given that teachers are responsible for the immediate care of students and must make decisions about this care constantly throughout the day (Dewey, 1975; Hansen, 1995, 2001; Noddings, 2003; Santoro, 2018), even the smallest teaching acts are loaded with ethical significance (Hansen, 1995, 2001; Jackson, Boostrom, & Hansen, 1993; Levinson & Fay, 2016). Put differently, we cannot divorce the actions and efficacy of a teacher from asking questions about to what end and for what purpose. Though certainly each strategy would work to get some children to class, they would also have other effects. For example, physically carrying a school-age child to class is sometimes done, but I think it is frightening and disrespectful.

Most management resources and books I've read position a child refusing to go to class as an issue around teacher control and student compliance (for one popular example, see Lemov, 2010). This pits the students and the teachers against each other. As my Anecdotal Recollection reveals, I too wanted Thomas to comply to save myself embarrassment. During an intense verbal or physical exchange, it can be hard to pause long enough to determine the teacher's motive. While Thomas was telling me he wouldn't go to class, he was doing so somewhat passively. In this relatively peaceful moment, I didn't need to respond immediately and could pause to think while Thomas lay there ignoring me.

Therefore, before responding, I quickly considered whether Thomas actually needed to go to class. In doing so, I asked myself, as I often do, whether this was about power or control—two teacher needs that often interfere with my ability to see the student well. I decided that my desire to get him to class went beyond my instinctive need for either power or control in this situation. As I quickly thought this through, I determined that Thomas needed to be in class for two reasons. First, I wanted him with his community learning and not alone in the office or the hallway. Because of behavior that scared them and resulted in frequent removal, Thomas had become increasingly isolated from other children, and he needed chances to reconnect. Second, I worried that if Thomas was caught not in class, someone might yell at him and there might be other repercussions such as losing recess. This would be hurtful to him.

I concluded that I very much wanted Thomas in class for his own sake, but this was tempered by my sense that, as discussed in the Introduction, the goal of getting to class was not worth getting him there at cost to his humanity. I had to get Thomas to class, and I had to do it in a way that respected him. Put more directly, I had to so in a manner that did not subject Thomas to dehumanizing punitive measures and would not risk escalation of this conflict.

ORIGINS AND KEY CRITERIA OF PRACTICAL WISDOM

For Aristotle (1999), practical wisdom did not translate into a concrete code of conduct. Had he mentored new teachers, I imagine he would have told them to put away the guidebook. He would have explained that because situations in actual life are complex and unpredictable, one's actions are highly situationally dependent. He would have then explained that practical wisdom requires three key criteria; the actor needs to

- be able to read the context,
- have clarity about personal values, and
- have some methods for acting appropriately.

To explore what these criteria mean in terms of teaching, I will explain each of the criteria and how it can be applied:

Context

The context with Thomas was complex, as it tends to be in schools. There was Thomas himself, a child I had come to know quite well through experience; observation; discussion with colleagues and the principal, Alison; and a Descriptive Review (a process described in depth in Chapter 3). Because many adults, including myself, found Thomas very hard to comprehend, I had spent hours in Thomas's classroom and at recess taking notes on his actions to try to understand him better.

The context was further informed by the physical setting. Thomas had been sent to the office because he was in trouble with his teacher. This meant that both Thomas and the adults he had just worked with were likely on edge. Thomas was lying in the hallway outside the office—breaking a rule in a highly public location. Given our school culture of taking responsibility for all children and our general policy of keeping children in class as much as possible, it would be hard to find an adult in the school who wouldn't try to get Thomas to his classroom. However, if they were rushed or irritated, the situation might deteriorate quickly. Finally, this was a school where sending a child to the office was not intended as punishment but as a chance for de-escalation with a different and sympathetic adult. Often, children were sent to me for the same reason.

The context also included me. I was someone Thomas and the teachers knew and trusted. After many years at this school, I had a reputation for being kind to children and unconventionally effective. I say this not to brag but because it influenced both my confidence and my capacity to act independently. Knowing my reputation, I was confident that if Alison or one of the teachers saw me in the hallway counting a child rolling, they would likely not interfere. If I were a new teacher or someone who picked on children regularly, my actions might at first glance have seemed erratic, irresponsible, and even mean.

Values

Values can be both personally and culturally derived. Aristotle's work rests on the assumption that there is a right way of seeing the world. Without delving into this complex topic, in our more relativistic time in this book we see values as more personal. Not only are there some differences in terms of what people value, but the priority placed on a given value is dependent on the individual. For example, in the hallway I found myself weighing two values: needing Thomas to feel respected and wanting him in class among his peers. Within my hierarchy of values, making sure that Thomas felt (and was) respected in the moment was more important than time spent in class.

In my college classes, preservice teachers think deeply about which values drive them and whether one weighs more heavily than another. They often comment that after engaging in coursework asking them to reflect regularly on their values, they discover that they have values that inform their pedagogy. In contrast to these new teachers, I had spent years determining what my core educational values were by reading, studying philosophy, reflecting on my practice, and practicing Descriptive Inquiry. Additionally, I was familiar with feelings such as loss of control that tended to pull me away from my values. This awareness helped me think through my values quickly in the hallway. After brief reflection, I determined that I had many reasons for wanting Thomas to be in his class that I felt were in his best interest. With this in mind, I then had to consider how I would act in a way that got Thomas to class in as empowering and respectful a manner as possible.

Methods

Again, as I mention in my Recollection, years of studying and being a teacher came to my aid. Though I had no rule book that instructed me to have children roll to class, I had a lot of experience with turning mundane tasks into a game. I had often walked my class through the hall silently by having them imagine they were different characters: royalty waving, dolls that can't bend their legs, the quietest creatures on Earth, and mice. Knowing that young children like these games helped bring rolling to my mind. Having set game-like challenges in the hall before, I had practiced my execution. Typically, when I had my class walk in particular ways, I wasn't stressed. The mood was playful. With Thomas, I was stressed, but I could rely on those earlier experiences and executions to perform in ways that made it fun and maintained calm when I enacted my "game" with Thomas.

I also knew that children often respond to challenges that feel like dares, including many children resistant to teacher rules. My sense is that the challenge allows them to be subversive or resistant while allowing the teacher to have some control over what is being resisted—in this case the teacher's pretend expectations. As noted, I knew Thomas from observation and time together and suspected he would be excited by a chance to "break a rule" by rolling where one should walk.

Finally, I knew from experience in the classroom that it can be fun and refreshing to shake things up. Asking Thomas to roll, something never done in the hallway, gave him the opportunity to violate expectations in a manner that was benign (our school floors get cleaned often) and of his choosing. Importantly, I would not have asked him to roll had he been standing. This would have felt disrespectful. That he had chosen to be on the floor was immensely important as I considered his dignity. In this way, what might have started as a personal act of rebellion, being on the floor, had turned into a shared game between us.

Interlocking Elements

As noted at the beginning of this chapter, practical wisdom requires that methods, values, and context inform actions. The practically wise teacher must find methods that speak to values and work for a particular context. Having many observations of Thomas wouldn't have been very helpful if I didn't have a range of methods to draw from. Methods and observations might lead to effective actions in the sense that they could have gotten him to class, but they wouldn't necessarily have fit with my values. Context matters too. My ability to act as I did was supported by being in a school that sanctioned play in the hallway and where people believed teachers knew what they were doing. In fact, as I have suggested throughout, cultivating each area of practical wisdom and having them operate in sync with each other is highly complex. It is this question of cultivation that motivates us in our writing. In the next chapter, I will frame our response to this question.

NOTE

1. Gratitude to David Hansen and Chris Higgins for a map of this terrain at the start of this project.

CHAPTER 2

The Cultivating of a Practically Wise Teacher Self

Cara E. Furman

Now that we've defined practical wisdom, make a list of areas where you deploy this capacity in your teaching. Perhaps you draw on it in your work with families, typically knowing exactly what tone to take in a difficult conversation. Perhaps you have practical wisdom when it comes to teaching math but are still developing your methods teaching poetry. Perhaps you had it teaching one grade level and are working toward it as you work with a different age of students. When I left the elementary school classroom, I was confident in my capacity as a teacher. When I shifted from teaching urban children to rural college students, I needed to redevelop practical wisdom. I was clear on my values but found the context required some different methods. Now consider, how do *you* foster that development? What does this look like on a yearly, monthly, and even daily basis? How will you tell this? Seek out colleagues and share. What themes emerge?

THE CULTIVATION OF PRACTICAL WISDOM

So what did you do over time to develop practical wisdom in various areas? What brought me to that moment of success with Thomas? The consultant referenced in the Introduction said that some people just have magic with kids, whereas most need the somewhat scripted techniques she offered. Others have called a teacher's facility intuition or talent.

Aristotle (1999) says little about how one might cultivate practical wisdom, and what he does say is relatively vague: "We must attend to the undemonstrated remarks and beliefs of experienced and older people or of prudent people, no less than their demonstrations" (LI1143b11-12). The prudent, it would seem, should serve as a model for our own actions. Though it is certainly possible to learn from watching another teacher, this approach is not always effective. Additionally, Aristotle suggests that practical wisdom comes from experience. I am hard-pressed to think of someone having practical wisdom without experience, but experience is also no guarantee. Aristotle also suggests that practical wisdom is supported through what he refers to as *friendship between equals*. What such a friendship looks like is left open-ended.

Contemporary writing is equally vague if not more so about the cultivation of practical wisdom. As Nona Lyons (1990) writes, "While the cases presented here offer glimpses of the dynamics of teachers' change, they do not precisely explain what precipitates change and exactly how it comes about" (p. 175). Lyons goes on to say that such an explanation is a "needed research agenda" (p. 175). Contributing to this agenda, we add to a small body of work showing how practical wisdom for teachers might be cultivated (Elbaz, 1983; Furman, 2014, 2016b, 2018; Halverson, 2004; Korthagen, 2001; Phelan, 2005; Sherman, 2013).

In considering the challenge of cultivating the interlocking criteria of practical wisdom—context, values, and methods—let's return to Thomas. Did I immediately and automatically know what to do? No. I was an experienced teacher, and yet, I felt momentarily brand-new. Thomas was acting in a way that surprised and even frightened me. I was flummoxed. In other words, I found myself in a context that resisted my typical methods and forced me to first closely reexamine my values and then rifle through my prior knowledge for methods.

To frame my preparation for this moment, I turn to three philosophical concepts: true friendship, the *polis*, and finally, and at length, the care of the self. Aristotle (1999) argues that people come together to support one another in a range of ways: as mentors, beneficiaries, and true friends. True friendship, he argues, is particularly relevant for developing practical wisdom as between true friends one gives feedback from a place of equality. In such friendships, one can be critical and supportive. We agree with Aristotle that learning from others, experience, and critical friendship play into our understanding of how practical wisdom is developed, but bringing these elements together is not necessarily straightforward.

Political philosopher Hannah Arendt (1998) has taken Aristotle's notion of true friendship and focused on the setting in which it occurs. Using the ancient concept of the polis (what was the Greek and Roman forum), she argues for a public meeting space in which ideas are presented and debated. An apt metaphor of a table helps to describe the features of this space. Arendt argues that the table is the common world among people, the ideas and things being discussed. She then argues that sharing one's perspective is like sitting at this table. Key to her notion of the table is that in coming together around shared ideas, one is both separate and together. Another important element, which will prove crucial in our discussion later in the book, is that in this public space, one has the opportunity to both be seen and see others. In other words, in this democratic space, not only are different ideas brought into the conversation, but in sharing one's ideas, one is sharing an important part of oneself. These interactions are marked by true friendship—a willingness to bring oneself honestly into the exchange with others. In participating in the polis, one leaves with some ideas strengthened, others expanded, and some even changed. In other words, one grows as a thinker through this engagement and, in doing so, in an ongoing way potentially develops practical wisdom.

Yet, as teachers, we care deeply about methods. This gesture to friendship and shared discussion, though compelling, still feels vague. What is the tone of these conversations, and how is it influenced? What does it look like to gather in these ways? Like the excitement Cecelia experienced when she first read about practical wisdom, when I first read about care of the self in a graduate course, I was thrilled.[1] Buried in the dense language of the philosophical text was a perfect description of how I prepared myself for teaching. When I shared it with Cecelia, she too felt that the care of the self as a means of cultivating practical wisdom had the potential to shed much insight on the permutations of our own project. To explain the care of the self, I will describe the concept contextualized again by my experience with Thomas. In Chapter 3, Cecelia will then bring together practical wisdom, care of the self, and Descriptive Inquiry to show how Descriptive Inquiry as an exercise helps a person care for the self and cultivate practical wisdom.

As I shared in Chapter 1, faced with Thomas in the hallway, I asked myself: Does he really need to go to class? I then considered the question quickly by weighing my values and decided, yes. Even with my acknowledgment that I considered this question relatively quickly, perhaps some readers find this pause to be an odd use of time (see Furman & Larsen, 2019, 2020, for a detailed discussion of interrupting to think in the midst of teaching). Perhaps it even seems implausible that faced with a child sprawled on the floor outside the school office, I would take the time to engage in such a dialogue with myself.

Certainly, many of my preservice students and the teachers I work with would find it surprising that my first response was to interrupt my actions and ask myself a question regarding my values and goals (Furman & Larsen, 2019). In fact, when I read journals about their teaching, I frequently ask my students to consider why they insisted on particular actions, and they often say that they are not sure and that the question itself is both interesting and new. I then implore them to get in the habit of asking "So what?" or "Who cares?" when they consider their actions in the classroom. I also explain to them, as I will explain in this section, that getting in the habit of asking these kinds of questions when one is not in the midst of teaching makes the teacher more likely to consider the purpose of actions in the moment of teaching. In fact, it was this kind of constant interrogation of purpose that made examining my intentions so instinctual that in the midst of a stressful moment, I stopped to reassess.

The rigorous examination apart from action to support reflection in the midst of action is one form of what some philosophers refer to as the care of the self: a way of approaching self-development that prepares us for action. The care of the self was written about by the ancient Greek Stoics and has many contemporary enthusiasts. The care of the self has been popularized in more current writings of Pierre Hadot (1995) and Michel Foucault (1997). In recent years, a few contemporary scholars have connected this discourse to education (De Marzio 2007a,b; Hansen, 2011).

Not to be confused with pampering or self-indulgence, care of the self refers broadly to activities that help individuals conduct themselves or to live well (De Marzio, 2007a). Fitting with educational philosopher Nel Noddings's (2003) conception of care as attention to someone for the sake of that person's development, care of the self is a means of developing the ethical self.

As with practical wisdom, my intention is not to provide a thorough and exhaustive discussion of the concept (for such an overview check out Foucault, 1997) but instead to consider the qualities of the care of the self that are most relevant to the cultivation of practical wisdom for teachers. I find the care of the self particularly exciting because it rather unusually argues that concrete exercises can amount to the cultivation of an ethical self, eliding nicely with the practical and philosophical aspects of Descriptive Inquiry (Furman, 2019a; Hansen, 2011).

For our purposes: the key elements of the care of the self are

- a predetermined set of exercises that correspond with a philosophy;
- the demand for hard, lifelong, and regular work; and
- cultivation within community. (Foucault, 1997)

So how did these categories come into play in relation to the development of my own practical wisdom as a teacher and my work with Thomas in particular?

A Predetermined Set of Exercises That Correspond with a Philosophy

A key element of the care of the self is that predetermined exercises correspond with developing a set of values (Foucault, 1997). Dewey (1975) similarly argued that daily actions mold our ethics. As one example, saying positive things to students tends to help teachers also see their students in a more positive light, whereas the more we criticize, the more we find to dislike. What makes the care of the self particularly interesting pedagogically is the idea that exercises practiced outside of our daily interactions prepare us to act according to our values in the moment. For example, perhaps a teacher wants to respond more positively to students. An exercise that strengthens one's ability to be positive about students is going through the names of students and writing a good quality about each one (Wood & Wrenn, 1999). Describing students regularly through Descriptive Inquiry helps the teacher find these positive and original qualities (Furman, 2019a).

descriptive inquiry, critical friends

In other words, <u>practicing a set of activities, one internalizes a way of seeing so that, faced with a challenge, one is prepared to draw on the strengthened perspective.</u> When I met Thomas that day in the hallway, as a practitioner of Descriptive Inquiry I had spent years describing my students and highlighting their capacities. Faced with a child who was behaving in a difficult way, I did not like what he was doing in the moment, but I was able to assume that with further study, he probably had a reason. Instead of judging the behavior, I tried to focus on what his purposes might have been. This made it easier for me to focus on finding an action that honored him. With a similar background, Alison, as principal, was also predisposed to patience with Thomas and acceptance of my practice. Faced with a teacher acting unconventionally, she was inclined to trust my motives and capacity and to follow my lead.

You too probably have exercises that you engage in that fortify you for daily life. Maybe you do deep breathing prior to meeting with a colleague who makes you agitated. Perhaps you make lists, as I have done, of the good qualities of students and colleagues who tend to make you angry to try to improve your next interaction. Perhaps at the beginning of the chapter you already identified some exercises that enabled you to develop practical wisdom. If you engage in exercises regularly to help you act in line with your values, these are likely examples of care of the self.

Demands Hard, Lifelong, and Regular Work

Returning to Thomas, I brought an underlying commitment to honoring all students, but when I encountered him in the hallway I also felt somewhat annoyed. My first thought was not loving but instead, "Really, Thomas, do you need to make this worse!" I share this to emphasize that as Foucault and the Stoics find, sticking with my values in daily life is hard! It felt natural to snap at him to simply go to class, an action that likely would have escalated the conflict. I also might have decided that while most children deserve respect, Thomas did not because he could be rude and wasn't being very polite when he encountered me. I might have rationalized that therefore harsh discipline would have been justified at this moment. For anyone in education, this kind of exceptionality talk is relatively common with phrases like "That sounds good in theory but with these kids, it will never work" or "Sure, I could have tried that with last year's class" or "That works for most of the class but Joey needs punishment." Again, this harsh approach likely would have escalated the conflict, which ultimately would have left Thomas more vulnerable to even harsher punitive measures.

The care of the self provides us with exercises that we can call on to act ethically in daily life. Though my first impulse was frustration, what allowed me to check those feelings and kept me from losing my patience with Thomas was another voice in my head saying, "He is being frustrating, but you believe in this child's good intentions." And that more patient but firm reminder came, as will be elaborated on in depth in the next two chapters, from years of practicing Descriptive Inquiry.

It is also important to note that though things went well with Thomas in the moment I described, earlier encounters had sometimes been scarier and not always gone as smoothly. In fact, earlier that year I'd felt burdened by the fact that every encounter with Thomas seemed to demand new wells of creativity from me, and his behavior in the school was often violent. Although many times he responded well to me as he did in this anecdote, many times he did not. I was afraid of a conflict escalating and leading to a physical response from Thomas—one that would then need me to locate one of the few teachers in the school trained in safe restraint.[2] Therefore, despite my years of practice, the daily challenges I encountered working with Thomas had threatened to corrode my ability to live up to my expectations for myself. This too is accounted for in the care of the self. Where content acquisition is typically looked at as something you master and then move on from, care of the self is "a constant practice" (Foucault, 1997, p. 94) that "has a function of struggle" (p. 97). Foucault offers the helpful image of a watchman, arguing that to be true to an ethos requires constant attention and self-regulation. Applied to teaching, the teacher does not simply master an ethos but must commit to working on enacting a philosophy daily.

In my case, while years of practicing Descriptive Inquiry gave me faith that I would find a way forward with Thomas, when I began working with him that year, I knew I needed help. I felt I needed to know Thomas better so that I could reliably calm him down and help my colleagues to do the same to ensure that he, his classmates, and his teachers were physically and emotionally safe. To get this help, I turned to Descriptive Inquiry, suggesting to Cecelia that I'd like to present my work with Thomas at our local inquiry group and asking her to chair the session. I went into the meeting not sure what I would learn about my work with Thomas but knowing that I would leave the group rejuvenated and better able to face new challenges. This, as my anecdote I hope suggests, proved true.

Requires Community

At the beginning of this chapter, I spoke about true friendship and how it occurs in the polis. The cultivation of the care of the self is democratic work. I drew from the exercises of Descriptive Inquiry to support my work, but simply writing a Review was not enough. I needed to share the Review with others and have their communal support. Because carrying out one's ethos is an arduous task, "it was a generally accepted principle one could not attend to oneself without the help of another" (Foucault, 1997, p. 9).

As Foucault (1997) explains, an unusual feature of the care of the self is that it occurs in a broad variety of social groupings. The support flows between groups and dyads, between peers, from mentor to mentee, and mentee to mentor. It occurs in letters and in person. As we will showcase in the following chapters, the nonhierarchical and different grouping structures of the care of self will prove extremely important. The community that came together earlier in the school year to do a Descriptive Review of my practice with Thomas included teachers from around the city, as well as some of the teachers at my school. Expanding this community of inquirers, I later shared what I learned from the group with teachers who worked with Thomas and the principal. As discussed in the next chapter, within the context of the Descriptive Review, every teacher (those who knew and who didn't know Thomas), regardless of experience, had equal say in the conversation. We came together as true friends.

CLOSING THOUGHTS

In concluding this chapter, I return to the opening of this book. What does it mean to teach for human dignity? In working with Thomas, I needed a way to help him find a path back to his classroom, but in trying to deescalate a volatile situation, I also sought to protect him physically and emotionally. Many of the teachers I work with find themselves in similar conundrums. This brings me to the opening question in Chapter 1, that is, what does it mean to prepare teachers and contribute to their ongoing growth? Put differently, what does it mean to develop practically wise teachers? Although much came out of my review of Thomas, one of the most important insights that came when hearing feedback from the group was that when writing about him, I was editing out my fear. In pushing aside the fact that I was frightened by Thomas at times, I lacked the capacity to address this fear more directly. Drawing on this insight, when I found Thomas in the hallway that day, I reframed our engagement humorously and, in doing so, reduced the tension likely felt on both sides.

I've argued that I demonstrated practical wisdom with Thomas, and I've begun to explore how this capacity was developed through care of my teacher self. As I suggest here, much of that ability was cultivated through having practiced Descriptive Inquiry for nearly 10 years and having recently refreshed my commitment with a Review of Thomas earlier that year.

So now, as a teacher educator, what would I do if a student-teacher came to me with a student who often refused to go to class? Would I instruct them to have their student roll on the floor? I hope by this point it is clear that my answer would be no. Would I ask them if they were afraid and suggest that they confront this fear? Again, my answer would be no. If our interaction was in the midst of class or a short conversation, I would draw on the features of practical wisdom to construct my advice. I would first ask them for context, having them describe both the child and the situation. I would then turn to methods: What do they know how to do? Perhaps I have some ideas about their strengths because I've observed them or read their teaching journals. If not, I might ask them to tell me some ideas they have. I would then go to values: What are they actually hoping to accomplish in this situation? What matters? Who cares?

I just described what I would do if I were pressed for time, and this solution might offer a modicum of support, but unfortunately much of the thinking would be dependent on me. Ideally, if I saw this teacher was willing and eager to give this question some time and space, I would suggest we do a Descriptive Review of this child. Perhaps I would build this into the class for everyone to participate. Perhaps the student-teacher would write one, and I would share feedback with them. Perhaps (and this happens occasionally), I would go to their school and lead the Review with their colleagues. In considering what such a care of the self through Descriptive Inquiry might look like and how it relates back to practical wisdom, I now turn this thread over to Cecelia to articulate.

NOTES

1. Thank you, David Hansen and Darryl De Marzio, for this introduction.

2. As I write this, protests across the country are calling for the removal of police from schools. At the time, I felt the stakes for deescalation were very high. If I could not calm Thomas down verbally and with affection as his teacher, the situation would draw the attention of school security, something I wanted to avoid.

CHAPTER 3

Cultivating Practical Wisdom Through Descriptive Inquiry

A Case of Caring of the Self

Cecelia E. Traugh

I begin this chapter by asking you to engage in one of the Descriptive Processes, the Reflection on the Word. Please take 3 minutes to write down all your associations with the word *value*. You may consider different forms of this word, such as *valuing* and *valued*. You may try to generate a definition of the word. You may consider ways the word is used in popular culture; for example, can you think of any song lyrics that mention it? You may consider the etymological origins. If possible, do this exercise with a few colleagues and then share what you came up with. Don't worry if some of your comments overlap. As you consider what you came up with (alone or with others), you will get a sense of what this word means to you. You will likely firm up what you already thought you knew about the word as well as discover some new elements.

I've asked you to enter this chapter with a consideration of the word *value* because, as we noted in the introduction, values are a central and often underdiscussed area of teaching.

As described in Chapter 1, practical wisdom is a value-rooted theory of action, and at its core, Descriptive Inquiry is values in action. Grounded in close description as the basis of making knowledge and in strong beliefs about human capacity, Descriptive Inquiry through its varied processes makes the phenomenon of that human capacity visible. Over my many years of experience with Descriptive Inquiry, I have learned that taking a descriptive stance toward one's work with children also has a very keen political edge. The trust in "human capacity widely distributed" (Carini, 2001, p. 20), the effort to see a person and their work in their terms, the shared authority of participants in the process, and the multiplicity of views and ideas that it invites result in democratic knowledge-making of a kind that supports individuals, builds community, and develops practical wisdom. The descriptive stance also helps individuals and groups work with the tensions that emerge in schools—for example, the tension of working to build a democratic school within a hierarchical system.

In this chapter, I discuss both the action side of Descriptive Inquiry—the Descriptive Process of this approach to inquiry—and its undergirding values and philosophical bases.

PUTTING VALUES INTO ACTION

The Descriptive Processes, the action side of Descriptive Inquiry, are described fully in several places, among them *From Another Angle* (Himley & Carini, 2000), the book that explores deeply the Descriptive Review of the Child, and *Prospect's Descriptive Processes: The Child, the Art of Teaching and the Classroom and School* (Himley et al., 2002), the online resource that lays out the history, values, and procedures of the Descriptive Processes. The work of Descriptive Inquiry is given shape and direction through the enactment of process. The core idea is that process is about making something new out of already existing things and/or ideas. It is a systematic way of making, doing, thinking, and working to reach a goal. There are steps, done in sequence, and for the process to be reliable, each step is done consistently.

There are tensions within the idea of process. One is between what is ultimately thought to be more important. Are the results, outcome, or achieved goal more important than the way, the process, through which outcomes were achieved, or vice versa? Another tension can be felt between being systematic and careful about procedure and being flexible and open to the unpredictable.

In the context of Descriptive Inquiry, process is understood as making new understandings from the ideas the group members bring to it; it provides an outline of steps that enable careful, rigorous, and collaborative work; the quality of the understandings produced depends on the care given to the descriptive nature of the procedure. As described by Himley et al. (2002):

> The descriptive processes all begin with immersion—observing a child or space or activity, exploring the many meanings of a keyword, drawing forth from teachers' own memories. They all have a focus or focusing question that the chair and the presenting teacher or parent or administrator work out thoughtfully ahead of time and that gives the participants a sense of how to listen and respond to the review. The processes are always collaborative. They have rules and roles necessary for making the inquiry process democratic and inclusive, and for guaranteeing respect and privacy for the individuals involved. . . . All the processes use descriptive language: language that is particular, concrete, ordinary . . . that avoids the categories, labels, and assumptions of educational theory or assessment. They are organized by a series of go-rounds, in which everyone speaks and no one is interrupted by cross talk. There are typically three roles: chair, presenter and note taker. (p. 4)

I briefly describe five Descriptive Inquiry processes here: Reflection, Recollection, Descriptive Review of the Child, Descriptive Review of Work, and Descriptive Review of Practice. All the processes share certain qualities:

- The group gathers in a circle and follows a go-round process with everyone contributing. Passing is possible but usually discouraged.
- A chair has worked with the presenter to plan the session. Deciding on the process to be used and the focus question of the session are key parts of the planning. The chair guides the group through the process, helping participants know what each stage of the process requires of them. The chair also does an integrative summary of the group's individual contributions at key times during the review.
- A note taker is prepared to document the session as fully as possible.
- The group tries to leave time at the close of the session to evaluate the process and the degree to which they were able to maintain a respectful stance toward the work, child, and presenter.

The Reflection asks the group to focus on a word that is relevant to the group's inquiry and to think expansively about its many meanings. The aim is to deepen and expand the group's thinking about the ideas contained within the word and to provide a context for the particular work of the group.

Recollections are structured stories from life experience that participants in an inquiry prepare in advance to share with their inquiry group. The purposes of the Recollection are to give the theme of an inquiry meaning and to help group members connect to that meaning by hearing how the idea has been lived and experienced by group members.

The Descriptive Review of the Child leads a family member and/or teacher to describe a child around five headings: (a) physical presence and gesture; (b) disposition and temperament; (c) connections with others, both children and adults; (d) strong interests and preferences; and (e) modes of thinking and learning. The aim is to create a full and complex picture of the child so that the child's strengths and capacities are more fully visible to those living with that child.

The Descriptive Review of Work, children's or adult's, aims to develop deeper understandings of the maker's "interests, perspectives and ways of making sense of the world" (Himley et al., 2002, p. 20). When the Review is of a student's work, the purpose is to generate ideas about ways to support the person as a thinker and learner. When reviewing an adult's work, such as a piece of published philosophy, the purpose is to develop a deeper understanding of text.

The Descriptive Review of Practice (or of Teaching as a "Work") aims to move a teacher's thinking beyond the "how" of it to what the work is; what in the person is being fulfilled through it; what of value is called out in the world through and by teaching; what outside oneself inspires it; where it fits in the bigger picture of the teacher's life; where it may connect with other work . . . ; what is central or indispensable to the work of teaching. (Himley et al., 2002, p. 17)

Here, I bring forward several aspects of the qualities named above that all the inquiry processes share in order to help the reader understand the inquiry stance that the Descriptive Processes develop. These elements are at the heart of the discussions of Descriptive Inquiry as it lives in the schools included in this book. The points I have chosen are (a) framing a focus question, (b) describing literally, and (c) creating an integrative restatement or summary.

Framing a Focus Question

One of the core skills of Descriptive Inquiry is that of asking focus questions. The focus question does what its name suggests—centers participants' attention on the issue that the presenter wants help thinking about. To be effective, the focus question needs to be one that will open up the issue at hand, help the presenter and participating group see the focus from multiple angles, and generate expansive thinking and so illuminate that issue.

Developing such questions is not a magical process. As we discuss in depth in Chapter 9, it does require the chair to listen carefully to the presenter as the presenter shares their concerns, questions, and stories and to keep track of what they hear and where they begin to see the connective tissue among the various pieces of what the presenter shares. The chair saying back to the presenter what they heard—both aspects of the presenter's content in the chair's words and the threads they are beginning to hear connecting the pieces—provides the presenter the opportunity to learn if they are making clear their real issue or if what they have said is leading the chair off in directions they do not intend. This back-and-forth process is critical for both the chair and the presenter in finding the focus, the meat of the matter. Once the significant issue is agreed on, framing a focus question or set of questions can follow, again looking for wording that will help participants break out of pat and habitual thinking and move to more imaginative possibilities.

Here I offer an example that I am wrestling with as I write this. I am struggling to find a strong focus question for the graduate faculty inquiry group I work with. The issue seems to be faculty being unsure how best to work with their advisory groups when they are discussing race and the conversation becomes emotional. However, it is the case that the faculty have done a good amount of work on how to hold productive discussions of race with people learning to teach and that many if not most faculty have strong

practice in this regard. I have selected the Recollection as the inquiry process to use because it can help participants directly address the issues, bring
nuances to the surface, and help us all see and think about the issue and our
practice more expansively.

The question needs to be one that invites public descriptions of practice
that include both strengths and vulnerabilities. As I have not yet settled on
a question, I share here two of the possibilities I am considering and my
thinking about their potential effectiveness.

One possibility is to ask faculty to think about a discussion they had
with graduate students at some time about how race surfaces in their work in
schools and to consider these questions as they prepared their Recollection:

- How did the discussion begin? Was it a student's issue or did you
  open it up?
- How did the discussion proceed? What ideas were generated? What
  feelings were expressed? What seemed easy to talk about? What
  were the difficult places?
- How did the conversation close? Has the topic reemerged?
- Where did you feel sure of yourself as the facilitator of the
  conversation? Where did you lack confidence?

The strength of these questions is that the request is general and would
probably be comfortable for most of the participating faculty. The group
would learn a lot about one another's experience, and there is an opening
for participants to name an area of vulnerability. The weakness of these
questions for my purpose is that they don't ask directly about the circumstance that gave rise to the issue we are trying to think about. They may
provide entry to a wider band of faculty, but the questions may lead to
responses that avoid aspects of the genesis of this inquiry.

A second possibility is to name the particular context of the issue
directly:

We recently had a large-group presentation during which a panel of
students shared their stories about their development of racial literacy.
When you met with your students, what happened? Describe the
discussion you had with students thinking about these questions:
- How did your students respond to the panel?
- What stories about their development of racial literacy emerged?
- What feelings about the topic did they share? What was the
  emotional tone of the group?
- How did you conduct the conversation? Where did you feel strong?
  Where did you feel vulnerable?
- How did the conversation close?
- What have the next steps been?

The strengths of these questions are that they are asking faculty to (a) think about a particular situation and the issues generated in terms of their practice when a discussion becomes tense, and (b) name both strengths and vulnerabilities of their practice as it was tested at this particular time. The two sets of questions share strengths. The problems with this set of questions rest in their particularity, which in this case is a two-headed coin. I fear that these questions narrow the focus so much that fewer faculty will feel able or comfortable in participating.

Which to choose? I will share these ideas with colleagues and get their responses. Perhaps my colleagues will find a way to merge the two approaches. I am confident they will let me know which will be more helpful to them as they work on their practice. The ultimate test will be the inquiry session itself when we implement the Recollection. If the questions do not help us move forward in our inquiry, they may at least help us know better where to begin next time.

Describing Literally

Whether we are describing a piece of work, a child, or our practice, Descriptive Inquiry asks us to "say what we see," to stay as literal as possible and avoid early interpretations or judgments. A longtime teacher and practitioner of Descriptive Inquiry, Alexander Doan, describes what it means to him to describe literally when studying children's writing. His description of his process applies to many aspects of this work: (a) what inquiry group participants need to do when describing work of all kinds, (b) what a chair asks a presenter to do when describing a child, and (c) what a teacher needs to attempt when describing their own practice. Here are Doan's thoughts:

> For me, describing a text literally involves, first of all, a mental shift, letting myself slow down, setting aside my usual assumptions—as much as possible—about writing and interpreting writing and instead trying to open to what is in front of me; to ready myself to take in features I often don't notice or that don't matter to me when I write and instead to look for what this writer has done. It means setting aside for a while any judgments or interpretations that are often already forming. (Sometimes it has been useful to reframe these as questions to consider later.) Also, since it is a collaborative process, it means not feeling like I have to notice everything, but relaxing into what I readily notice and being prepared to have my seeing also guided over time by what others notice.
>
> Having made this mental reframing, describing literally means paying as close attention to the text as possible and simply putting into words what I notice is there. That can involve noticing the kind of paper (if paper) it is written on and how the text is located on the

page and what it appears to be written with. It can involve graphic features such as handwriting and its variations and its lines, letter formation, upper or lower case use, or its font if word-processed. It can involve naming words used as well as kinds of words used. It can involve naming punctuation and how it is used (if at all). It can involve obvious elements of syntax, for example, the type of sentences used. It can involve some basic form of genre noticing, that it is a letter or a paragraph. It can involve any meanings I am noticing, or any ambiguities. Eventually I notice things such as the rhythm of the language, but that usually comes later. I am not trying to interpret the text in any full way at this point; there hasn't been enough description yet to enable any such interpretation to be grounded in anything other than my usual ways of interpreting, which won't help me to see this text more fully. I'm just looking at the text and also listening to what others are noticing (and often being amazed at what I don't notice that they do). Usually there are several rounds of this kind. After as much of the "literal" features of the text have been put into words, the group either spontaneously or at the chair's direction moves into naming other elements of the text that have now become visible through the time spent looking at and reading the text, such as the rhythm and sounds of the language, the style, the uses of syntax through the piece, the way meaning develops through the piece. New questions also emerge as people name tentative thoughts about what they observe. The goal of the description is not a complete explanation of the piece, but a deeper look at the text and its meaning and perhaps a greater sense of the author and her intentions.

Several of the necessary qualities of taking a descriptive stance are named here. Slowing down, setting aside quick interpretations, paying close attention to what is being described, using language to name what you see, and listening closely to what others see are some of the key shifts away from habitual ways of seeing that support the new ways of understanding that emerge through description and Descriptive Inquiry.

Creating an Integrative Restatement or Summary

Descriptive Inquiry is a knowledge-making activity. Through the process of preparing a Descriptive Review of the Child or of Practice, the presenter begins to deepen their understanding of themselves and the person or practice they are describing. In the inquiry session itself, the chair can make periodic summary statements that pull together a group's description. This is particularly helpful when describing work. The chair also makes an integrative restatement at the close of the session. By sharing with the group the threads and themes the chair thinks run through the descriptive conversation and suggestions of other ideas that might sit alongside those generated by the group, the chair's integrative restatement has the potential of helping the group see the new understandings they have created, the new ideas they may have generated.

The process of creating the restatement is an important aspect of Descriptive Inquiry. It requires the chair to listen carefully for both details and larger themes and issues with the aim of helping the group relate the descriptive information to the focus question. As stated in *Prospect's Descriptive Processes*,

> The restatement is not about defining or closing down the inquiry. It's not about finding answers or solving problems. Its value lies in what it can evoke from the participants—what new possibilities we can imagine, what further questions may arise from how the ideas overlap or diverge, what meaning this review has for [group members'] work in [their] classrooms and . . . schools. (Himley et al., 2002, p. 86)

In a faculty reading group that Cara led, she asked her colleagues to put together an Anecdotal Recollection of a time when they felt re-moralized— able to reconnect their values to their teaching after a period of disconnect (see Santoro [2018] for the book they studied and from which they drew this idea). As people shared stories, a theme of relationships emerged and was noted by participants, some of whom would begin their story by saying, "Well, mine is all about relationships too." As Cara took notes, she looked both for themes and outliers in the conversation. In doing so, she found that while many of the stories were about relationships, other themes emerged as well, such as moments of leadership and passion for a particular activity. As she pulled together themes, she also saw that although relationships were central, a particular kind of relationship came to the forefront: those that involved true friendship (as defined in Chapter 2) in which people came together around a shared interest, problem-solved, noticed one another's work, and gave respectful pushback. In sharing this as a restatement, her colleagues were able to pinpoint what they meant by relationships and to think more deeply about what reinspired their own work.

VALUES SHAPING DESCRIPTIVE INQUIRY

At the start of the chapter, I described Descriptive Inquiry as values in action. I have focused so far on some of the actions involved in Descriptive Inquiry. Here I describe what I believe are core grounding values of Descriptive Inquiry. I elaborate the idea of description, move to inquiry and the authority of questions, and close with democratic knowledge-making. Running through my discussion of these ideas is their relationship with making visible human capacity. These ideas and the values they hold provide the animating spirit of Descriptive Inquiry. It is this spirit that helps Descriptive Process–Based Inquiry maintain the life of the person or person's work described by opening up the describing group to the object's meaning. To illustrate the movement and animating spirit of the work, throughout this chapter I both discuss values underlying Descriptive Inquiry and provide examples of how I came to explore these ideas in my teaching and work with educators. In doing so, I particularly emphasize how the Descriptive Process when used within a school builds the community's practical wisdom and democratic practice.

Description

Description is the core discipline of Descriptive Inquiry. As stated earlier, descriptive language is "particular, concrete, ordinary . . . [and] avoids the categories, labels, and assumptions of educational theory or assessment." As Doan shared earlier, description is a mode of thinking and expression that also serves as an exercise that helps you to say what you see and to work against the tendency to make quick judgments and use language carelessly. Carini (1979) names this basic human capacity as a "gift of vision" and lays out the need for practice if we are to hone this skill. She writes

> The gift of vision . . . through which observing lays claim to its fullest possibilities, requires exercise to realize its power or it relapses into a kind of blindness, in which the things in the world are perceived only as objects-of-use; that is, in terms of personal needs. In its most benign form, habituated perception is reassuring and indeed useful. . . . But there are limitations and implicit dangers in habituated perception. . . . when habituated perception is carried to an extreme of circumstance (*e.g.*, extreme physical need), or through a failure to exercise the gift of vision (*e.g.*, ordinary "busy-ness"), the world may come to be seen only from the frame of reference of personal need. Then both viewer and viewed are impoverished, detachment replaces interest, and the world loses its power for calling forth meaning. (p. 11)

This passage tells us much about description and what it means to learn to describe and underlines important aspects of the idea of care of the self discussed in Chapter 2. Most basic of all, this passage should make clear that we are talking about an ordinary human capacity, a capacity that must be practiced or we lose it and become blind to the world and everything in it—not blind in the physical sense, but blind in the sense of habit, of seeing everything in terms of its use to us or in terms of how it is seen conventionally.

The blindness Carini names, this failure to see, often results from our being too busy, too pressed by the demands of our lives to do the kind of practice necessary for true care of the self. We end up seeing only what we need or want to see because a deeper level of attention is not reasonable or productive. Habitual ways of seeing help us get through our days without having to think about everything. For example, when we do not attend to who we are racially, we may not recognize the limits of our seeing and how we are relying on stereotypes. When we do not take the time to know a child in their complexity, we can rely on the casual use of labels to describe them. When we have set definitions of a role in a school, the work a person in that role actually does can be invisible. In a meeting of a leaders' inquiry group, a principal raised this focus question: "How can I make the parapro-fessionals'[1] work visible to themselves, teachers and the school so that they can be brought in as partners, especially as we engage in equity work in the school?" In the inquiry meeting, the principal shared examples of how para-professionals work with teachers, and through their responses to the focus question, the group expanded the principal's vision of the role and shared ideas about how to open their work up to the school community.

Through our failure to use our gifts of seeing to their fullest, we and the world around us are made small. Not letting the world and its people fully into our range of vision results in a kind of stasis in terms of our points of view and understandings. The world and its people are only what our version of them allows them to be. Seeing only what habit and the powers that be allow us to see, we lose interest and have no reason to explore new avenues, create new connections.

There are so many examples of how blindness works in our world today. On the local scale—continuing to call a student a "misbehaver" keeps the namer in that narrow mode of seeing that child and boxes the child into a corner with no way for either person to get out. On the national scene an example is how we assess the worth of children in the public policy sphere. As Polakow (1994) reminds us, "Poor children, it seems, are deserving of public money only if investment in their early lives has demonstrable eco-nomic payoffs. They matter instrumentally, not existentially" (p. 101). On the international scene, we see the growth of extreme views that refuse to acknowledge the humanity of the opposition and leave no room for peaceful solution.

Practicing description makes us practice seeing. It makes us practice trying to see people in their terms, trying to hear what their version of the world is, trying to learn what sense they make of their work and life. Prac-ticing description can result in a kind of double vision, alert to the immedi-ate situation and the quick action that may be required and aware that there is more there than meets the eye, to be uncovered with careful watching and increased awareness of the larger social systems that may be at play. In these times of "one size fits all" solutions, practicing descriptive seeing runs against the grain and so is difficult. But that difficulty tells us that it is ever more important to do if we are to engage in the kind of care of the self that helps us build our ethical selves.

The work of seeing others in their terms requires imagination. I share here a story from my own teaching to illustrate this point:

Many years ago I was the director of a middle school, grades 5 through 8. As director, I always taught a class, and one year it was 6th-grade English. In that class was a child who struggled with classroom learning. He was not a strong writer or reader. He would frequently get up and dance, gaining the appreciative attention of his classmates and a firm "Sit down, Dajay" from me—which he sometimes heeded and sometimes didn't. He was a source of frustration.

One of the activities my 5th/6th-grade English teacher colleagues and I developed that year was a once-a-week observing and describing activity we called "tree." Each week we walked to a sheltered spot and observed and described a large Norwegian maple. We wrote, drew, painted. In that place, Dajay had room to exercise his very active ways. For example, in the fall we were outside on a day when the maple's leaves were floating and flying from their branches. Dajay spent his time running around with his arms extended straight out, bending and swaying as he ran. Slowly, I began to see what he was doing—he was being the leaves. Through his imagining, I began to reimagine him. I began to look more closely at his classroom behavior and the possibility that Dajay was a child who put his learning through his body. Dances happened when ideas caught him. In response, I had to begin to rework my classroom practice, making it more welcoming of physical movement, much to Dajay's benefit and the benefit of the other 6th-grade children I was teaching.

In closing this story, I must add that through Dajay's being the leaves I have never seen leaves falling to the ground in the same way. Their fall has become the floating, soaring dance my student did long ago during "tree."

What does the act of describing do that supports imaginative re-seeing? Description asks us to hold off as best we can on quick interpretations and surface judgments and to put language to what we see. In the careful work of Descriptive Processes, we slowly allow ourselves to be immersed in what we describe, to see it more fully from our own perspectives, to see it yet more fully from the perspectives of others, and to begin to see it on its own terms, enabling the meaning of the person or work to emerge.

Concluding this discussion of description, I return to Carini's idea of "the gift of vision." In order to move beyond the status quo of our understandings, we need to learn how to "say what we see." We need to learn how, through our fresh seeing, to reimagine and rethink, to ask new questions, and probably to challenge the conventional.

In her writing on practical wisdom, Martha C. Nussbaum (1992) argues that contrary to popular opinions, ethical decisions tend not to be resolved by weighing the value of multiple choices. Instead, she maintains that the way forward comes from reframing the dilemma in an entirely new way. In other words, by her reasoning, in studying Dajay I did not find a way to control his movement. Instead, through this new way of seeing, I resolved my negative response to his movement and found ways that he and I could both be more at ease in the classroom together.

Inquiry and the Authority of Questions

Alongside learning how to "say what we see" is the value of learning how to ask questions of the work we do with children and colleagues. Learning how to raise one's own questions and open oneself to generating new possibilities through the inquiry process is core to Descriptive Inquiry. Descriptive Inquiry is not a program that gives step-by-step directions to follow when teaching reading. It is not the "silver bullet" that Michelle notes later in this text that teachers can wish someone would provide. In fact, it is a process that results in more questions rather than firm answers. I have several colleagues and teacher friends who inevitably after an inquiry session with me say, "I have more questions now than when I came." When I hear this response, I think I hear some discomfort with the implied uncertainty of asking questions and a wish for answers. I also feel the hardness of that place defined by questions when the teacher is returning to a classroom filled with immediate demands, which require decision and action now. But I also feel the energy that has been renewed by the possibilities we have uncovered together. From my many years in schools, I am sure there is no silver bullet and that this, in fact, is one of the wonderful things about teaching. Without any one answer, we must stay alive to the questions.

So, how do inquiry and close description actually fit into the process of teaching and growing as a teacher? How can asking questions about students and teaching practice be important when individuals new to teaching are just putting all the pieces together—for example, their beginning pedagogical knowledge, the curricula they are required to use by their school, the questions and demands of families. How can asking questions about students and teaching practice be important when most teachers, new and experienced, work in a system that prefers set practices that are deemed "best" by some, often distant, educational authorities?

Authority

Here I want to think about the idea of the authority of questions. First, the idea of authority. At the start of this chapter, I asked you to reflect on the word *value*. A Reflection on a Word as I've noted helps people to better grasp the possibility of particular words. As a chair and a presenter, I look for words that I sense I need to slow down for, to see better.

Authority is one such word that I often feel both I and the teachers and principals I work with need to take more time to think about. I therefore have done Reflections on this word with several groups and found there is much complexity to this idea. As you study this word with me, I urge you to again take a few minutes to jot down your own perceptions alone or with colleagues. Then, as you read my summary of the word (based on many people's takes) consider how your own ideas fit. You may find they challenge, complement, contradict, deepen, or take my work in a different direction.

Different roles are vested with different authority. There are many varieties of authority. People convey their authority in a range of ways. There is a kind of dynamic within the idea that is related to the sources of authority and where it lives, and there is discomfort with this dynamic. Does authority come from within? Somewhere external to us? What is the relationship between these sources? What is the relationship of authority to power?

The idea of author is part of authority. Seeing this word within the word gives us an idea about an internal source of authority. From this vantage point, authority is about the person being a creator/shaper/maker, the active agent in their life. It is about "ownership" of ideas and the power that ownership brings.

There is also the authority the sources of which raise questions—for example, the entitled authorities of gender, race, class, celebrity.

In the education world, we do continue to live and work in a time of authoritative answers and solutions. These answers can often be presented as universal. For example, national standards, standardized tests, and charter schools seem to be the promised fixes for the nation's educational issues and problems at this time.

All these framings of authority have different expectations for the relationship people have toward it and the power that comes with it. For example, should we submit to authority? Are people supposed to stand in awe of it? Do we recognize, respect, and trust it? Should we resist it? Should we speak truth to it? Can we sometimes be complicit with it? Do we responsibly "own" it?

Living and Meeting at the Question

Alongside the ideas embedded in authority, I put the idea of question. In the context of a quest for answers that will solve all our problems and an authoritarian educational system that sees itself as having these answers, what can I mean when I talk about the authority of the question? What can I mean by the possibility of authority resting on a recognition that all knowledge is partial and needing continued questioning in order to develop and deepen? To explore the idea of question, I turn to two poets, Rainer Maria Rilke and Muriel Rukeyser. Rilke first. A young poet wrote Rilke a letter in July 1903, with a question about love. Rilke (1987) didn't respond until May of the next year, saying

I would like to beg you, dear Sir, as well as I can, to have patience with every-thing unresolved in your heart and to try to love the questions themselves as if they were locked rooms or books written in a very foreign language. Don't search for the answers, which could not be given to you now, because you would not be able to live them. And, the point is, to live everything. Live the questions now. Perhaps then, someday far in the future, you will gradually, without even noticing it, live your way into the answer. (pp. 34–35)

"Try to love the questions." They are your own, children of your mind. Keep them close to you; don't lose them. Appreciate, respect, and enjoy the questions. Be curious and wonder about them. Spend time with them; give them your full attention. "Don't search for the answers . . . because you would not be able to live them." Don't try to get rid of your questions with answers someone could give you. That act of disrespect won't do you any good because you would not be able to understand the answer anyway; you would not be able to make it part of you, to act on it authentically.

Instead, "live the questions now." Bring them to all the contexts of your life. See what they look like from the different vantage points parts of life bring to you. Let them help you to be open to life's variety and possibilities. See how the questions both expand your experience and are expanded by it.

Then, sometime far in the future, without knowing it, you may "live your way into the answer." Watching Dajay, I wondered, wondered about his movement, wondered about his purpose, wondered about the sense he was making. Living with those questions in the classroom and then outside, I lived my way to an answer, a way of respecting Dajay's meaning-making and, in doing so, listening better to other students as well.

A second large idea about questions I found in Rukeyser (1996), a poet and writer about poetry: "Art and science have instigated each other from the beginning; sparsely when the conclusions, the answers, were translated from one form to the other; always more fruitfully when the questions were used. . . . They make a meeting place" (p. 162). Rukeyser puts two human enterprises we typically see as fairly separate together in a surprising way by saying that art and science each began the other, that they are connected through their historical beginnings in human thought. She goes on to say, however, that the connections between the two modes of thinking thin out and become hard to see when they are brought together around end points, when efforts are made to apply one field's answers to the other. Working with conclusions, scientists and artists don't have much to say to each other. The relationship between the two ways of thinking about the stuff of the world is most productive, most rich when their questions are used as the connecting points. Questions "make a meeting place." In other words, it is in questions that the polis, described in Chapter 2, comes into being—two disciplines meeting around the shared table of an inquiry.

I love the line "They make a meeting place." It expresses an idea close to my heart and serves as a guide for my work in schools and in teacher education. It speaks to the power of questions to create possibilities. Let me give one example of what I mean by using a questioning stance to create a meeting place where win/lose, either/or is not the governing stance.

Oftentimes when parents and teachers get together, talk that will be helpful to children's education is difficult. The tone can become tense in a short time. In each other's ears, a parent's questions become a criticism; the teacher's response becomes a defense. An example of an effort to create the setting for and engage in another kind of conversation was a parent-teacher day held at the Neighborhood School. The day was built around children's work and these questions: What is children's work? And what can we learn from it together? Teachers and parents sat around the table—five tables actually—to look closely at writing, drawing, and block building to see what was there. I chaired the block-building group. At those child-size tables, a polis came together around the work. Everyone participated with equal authority. We were not seeking answers; we were expanding the possibilities for thinking about what the children had made and thought about as they worked with the blocks. The spirit generated through the descriptions carried into further conversations about implications for parenting and classrooms, and some important questions were raised. For example, a parent said that the transition from kindergarten to 1st grade was a bit tough for her child. Why, she queried, is there such a sharp break between what is allowed in kindergarten and what is expected in 1st grade?

This is an important question for a school. Creating a forum that brings parents and teachers together for some real thinking about it was an important next step; however, as asked, the question felt potentially divisive, the tone accusatory. In Chapter 2, we argued that true friendship requires that we both affirm and offer frank critique. To create the polis in which such disagreement can occur, to make a meeting place, to give the question authority for both teachers and parents, the question needed to be reframed to remove the polarity and seek instead the common concern at the center—that is, the child's transition experience from the child's perspective. I suggested this reframing: How can we come to understand our children's experience of the move from kindergarten to 1st grade? What possibilities for supporting our children do these understandings open up to us teachers and parents?

So, after this exploration of the two ideas, what am I saying when I say that questions have authority? One point is that if we can see questions as meeting places for difference we make room for multiplicity, for thinking that gets us out of the trap of either/or or only seeing in the way our theories and assumptions tell us "It is supposed to be." While recognizing the authority of questions makes it clear that there are limits to what we can know about other people and about the world around us, this same recognition can mean that we have to know our fellow humans through a process that vigilantly allows voice to others' authority—the child's and our colleagues'—and builds relationship.

The authority of the question rests in our living the question and in the connections questions can allow us to make. Our living of questions allows us to both contextualize and deepen any understandings, which come through that living. Our living of questions leads to the ongoing process of trying things out and looking at their effects. Our living of questions allows us to maintain wonder and keep things open to possibility. Our living of questions allows us to grow in our capacities to enact our values and act ethically.

Democratic Knowledge-Making

Description, giving authority to questions and following the guidelines of the Descriptive Inquiry processes leads to a kind of knowledge-making. To help describe the kind of knowledge made through Descriptive Inquiry, I first distinguish it from the nature of the knowledge needed by all large bureaucracies and provided to schools' bureaucratic machines by the standardized testing required of all public schools. James C. Scott (2008) writes:

> Certain forms of knowledge and control require a narrowing of vision. The great advantage of such tunnel vision is that it brings into sharp focus certain limited aspects of an otherwise far more complex and unwieldy reality. This very simplification, in turn, makes the phenomenon at the center of the field of vision more legible and hence more susceptible to careful measurement and calculation. Combined with similar observations, an overall, aggregate, synoptic view of a selective reality is achieved, making possible a high degree of schematic knowledge, control, and manipulation. (p. 11)

To do the work that bureaucracies need to do, the knowledge they gain from standardized testing meets the criteria that Scott names. Namely, it simplifies what is defined as learning; it provides information about narrowly defined and thus simplified areas of learning; it brings those particular areas into sharp focus and leaves the rest outside its lens; it creates a picture of a selected reality. This kind of knowledge is useful for many purposes. For example, it supports big picture accountability and enables comparisons of schools across the cities and states. Detailed knowledge of the individual person is not the aim of this kind of knowing. That would be too messy. However, individuals are labeled and known by its results—1s, 2s, etc. And, because this kind of knowledge has become the "coin of the realm," the "selective reality" described by test scores is given credence and value, what is outside its scope can be forgotten and devalued, and the worth and long-term lives of schools and children can become dependent on the narrowed vision.

Descriptive Inquiry puts other ideas about persons and their learning and work into play. The detail and resulting complexity of these ideas can "open up . . . new possibilities of thought, reflection, and action" (Himley & Carini, 2000, p. 207). As Carini writes:

> Through description, the person becomes more visible and real education begins, and it is, finally, this *taproot of the person* that characterizes [the] particular educational stance [of Descriptive Inquiry] and that gives meaning to the descriptive processes. It is the ethical insistence on the hard work necessary to accord to others—*all others*—the status of person, with all the complexity, capability, range of emotions and desires, and possibilities that we know ourselves to have. [Descriptive Inquiry] seeks to start from the most spacious understanding of the person in thinking about children and education. (p. 131)

Description as knowledge-making serves purposes different from those of bureaucratic and standardized forms. The knowledge created through description, because it is grounded in persons, is particular and local and aims for complexity and spaciousness. This knowledge argues with the sureness of a test score or level of reading and instead suggests that all knowledge is tentative and partial.

Drawing on ideas from "Creative Democracy—The Task Before Us" (Dewey et al., 1939/1991), I cite Dewey here to underline the value of the person as basic to democracy. In doing so, I emphasize two key points:

- "Democracy is a way of life controlled by a working faith in the possibilities of human nature" (p. 226).
- "Democracy is a way of life controlled not merely by faith in human nature in general but by faith in the capacity of human beings for intelligent judgment and action if proper conditions are furnished" (p. 227).

In considering the first point, a "working faith" is definitively not an abstract, theoretical faith. It is a faith that is put to work, put into practice, tested. Schools can be powerful arenas for the enactment of this aspect of democracy as a way of life. Practice grounded in human possibility is important but often not supported in schools. Few of us are fully realized, but teachers often look only at what a student is and can do in the present, ignoring the possibilities that are there that could be seen and brought forth. The same is true of teachers and administrators. To base the work of schools on the possibilities of human nature is to take a longer, fuller view. To work democratically, at a minimum, we must have faith in the possibilities of children, of fellow teachers and administrators, and of parents.

A working faith in human capacity is not always easy to hold on to or to base one's teaching practice on. So much pulls us off this center, for example, the press for high test scores that makes narrow bands of academic learning the main way we see who children are and leads us to use the shorthand description of children as 1s, 2s, 3s, or 4s or the shorthand description of children as readers as level C or G.

"On the ground" in schools, the bureaucratic and descriptive ways of seeing people and their learning when put alongside each other create tension. This is uncomfortable, but that discomfort can have the benefits of raising questions and exploring possibilities.

Here I share an example of people working to do this. The example is from a school, the Earth School, that was grappling with the tension they felt between the standardized and descriptive ways of knowing. At the time of this tension, the Earth School had used Descriptive Process for a number of years to help them think about children and teaching practice, but as a New York public school, it must pay attention to the needs of the bureaucracy for standardized measures and reporting.

Teachers adopted the use of leveled books[2] as one way to evaluate children's reading. This mode of working had much to say for it in the setting of this school. The Department of Education approved its use because it provided a way of documenting a child's progress as a reader easily and uniformly across the system, and it provided data on which decisions about a school's and its teachers' quality can be made. Most teachers liked it because it (a) was easy to communicate to families, (b) could make it easier for children to choose books they could decode, (c) made working with children on their reading feel systematic, (d) gave everyone an easily understood vision of learning to read, and (e) was supported by major names in literacy education.

However, the teachers were having problematic experiences stemming from this mode of assessment. First, something was happening among children. They were telling one another that they were level C readers and so couldn't choose a book from the D bin. Teachers were also noticing that the first question parents asked about their children was what level book they were reading. In addition, this school was part of a Design Your Own Assessment project[3] that used Descriptive Inquiry as a form of assessment, and they had been trying to systematically describe their students' work. In combination, these experiences were coming together, and the teachers were beginning to ask, "When did reading become about leveling and a child become their level?" Another set of values that had always existed in these teachers' thinking but had been submerged was beginning to percolate back into the discussion. Alongside the ease that the leveling of books provided, these teachers also recognized that most books written specifically as leveled readers are not interesting and have little literary value and that assessment of levels gives only a partial picture of a child as a reader. The children's and parents' learned responses to leveled books and the collection of descriptions of children were making the teachers ask about what they could do to counteract the idea that reading is about levels rather than literature or a child's learning about an interest or enjoying a story.

Himley & Carini (2000) provide a way of thinking about the pressure on an individual teacher to use shorthand such as leveled libraries to assess children. Himley writes

> All too often we are too tightly held by the ways of the world, too embedded in the discourses and technologies of thought and the regimes of truth, and too involved in moment and place and self really to take notice and give our full attention. . . . By holding off that discursive power, we open up space to reflect on word choice, identify assumptions, play out fuller meanings, look at connections and implications and effects, recognize and understand one another—see things differently. (p. 207)

The Earth School teachers were trying to both create the kind of expansive space to reflect on meaning Himley advocates and reassert the value of the persons they taught.

Here I add two more ideas to this construct of democratic knowledge-making through Descriptive Inquiry. First, as noted, Arendt (1998) describes a polis in which people can reveal themselves through word and deed and in which the protections of democracy—that is, inclusion of a variety of perspectives and a slowing things down—are in force. As a complement to these ideas, I bring in Dewey. Both Arendt and Dewey are concerned about how citizens enact democracy in their daily lives. When Dewey writes, "Democracy as a way of life is controlled by personal faith in personal day-by-day working together with others" (Dewey et al., 1939/1991, p. 228), he asserts this idea to contrast with the machine-like definition of democracy that emphasizes its structures and mechanisms. My interest is in how Descriptive Inquiry enacts the possibility of making democracy a "commonplace of living" in schools.

As we have already seen, one facet of making democracy a "commonplace of living in schools" is holding on to and deepening our "working faith in the possibilities of human nature" (Dewey et al., 1939/1991, p. 226). A way to this end is to make the humanness and human capacities of our fellows visible to us. An example of a vehicle that can move schools to this goal is the Descriptive Review of the Child. The descriptive and respectful stance toward children that the Descriptive Review of the Child holds us to allows us to see a child, to make the child more knowable to us, to develop a working faith in that child. I illustrate this point with a story from a Descriptive Review I chaired at the Neighborhood School that was presented by a paraprofessional, Aaron, in that school who was also an undergraduate student in teacher education. Aaron worked in the classroom taught by Mary.

Chris, a 2nd-grader, seemed invisible in his classroom. He entered so quietly that Aaron had to remind himself to look for him in the morning. Chris did nothing to draw attention to himself. He talked softly, obeyed the teacher's directions, seldom raised his hand to be called on, didn't show anger, kept to himself, and often seemed to be lost in his own thoughts. Mary described him as a young 2nd-grader having a December 31 birth date, and she felt that, as the youngest child in his grade group, he was always behind his 2nd-grade peers. She saw him as knowing what he was doing in math, say, but as very slow in being able to tell her what he knew. She also acknowledged that Chris told her in a parent conference, "You don't see me."

What was striking about this Descriptive Review was that it made this child, a child who was previously identified by himself and others as invisible, visible to the full staff of the school. In contrast to typical school discourse, it wasn't his academic strengths or weaknesses, his ability to reach preestablished milestones, that we focused on; it was his qualities as a person that the paraprofessional made visible to us through his observations.

The description helped us see that Chris's quietness disappeared when he recognized other children's work and successes. Aaron writes:

It's not that he doesn't know how to use his loud voice. When he's in smaller groups, his voice gets so much louder. A friend of his made a deck of action figure cards, which Chris saw from across the table. Chris says, "Wow!!!" I was surprised because I thought someone had done something extraordinary with the way he responded. His voice is also much louder than usual in the block area when he sees that his peers' ramps for marbles are functioning for them. Here he also lets out a loud "Yeah!!" and "Super!!"

Chris's sense of fairness and justice became visible to us in a story Aaron tells from the block area:

The only time I saw him get a little upset was when a boy, Jay, needed a marble for his marble maze in the block area. Four other boys had all the other marbles, about 20. They didn't want to share one marble with him. Jay cried and Chris said to the group, "He only has one marble," pointing to Jay. After Chris's comment one of the boys gave Jay a marble. Soon after, he asked me if he could switch from blocks to the art shelf. It seemed to me that he felt it was unfair how they treated him. He didn't want to be around the boys anymore, and leaving was probably his way of telling them they were wrong. They all noticed when he left but continued to play as if nothing happened, including Jay.

Through the Review, Chris came to life to the teachers and to the forefront of their thinking. The group of teachers hearing the Review began to imagine ways to respond to the focus question: How do we help Chris and all members of the classroom community identify his strengths and abilities? They saw him as a child who uses one-word utterances to express his appreciation. Could he be recognized as a person who knows the right word to say? Fairness is a major issue for this age. Could his sense of fairness be highlighted by making him a "fairness expert" for his class? He expresses himself more easily in small groups. Would putting him in a range of small groups help others see his tenderness and let his animated side be more visible to himself and others? In these ways, the school was able to see possibilities in Chris that they had not before and were able to take steps to develop them and to work on the basis of his human capacities that had been invisible before.

How is this activity democratic knowledge-making? On the most basic level, this Review was a democratic opportunity for the voices of the full group to be heard. A paraprofessional, one of the usually silent partners of classroom teachers, presented the Review. Turning to Dewey's ideas to push me deeper, I see the teachers' confidence in the practice of Descriptive Review and their regular sharing of Reviews of children about whom they had questions as illustrating Dewey's idea that "democracy as a way of life is controlled by personal faith in personal day-by-day working together with others" (Dewey et al., 1939/1991, p. 228). I see making this child's capacities visible to this school's teaching community as helping the teachers see Chris's human possibilities, and perhaps his humanity. Through that seeing they practiced their "working faith in the possibilities of human nature" (p. 226). I see their participation in the Review and their recommending to Mary and Aaron ideas about how to change the classroom environment to better serve Chris and let his capacities better come forth as evidence of the group showing Dewey's second point, faith in the "capacity of human beings for intelligent judgment and action if proper conditions are furnished" (p. 227). In the "proper conditions" created by the Descriptive Review, I also see these teachers working to more adequately base Chris's education on, as Carini says is necessary, "the most spacious understanding of the person" (Himley & Carini, 2000, p. 131).

Dewey's ideas help me understand the depth of what it means to enact the idea of democratic knowledge-making as a way of life within the school. Historically and currently, schools have developed into hierarchical organizations usually with top-down decision-making processes. Mandated curriculum and assessment are the rule. These large systems are capable at best of a faith in human nature in general, not in seeing or having faith in the capacity and possibilities of individual human beings, certainly not the close looking that made Chris's possibilities and capacities evident to his school community.

Furthermore, Dewey's idea about democracy requires schools to acknowledge the necessity to provide "proper conditions" for teachers to develop intelligent judgments that can be used as the basis for sound action. Teacher and parent knowledge of children and how best to educate them are not primary resources within the current system. Descriptive Inquiry is one way to provide the conditions needed for teachers and parents to build their faith in human capacity and use each other's capacities for intelligent judgment to chart courses of action around a child or an issue confronting them. Descriptive Inquiry is a way for us to develop the trust in others we need in order to carry out our "day-by-day working together." This Descriptive Review enabled the slow-going sharing of a multiplicity of perspectives that helps us better protect the humans in our care.

I know from conversations and work with teachers in schools that we don't have many opportunities to practice the kind of "creative democracy" that Dewey describes for us. It is frightening to know that many teachers will say that their "hands-on"/firsthand experiences of being a part of a democratic community are few and far between in any aspect of their lives. Interaction between teachers tends to be what Arendt (1998) refers to as social at best: moving through the shared space as opposed to a polis in which people come together around shared ideas. This does not bode well for the quality of life in schools, for education, or for our continuing as a democratic society. In contrast, teachers participating in Descriptive Inquiry move toward the shared purpose that a democratic polis demands.

In these times of "one size fits all" solutions, drawing on Descriptive Inquiry is especially difficult when pressures abound to narrow our lens, to let a label stand for a person. But that difficulty tells us that it is ever more important to do. To create the particular and spacious knowledge needed for democratic schooling, I return to our foundational commitment in this project to human capacity. We must first hold on to our humanity, and second, we must make that effort in knowledge-making collaboration with others.

CLOSING COMMENTS:
DESCRIPTIVE INQUIRY AS AN ETHICAL ENDEAVOR

Descriptive Inquiry is an exercise tasked with deep ethical import. I quote Robin Kelley (2002) to name one value-laden purpose of this work: "Freeing our imaginations from slavery [to preconceived notions] may be the most difficult struggle we have ever faced. . . . [and] we . . . must do the complicated intellectual work of dreaming and imagining" (p. 62). As the Stoics discovered thousands of years ago, our minds are tricky and elusive. Gaining control of our minds and subsequently our actions, "freeing our imaginations from slavery," is extremely difficult. It can be tempting to label, to dismiss, to not see, because sometimes this path feels easier. Yet going that route risks missing the complexity of the person and, in doing so, missing their humanity. Much is at stake.

Undertaking Descriptive Inquiry serves as an exercise in the Foucauldian sense, engaging us in the difficult struggle and the complicated intellectual work Kelley names. Imagining and dreaming possibilities can run counter to many of the workplace values and expectations to which we are accountable. However, our powers of imagining are a human capacity we need to be in real relationship with children and with the work of educating.

Descriptive Inquiry draws on several sources of energy to power the doing of this complicated yet basic work. Valuing our humanity and the humanity of children and colleagues, generating questions that matter to one's work, and using a process that encourages inclusion and agency, as has been described in this chapter, are the enabling forces.

My many years of doing descriptive work in schools spurred questions of meaning. What has it meant over time to do Descriptive Reviews of Children that ask teachers to look closely at the particularities of a child and to do that descriptively and not judgmentally? What has it meant over time to do Descriptive Reviews of Teaching Practice on issues teachers want to explore with colleagues, and again, staying descriptive and particular and not judging a colleague's work but instead joining with that colleague in real thinking about practice? What has it meant over time to do Descriptive Reviews of Practice with principals of schools focusing on questions they want to explore with their teaching staffs? Each separate Review had meaning for the presenter and the group, but did all the individual pieces add up to anything larger? I intuited that it did, but it wasn't until I read *Practical Wisdom: The Right Way to Do the Right Thing* that I had a frame and language to help me describe how the Descriptive Inquiry work I was doing supported both the development of individual teachers and principals and helped create the kind of school culture that supported individuals' growth. The power of the connection of practical wisdom and Descriptive Inquiry is illustrated in the following chapters.

NOTES

1. The term "paraprofessional" is used in New York City for persons in classrooms who may be otherwise titled "teachers' aides." They provide many types of services in schools—for example, one-on-one support for children designated as needing such services.

2. These are books that have been coded, in this case alphabetically, based on difficulty.

3. A Department of Education project that gave schools an opportunity to apply to develop assessments of children's learning that were in keeping with the schools' beliefs about learning and potentially could be used as alternatives to standardized testing. We asked for and received permission to use Descriptive Inquiry as the means that five small schools could use for this development.

Part II

HOW DESCRIPTIVE INQUIRY LIVED IN THE SCHOOLS

PROMOTING HUMAN DIGNITY WITH CHILDREN AND TEACHERS

CHAPTER 4

City-as-School

Building a Collaborative Culture
Through Descriptive Inquiry

Rachel Seher

Please read the following passage. When you finish, go back and read it again aloud, noting the sound of the words and phrases as well as the meaning.

> Collaborative cultures require broad agreement on educational values, but they also tolerate disagreement and to some extent actively encourage it within limits. Schools characterized by collaborative cultures are also places of hard work, of strong and common commitment, dedication, of collective responsibility, and of a special sense of pride in the institution. . . .
>
> Ironically, disagreement is stronger and more frequent in schools with collaborative cultures than it is elsewhere, as purposes, values and their relationship to practice are discussed. . . . In collaborative cultures, the examination of values and purpose is not a one time event, as when staff participate in writing a Mission Statement. . . . Purposes in collaborative cultures are not entirely idiosyncratic, but gain much of their strength from being developed with and shared by other colleagues.
>
> Collaborative cultures facilitate commitment to change and improvement. They also create communities of teachers who no longer have the dependent relationship to externally imposed change that isolation and uncertainty tend to encourage. . . .
>
> *Within these schools the individual and the group are inherently and simultaneously valued.* Individuals are valued, and so is interdependence. (Fullan & Hargreaves, 1996, pp. 48–49)

What does a close reading of this passage say to you? What words and/ or phrases stand out? What words or phrases are repeated? What meaning comes forward through this repetition? What do you see about the relationship of individual to group in this passage? What argument is conveyed? What is the tone?

This chapter focuses on the process of bringing Descriptive Inquiry to City-as-School, a progressive public high school in New York City, and on how Descriptive Inquiry supported our efforts to become a school with a collaborative culture. I developed this description from my perspective. I was an assistant principal of the school at the time of this story and now serve as principal. I worked closely with our then principal, Alan Cheng, who subsequently transitioned to the superintendency. The decision to bring Descriptive Inquiry to City-as-School was very deliberate on our part. We strongly believed that this unique inquiry process could help us, as a staff, work together more productively, better understand our students, deepen learning and growth for young people and adults, and more fully live our values as a school community.

This chapter focuses on our first year working with Descriptive Inquiry. It shows the evolution of the work and of me as a school leader. The story reveals not only that Descriptive Inquiry helped us build a more collaborative culture in the school but also that I learned how to be a different kind of school leader. I learned how to work with colleagues in a way that was structured, principled, and disciplined, on the one hand, and open, collaborative, and emergent, on the other. I learned how to approach my work as a school leader in a way that fostered a more collaborative culture.

I briefly outline Fullan and Hargreaves's (1996) ideas of collaborative culture and use them as a lens through which to view our work with Descriptive Inquiry at City-as-School. I describe our efforts to foster a collaborative culture before using Descriptive Inquiry and then turn to the process through which we began to use Descriptive Inquiry, focusing on key moments and critical incidents. It is important to note that we have expanded our use of Descriptive Inquiry at City-as-School since introducing it in the 2016–2017 school year.

COLLABORATIVE CULTURES

Since we began working together, a central focus for Alan and me was to build a more "collaborative culture" in the school (Fullan & Hargreaves, 1996). To our chagrin, this work was initially top-down, largely driven by the two of us. The introduction of Descriptive Inquiry contributed significantly to our efforts to broaden understanding of what it takes to develop a collaborative culture and to make this a community effort increasingly led by staff. Four elements of a collaborative culture outlined in the passage above serve as touchstones for reflecting on our work.

First, schools with collaborative cultures are values driven. Second, collaborative cultures not only "tolerate disagreement" but "actively encourage it" within "broad agreement on educational values" (Fullan & Hargreaves, 1996, p. 48). Third, purposes and values are not "idiosyncratic" but "gain strength from being developed with and shared by colleagues" (p. 49). Lastly, collaborative cultures encourage a positive relationship to change.

Fullan and Hargreaves contrast this to a culture of "individualism," which is "a state of professional isolation" (p. 38). In such a culture, "teachers and principals become so professionally estranged in their workplace isolation that they neglect each other. They do not often compliment, support and acknowledge each other's positive efforts" (Rosenholtz, p. 107, as quoted in Fullan & Hargreaves, 1996, p. 39). Teachers "learn little from their colleagues" and "are not in a position to experiment and improve," and student learning, in turn, suffers (p. 39).

Fullan and Hargreaves (1996) also contrast a collaborative culture with one of "comfortable collaboration." Comfortable collaboration takes "bounded rather than extended, forms . . . in the sense of not extending into classroom settings" (p. 55). Bounded collaboration "restricts the extent to which teachers can inquire and advise one another about their practice" and "keeps the tougher questions about their work and how to improve it off the agenda" (p. 55). It remains at the "comfortable level" of celebrating, supporting, coordinating, and exchanging and rarely reaches into inquiring, questioning, criticizing, and dialoguing with respect to the "principles or ethics of practice" (pp. 55–56). Comfortable collaboration results in little instructional improvement.

CITY-AS-SCHOOL[1]

City-as-School is a unique, values-driven school with a focus on reengaging older adolescents in formal education through experiential learning. It was founded in 1972 as a school-without-walls and is a member of the New York Performance Standards Consortium. All students participate in credit-bearing internships for half of the school week and take classes that build to graduation portfolio pieces, known as performance-based assessment tasks (PBATs), for the other half.[2] Core values of the school that have been articulated in various documents and verbally over time are freedom, trust, and mutual responsibility.

The stated purpose of the school is to provide exciting learning opportunities in a highly supportive environment so that young people who have disconnected from their previous school settings will reengage with formal education, earn a high school diploma, and pursue meaningful postsecondary plans. We serve approximately 570 youth ages 16–21 who come to us from across the city. Our student population is racially, culturally, and economically diverse and mirrors the makeup of New York City. Some students hail from highly competitive selective schools that they experienced as pressure cookers, others from large comprehensive high schools that did not serve them well, some from small schools that nevertheless enact a more traditional educational model, and many others from outside of the New York City Department of Education, including independent schools, home-schooling, and mental health settings. All of our students encountered a significant obstacle along their path in high school, ranging from the mode of education itself to personal and familial crises, such as illness, economic insecurity, housing instability, and childcare responsibilities. Our physical school building sits in Manhattan's West Village, and students travel to us for class days but can choose internships in their home boroughs.

The school staff consists of approximately 50 full-time educators, including 26 advisers, 14 internship coordinators, 7 guidance counselors/social workers, 3 career and college counselors, 1 full-time restorative justice coordinator, 8 support staff members responsible for daily student outreach, and a 4-member leadership team. Internship coordinators are licensed teachers who facilitate internships, and advisers are classroom teachers who serve as academic advisers. Each student is paired with an adviser who supports them through their time at City-as-School and sees them through graduation. Students meet with their advisers in a group once per week and check in individually often. Each student is also connected with a guidance counselor or a social worker as well as a career and college counselor.

Unlike many other public schools in New York City, staff stay at City-as-School, and we benefit from having an intergenerational, multicultural staff with diverse experiences and interests. Alan hired me shortly after he became principal, and we worked together closely, especially in the area of instructional leadership. At the time, most of the staff had been at the school longer than either of us and in some cases significantly longer. A number of faculty members were within retirement range and did, in fact, retire after the new contract incentivized retirement. The founding principal, Fred Koury, was an early leader in the teachers' union and active in the civil rights movement, and our two longest-time staff members knew and were hired by Fred. Staff longevity and organizational history is therefore an important context for the story of how we used Descriptive Inquiry to change our school culture for the better.

BEFORE DESCRIPTIVE INQUIRY

A practically wise leader must enact values in a context-appropriate manner. As described earlier, Alan and I initially took a directive approach to fostering a collaborative culture at City-as-School. When we first began working together, the professional culture had elements of individualism and comfortable collaboration, as the examples below illustrate. To facilitate culture change, Alan and I initially relied on our bureaucratic power, knowledge as educators, and relationships with colleagues. We made significant inroads to foster a more collaborative culture, but the work could go only so far because it was driven by the two of us.

When I first joined the staff, Alan and I devoted our first six months together to visiting classes and internship seminars and having individual conversations with colleagues about their goals, priorities, and practice. We learned that some faculty members sought to engage students in challenging and interesting project work, some used textbooks and gave tests, and others simply required students to complete enough worksheets or journal entries to justify awarding credit for the learning experience. We also noticed that some staff were more inclined to build relationships with students and their families than others. We believed that such variation undermined our mission as a highly supportive experiential learning school and member of the Consortium and, ultimately, the quality of the student experience and learning.

In collaborative communities, shared vision is not top-down or simply dictated from an external mission but evolves from work in the community. At the time, faculty members did not have many opportunities to work toward a shared vision or improve their practice. Teachers spoke informally about teaching, students, and many other topics. Whole-faculty meetings occurred every other week and often involved announcements and business items, birthdays and other celebrations, and the coordination of events like the school's 40th-anniversary party. In other words, there was a lot of "comfortable collaboration" in place.

On the other hand, there were no established systems for problem solving together. We did not have teacher team meetings at the time. The advisory and internship departments met bimonthly and had a similar focus as faculty meetings, except at the level of the department. In the advisory department, I witnessed firsthand harmful and unproductive conflict. Members of the department made hurtful comments toward colleagues, did not follow the agenda created by the department chair, and verbalized complaints about various aspects of the school life and leadership. A longtime staff member described advisory department meetings as follows: "When I first started teaching here, I felt like an abused child in meetings. People would curse at each other and take each other down. Then, I accepted it. Now, I wait for the crescendo, when someone goes off. It's the most interesting part of the meeting."

Some staff members wanted deeper, more meaningful collaboration, and others were comfortable with the status quo. A teacher with 30 years of experience expressed appreciation following an observation that first year, saying that it was the first time she could remember someone seeing her class and then talking with her about her teaching. In contrast, another staff member expressed pride that she had convinced a previous principal to do away with weekly faculty meetings, which had resulted in the bimonthly meetings.

Regardless of the staff's mixed opinions, Alan and I agreed that professional learning and building a culture of collaboration should be our focus and worked toward that goal. We began by identifying a yearly instructional focus based on input from our superintendent, which was a requirement for us as a school in the Department of Education. In our first 3 years working together, Alan and I decided to make project-based learning our instructional focus in order to foster curricular and pedagogical coherence. We believed that we needed a schoolwide framework for learning that reflected our identity as an experiential learning school and member of the Consortium. We also believed that greater coherence in this area would benefit our students. Alan and I concentrated on project-based learning as the particular focus in light of our use of PBATs. We introduced this to the staff and then added weekly faculty meetings during which we led several sessions on project-based learning. We did the same on full professional development days. We also reinforced project-based learning through classroom observations and individual work with teachers.

This decision met with resistance from some faculty, including active members of our United Federation of Teachers chapter, who argued that teachers should be able to teach however they wanted; even faculty who already used project-based learning argued for individual autonomy. Alan and I maintained that we were a unique school with a unique vision and that our curricula and pedagogy should reflect that. He and I also maintained that working within a unified framework for learning would benefit students by deepening learning in classrooms and internships and improving the quality of PBATs. We held voluntary meetings in which we discussed this with faculty, but we never reached consensus.

Alan and I continued to reinforce project-based learning over our first few years together and explicitly hired teachers who wanted to work within that framework. We also asked department chairs to integrate opportunities to share curriculum, student work, and promising practice into meeting times. By the end of those first few years, all classes and internships built to final projects that were aligned to Consortium rubrics. At present, longtime faculty still vary in terms of skill and commitment to project-based learning, and a few still rely on teacher-focused, direct instruction primarily and worksheets. However, all try to use project-based learning to some degree.

In addition to supporting project-based learning, Alan and I reinforced collegial meeting participation. We regularly joined advisory and internship department meetings, reviewed meeting agendas with department chairs, and met with faculty who did not follow the agenda, used hurtful language, or refused to attend (or stormed out) of meetings. This increased the likelihood that faculty followed the meeting agenda created by the department chair and reduced the use of hurtful comments during meeting time.

We also formed an English teaching team that I facilitated in order to create a space for that group of teachers to look at student work and talk about practice in their subject area. The English Regents is the only exam required in Consortium schools, and our students struggled with it at the time. This led to great stress for students and teachers, since the exam is a graduation requirement. The English team began to meet weekly to develop curriculum and share practices for supporting students in reading and writing. We also examined student work. I participated in the meetings as an English teacher, facilitator, and school leader. Teachers reported that they valued these team meetings as a learning space. Based on this, we expanded teaching team meetings to all subject areas the following year. We eventually identified teacher leaders to facilitate the teams and gave them copies of the book *The Power of Protocols* (McDonald, 2003), and often used similar protocols from the National School Reform Faculty (NSRF) and School Reform Initiative (SRI) in meetings ourselves. Eventually all teaching teams and departments came to meet weekly, and teacher leaders facilitated the meetings. We also formed a professional development committee, facilitated by Alan and me, to guide the use of our Friday morning faculty meeting time.

This early work felt essential in terms of establishing a basic foundation of pedagogical coherence and collegiality, but we wanted to move toward a collaborative culture with deep roots in the faculty, not one that was imposed by the formal school leadership. To move closer to a true collaborative culture, we needed to develop our and the school's capacity to engage in disagreement productively.

STARTING DESCRIPTIVE INQUIRY

I learned about Descriptive Inquiry my fourth year at City-as-School. I had read Cecelia's (Traugh, 2005) essay, "Trusting the Possibilities: Giving Voice to Vito's Ideas" and immediately made a strong connection. In the piece, Cecelia describes how she worked with teachers at Central Park East 1 to use Descriptive Inquiry to show the value of project time, a defining practice of the school with indirect and nuanced effects on student learning, in a larger climate marked by bureaucratic legibility and control in which standardized test scores were valued.

I brought the article to our subject team facilitators and shared it with them. They were intrigued to see another values-driven progressive school use Descriptive Inquiry to sustain and protect defining practices in the context of a larger culture of bureaucratization and standardization. Based on this initial interest, we explored some of Carini's writings as a group of teaching team facilitators and identified ways that we might use Descriptive Inquiry. The team facilitators expressed interest in the idea of a Descriptive Review of the Child and also in looking at student work and teacher practice through a descriptive lens. The idea of coming to know our students better and then using what we learned to make decisions about educational practice appealed to me and also to members of the team facilitators group.

That summer, I immersed myself in Descriptive Inquiry. I attended the weeklong Summer Institute on Descriptive Inquiry and read all of Carini's writings. Alan and I met with Cecelia at the end of that summer to discuss ways that she might support us in using Descriptive Inquiry to deepen professional learning and collaboration. Cecelia immediately helped us negotiate a significant tension around our school's instructional focus. That summer, our superintendent had offered a summer workshop on "cognitive engagement" using literature on "flow" and materials from the Coalition of Essential Schools on "using one's mind well." Based on this, Alan and I had made cognitive engagement the coming year's instructional focus. I shared with Cecelia that the idea of "using one's mind well" appealed to me but that I worried that the term "cognitive engagement" would seem removed from the language of the school and that the faculty would reject it. Cecelia agreed and suggested using the term "meaningful work" instead, noting that people are cognitively engaged and use their minds well when involved in meaningful work. She also suggested including a Recollection in the facilitators' retreat on a time when we, as teachers, had engaged students in meaningful work. The purpose was to illuminate the qualities of meaningful work and help us understand it better. Cecelia also suggested looking at the concepts of "meaningful work" and "cognitive engagement" alongside each other so that we could identify similarities and points of divergence. This made sense to me as a way to negotiate possible tensions between the external and local, and I quickly agreed.[3]

By the end of this conversation, I was convinced that Cecelia could help us work with the staff of City-as-School more effectively and in ways that reflected my values and that Descriptive Inquiry could help us, as a whole staff, do the same. I was convinced that she could help us use Descriptive Inquiry to build a more collaborative culture. She had quickly reframed what we, in the school, experienced as a conflict between the school leadership and staff to an external tension around which we could and should work together productively. She also offered Descriptive Inquiry as a way for us to do this; it could help us have meaningful professional conversations, build more collegial relations, and better ground our decisions in a diversity of perspectives within broad consensus around values and purpose.

Cecelia agreed to lead a 2-day retreat on Descriptive Inquiry with our teacher leaders. The formal school leadership, teaching team facilitators, and professional development committee members would all participate. We agreed to introduce key Descriptive Processes: Reflection on a Word, Recollection, Review of Visual Work, and Review of Written Work. We would then close the retreat by generating ideas as to how we might use Descriptive Inquiry to deepen our work with one another in support of our students in "meaningful work."

The facilitators' retreat went well, and we were able to move forward in using Descriptive Inquiry with the whole staff. At Cecelia's suggestion, we decided to begin the work by using Descriptive Inquiry during our faculty meeting time. During this time, faculty would be part of study groups that would meet every 3 weeks and use Descriptive Inquiry to focus on our students and their work. We asked all teacher leaders to co-facilitate these study groups and participate in weekly planning meetings. Alan and I facilitated the planning meetings, with Cecelia joining us once a month to guide the planning, make suggestions, and support us in using Descriptive Processes. Cecelia also provided guidance and insights to Alan and me through regular phone calls.

For the first half of that first year, we formed study groups around particular students. Alan and I worked with Cecelia to plan this first round of study groups and then brought our plan to the facilitators to refine. The students were identified through an algorithm that Alan created, which prioritized attendance (meaning the students had attended school enough that staff would know them) and that also ensured that each faculty member would be in a group focused on a student with whom they had worked. In the groups, we took turns bringing work from our focus student that we examined using a Review of Work to learn more about the student as a person, thinker, and maker and then reflect on the implications for our practice, both in terms of working with that particular student and in general. Halfway through our first year using Descriptive Inquiry, we shifted from student-focused study groups to practice-focused study groups. Doing so was an example of being responsive, adapting to a challenge that arose with our initial work. First, even though Alan's algorithm identified students with relatively high attendance for our school, not all of them had produced enough work for teachers to bring. Additionally, students choose a new program of classes and internships at the start of every 8- to 10-week cycle, and most of us had worked with our focus student the previous cycle when the groups were formed but no longer worked directly with the student. Perhaps most importantly, the lack of choice for staff in identifying students and choosing which group to join diminished investment.

We closed out the student-focused study groups halfway through that year by sharing what we learned about our focus students, ourselves, and our practice. Cecelia led this process with the facilitators first, and then the facilitators led the same process with small groups of faculty during a Friday morning faculty meeting. Each group had at least one member from each of the original student-focused study groups.

Cecelia then led the facilitators in a Review of the notes from the faculty small groups. Showcasing our increasingly collaborative relationship with our staff, Alan and I participated alongside the facilitators. We identified themes, patterns, and important insights as well as topics or questions of practice that emerged. Cecelia suggested that we re-form the study groups around the questions about practice, and we (the facilitators with Alan and me) worked to identify, clarify, and refine the questions of practice. This allowed us to form study groups around questions that faculty members had initially surfaced by looking at student work. In this way, we were moving away from top-down reform to include teachers in goal setting. As facilitators, we synthesized the questions and articulated them in a way that would connect back to our instructional focus—meaningful work—while still capturing faculty thinking and learning. Each facilitator then chose a specific question on which to lead a study group, and faculty members chose which study group to join. As such, we were increasingly able to provide guidance as leaders in a manner that honored teacher voice.

The questions of practice were all about meaningful work and fell into two categories: (1) student work and meaning-making and (2) pedagogical process. In the first category, faculty asked questions such as: How can we help students discover meaning in formal writing (e.g., essays, research papers)? What do we already do that helps school-resistant teenagers find meaning in their work? How can we build on this? Thinking about pedagogical process, faculty asked, for example, how they could help students engage in meaningful inquiry and find meaning in what they learn through inquiry.

When the facilitators reported back at our weekly planning meetings, they said investment in the new study groups was much higher among faculty and also the facilitators themselves. As one person noted, "The energy has shifted." Faculty shared work more eagerly and found the Reviews more useful. We were able to hold one more share at the end of the year during our faculty retreat, and the themes and questions from this informed our professional development planning and inquiry work the following year.

This way of working as a facilitators group and a faculty was much more collaborative in the sense used by Fullan and Hargreaves (1996) than previously. We had more successfully made decisions based on shared values, resolved conflicts productively, made changes together, and valued the individual and the whole. We also found productive ways to disagree and then find common ground. Alan and I did not insist that we maintain the student-focused study groups, and the teacher facilitators did not insist that we abandon Descriptive Inquiry. We also came to agreement about the questions of practice and connected them to a schoolwide instructional focus; within that, both facilitators and faculty chose their question.

As usual, we closed that year with a June Faculty Retreat; however, this retreat was qualitatively different from previous years'. In the past, Alan and I had co-planned and then facilitated the retreat. This year, however, the retreat built on our inquiry work, and Cecelia worked with Alan, me, and the teacher leaders group to plan. We met three times to plan with Cecelia's support and ultimately agreed to use the retreat to close out the study groups from Cycles 3 and 4 and collect threads—themes and questions—to use as the foundation for the following year's study groups. The teacher leaders also wanted to ensure that lighthearted fun was included alongside the work they needed to do. We agreed to a three-part agenda:

- Community building with an ice-breaking activity,
- Closing out the study groups, and
- Collecting staff ideas and feedback about professional development.

Showcasing our increasingly collaborative environment, we also agreed to divide up the planning. Alan, Cecelia, and I would plan the inquiry portion, and different teacher leaders would plan different community-building activities. We all brought drafts of agendas to the whole group for input and revision and then collaboratively worked to implement the plan the day of the retreat.

For the inquiry portion, we again used small groups with members from each inquiry group. The day of the retreat, each study group had a chance to meet to review their notes from the semester and to identify key ideas, which were then shared in *jigsaw groups*.[4] Finally, each of the jigsaw groups shared two or three key takeaways and implications for next year's professional development time. We sat in a whole-faculty circle for this portion, and after each jigsaw group reported back, faculty members were able to add and build on the ideas.

I took on the role of chair. I took handwritten notes and reflected back themes, patterns, and important ideas and questions. I compiled the notes into a summary that I shared with the whole faculty that evening and that we returned to the following year. Of note, my role had morphed from the beginning of the year. I was no longer dictating the goals but synthesizing what the teachers had identified. Further, in taking and then sharing notes, I was making transparent exactly where these ideas came from and giving opportunities for others to add any themes I might have missed.

This shift toward a more democratic community was immediately apparent. The whole-faculty circle at the end of the retreat was the first time we had a circle like this with equitable participation and productive conflict in my time at City-as-School. People took turns speaking, built on one another's ideas, and disagreed collegially. It was also the first time that we left a June faculty retreat with ideas that most faculty seemed invested in pursuing the following year. For their part, the teacher leaders seemed confident and comfortable as they facilitated their study groups and jigsaws. Faculty even thanked and hugged us after, saying that this retreat felt very "grounded" and that they appreciated that we built on the year's ongoing work.

Based on the June 2016–2017 retreat, Alan and I worked with teacher leaders to plan and facilitate our first three professional development days in September 2017–2018. In the interest of transparency and highlighting the teachers' ideas, we projected the notes from the June retreat each morning and indicated exactly which portion of the notes had inspired the session. We continued to use Descriptive Processes each day. This represents a shift toward greater faculty involvement in generating ideas for and leading our start-of-the-year professional development that was made possible through our inquiry work.

LESSONS FOR SCHOOL LEADERSHIP

At the time of publication, we continue to use Descriptive Inquiry at City-as-School. Our practice has deepened and our use of Descriptive Processes has expanded exponentially. We continue to meet in faculty study groups every 3 weeks and use Descriptive Process to explore specific aspects of our practice. Fullan and Hargreaves (1996) argue that in collaborative cultures, disagreement occurs more, not less. Showcasing our increased capacity to take on difficult issues, we are now using the processes to navigate culturally responsive pedagogy and racial literacy. This topic emerged from past faculty study groups and faculty retreats during which we used Descriptive Processes. Our teaching teams also use Descriptive Inquiry to examine student and teacher work, and we use Descriptive Processes in all of our leadership and committee meetings. Through Descriptive Inquiry, we have examined the process through which students choose internships and classes, our policies and practices toward substance use, and the ongoing challenge of student attendance. We have also begun to create a student survey so that we can learn from our students about their experience with specific aspects of our program and make adjustments and additions so as to provide as much support as possible. In other words, through Descriptive Inquiry we are consistently able to take hard and honest looks at our teaching, our students, and ourselves to better support student development.

We have a much more collaborative culture in our school. Values are clearer and more universally held. We used Descriptive Processes to create a one-page overview of the City-as-School model that has general consensus among the staff, and we also work within a set of community agreements during our faculty meeting time. Disagreements and tensions inevitably surface because we are a values-driven school filled with staff who care, but we have productive ways of handling them.

As Cecelia will argue in Chapter 7, any discussion of democracy must include an exploration of leadership. As a school leader, I have become much more comfortable and confident largely because of our work with Cecelia to use Descriptive Inquiry. I am better able to (a) attend to the needs and ideas of a group because Descriptive Inquiry provides a structured and egalitarian way of working, and (b) sit with conflict and tensions because I recognize that these can be productive sources of growth now that we have Descriptive Inquiry. I have also become a better listener and am able to better surface questions and ideas from a group and to take in multiple perspectives and hold them alongside each other. This allows me to better work with groups and move them toward decision for action.

A collaborative culture matters at all times in schools, but the strength of a school culture is often tested in times of adversity. I write this chapter on April 18, 2020, in the midst of New York City school building closures due to the coronavirus pandemic and can see from this vantage point that our work with Descriptive Inquiry has laid the foundation for the entire faculty to manage the transition to emergency online teaching in ways that are collaborative, inquiry based, and student focused. All of the work we have done with Descriptive Inquiry to build our community has, of course, increased trust and habits of listening among the staff, to which I attribute our ability to handle this current crisis as collaboratively as we have.

ADDENDUM

Reading Rachel's description of our work together has led me, Cecelia, to think about what that work has been, what I have contributed to the school's growth, and what I have learned from it. Although my role is the focus of Chapter 9, I want to emphasize a few elements here. First, working in this high school has been different from working in elementary schools. For example, while very committed to and interested in their students, doing Descriptive Reviews, the centerpiece of work in elementary schools, has not been, for many reasons, a go-to process. We have not yet found a way to collaboratively build a Review among teachers who know the student or bring the student into a Review. I think doing so would build the sense that all students belong to all teachers, a feeling that, as showcased in the next two chapters, exists in the elementary schools that do descriptive work.

I am also interested to see described here how my work with City-as-School has primarily focused on building the leadership of both principals and teachers. I don't work directly with all faculty as I do in the other schools in which I work. What I do is work with Rachel to help her learn how to frame and reframe issues and questions so that they can be entered from various vantage points and are generative of discussion, and I do inquiry sessions with teacher-leader groups, using processes they can, in turn, use confidently with their groups. This has enabled a gradual release of authority, giving teachers more shaping power over their work. This process is not so different from what happened over time in other schools, as they created PD committees that shaped the inquiry and other PD work they did. However, the starting places have been different. At City-as-School, Rachel and I began with the leadership and my contributions focused on the teacher-leader groups; at other schools, though the principals made the invitation, my work was largely developing Reviews with teachers. No matter the entry point, as the work deepened, teachers contributed more strongly to school decision making.

NOTES

1. Each of the schools featured is a progressive mission-driven school with commitments to inclusion. To give readers a sense of this, we've described City-as-School and Central Park East 1 in depth.

2. The 38 Consortium high schools have a standardized testing waiver and use PBATs in lieu of NYS Regents Exam as high school graduation requirements. The PBATs in all the schools are aligned to common rubrics, and teachers meet for moderation studies to norm their assessment each year. Consortium PBATs "meet or exceed" the state Regents Standards. See www.performanceassessment.org.

3. An elaborated version of this story is told by Rachel in Chapter 7.

4. A participation structure in which people first work in small groups. Then, they are redistributed, with one member of each original group placed in a new group. In this way, the work of different small groups can be efficiently shared throughout the larger community.

CHAPTER 5

Curricular Values

Exploring the Place of Children, Teachers, and the Culture of School in Building Curriculum

Cara E. Furman and Cecelia E. Traugh

We begin with a Descriptive Review of Work. Identify a piece of student work that surprised or drew your attention and that you currently have available to look at. Begin with first impressions, what is your initial, unguarded or perhaps guarded, response to this work? Now describe. If it's a piece of writing, read aloud, then paraphrase, then focus on details in the text such as sentence structure, punctuation, word choice, sounds. If an image, think about placement on the page, colors used, the shapes and thickness of markings or brushstrokes, the markings themselves and how they interact. Try to avoid naming what you see. For example, you might say, "A round circle with two dots in the middle is placed on top of a straight line" as opposed to your inference that this is a face on a neck. After describing, what inferences might you draw about this student as a maker? What about this student does describing this piece of work make more visible to you? What questions does the work bring up? Finally, how does this piece of work relate to your teaching and the curriculum? Do you see the student inspired by the curriculum, growing their capacity within or alongside it? Was this work in opposition to or in spite of the curriculum? For example, later in this chapter Cara describes an exuberant image a child doodled on the back of a writing prompt that contrasted with his rather flat and unenthusiastic response to the prompt itself.

This chapter focuses on curriculum, knowledge and recognition of the child and the teacher, and how the school's curricular value stance can influence its content and shape. Of note, we use the term "curriculum" broadly to refer to a course of study. We are thinking about the shared curriculum developed for a school, grade, and class; individualized curriculum that has been modified or created for or by a child; and even the hidden curriculum—what is being taught in school that may not be intended, planned, or directly acknowledged. Key is the recognition that all curriculum reflects values and that working to understand the value choices individuals and schools express through curriculum is basic to care of the teacher self.

The connection between Descriptive Inquiry and curriculum development came up throughout the interviews. In each school, the teachers were curriculum developers, though variation occurred even within a particular school. In some cases, teachers were grounded in a preestablished published curriculum such as Investigations (TERC, 2008) or Lucy Calkins's (2003) Writing Workshop Model and modified based on limitations in the content overall as well as the needs of individual classes and students. For example, the Earth School used the Investigations math program, but teachers found that it moved too fast between lessons and didn't have a robust approach to numerical development. Responding to this, teachers worked in grade teams and sometimes as a whole staff to integrate other programs and also built on their own math understandings to supplement.

Teachers were also responsible for creating curricula. Again at the Earth School, each grade followed an integrated social studies and science curriculum referred to as Core. Although content was loosely based on state standards, grade teams developed these curricula largely based on their own research into a topic.

Regardless of who developed the curricula, modifying it to support individual and/or groups of children was necessary and challenging work. Speaking to the challenge, during Cara's masters in elementary education, she wrote a child study—close analyses of children based in part on Descriptive Inquiry. At the conclusion of the paper, she was to say how she would use what she knew to teach the child. Cara, frankly, didn't have a lot to say. Her grade reflected both her ability to describe and her inability to apply her understandings. A few years later, when she was the faculty member assigning this work, she found her students also struggled with this final and crucial link. But now, as the professor, she was uncomfortable docking points, believing that the link between description and methods is not intuitive and that she had not taught it well.

Some of the challenges determining how to adapt and develop curriculum around an individual child can be attributed to being a new teacher without a host of methods. Yet, in our work as teacher educators, we often find teachers who can talk in-depth about individual children, but this knowledge doesn't make its way into their planning. Sometimes the disconnect happens because teachers lack the space in their schedules or the autonomy to follow what they know about children. That said, even in the schools featured in this book where teachers have that freedom, it is not always productively exercised. One issue is that teachers often consider curriculum to be relatively fixed. Responding to individuals or groups of children based on observation tends to occur only in small adaptations. Put differently, the curriculum is tweaked in response to the child as opposed to the children's needs leading the curriculum. Further, though much has been written on the value of developing curriculum (Meier, 2015), the links between curriculum and studying individual classes and students are not always explicated.

To look at how Descriptive Inquiry helps teachers develop curriculum that is more deeply responsive to students' interests, cultures, and ways of thinking and learning, we first describe Cara's journey to showcase how Descriptive Inquiry helped her modify her writing curriculum.

We then turn to the principal interviews with Alison, Jane, Judith, and Michelle to explore some key themes in how the principals saw Descriptive Inquiry supporting important values of their schools in curriculum development. After, we describe how faculty at City-as-School are learning to use Descriptive Inquiry to make their curricular culture more fully reflect their student body of color to better enact values of inclusion both for students and faculty of color. Finally, we close by describing how studying children, curriculum, and values as a community through Descriptive Inquiry affirms both students and teachers.

INQUIRIES INTO WRITING CURRICULUM—CARA'S STORY

In my second year at the Earth School, the faculty launched an exploration into the writing curriculum. For the previous 2 years, professional development had focused on many different areas: assessment, inclusion, implementing Responsive Classroom (Anderson, 2015) schoolwide, improvement in math instruction, and other subthemes. Reviews from the previous year had looked at how to assess children more holistically and how to support children who stood outside of the norm of a given classroom. Typically, though not exclusively, these were children whose strengths were not visible using more traditional assessment measures. At the close of my first year, staff expressed interest in focusing professional development narrowly and thematically.

In Chapter 4, Rachel describes how teachers increasingly took ownership over professional development. When I came to the Earth School, a number of systems enabled teacher voice. A biweekly planning committee made up of Cecelia, the principal, and a number of staff members set much of the professional development agenda. Additionally, the rest of the staff frequently voted on topics, filled out surveys, and made suggestions informally. Staff influenced what they studied, the resources they drew on (such as books and consultants), and how they studied (Descriptive Inquiry, guided exploration of materials, direct instruction).

The year before the study of writing launched, many teachers requested that we focus on a content area and we were given a survey on topics that could be addressed the following year. In addition to teacher interest, this focus also shows the intersection between citywide policy and school. Liberated from following the mandated Reading and Writing Project curriculum, some teachers continued to follow that curriculum whereas others were beginning to experiment with different approaches in their classes. Many felt that writing instruction could be improved and were eager to start experimenting now that we had the freedom to do so.

Additionally, as referenced in Chapter 3, the school had recently entered into a network with other progressive public schools and Cecelia to develop interim assessments, Design Your Own Assessment, as part of an initiative launched by the city to promote school autonomy. Through this group, schools developed and implemented assessments that reflected their values and were able to opt out of citywide interim assessments. A focus of this group at the time was on how to assess student writing in a manner that fit with the values of the network of schools.

At the Earth School, the look at writing went in a variety of directions. Over the summer teachers read Ron Berger's (2003) *An Ethic of Excellence: Building a Culture of Craftsmanship With Students* to think broadly about the multistep process of creating meaningful work. To develop a culture of craftsmanship before launching the writing curriculum, all classes began the year with students creating self-portraits, projects worked on over many days (and in some classes weeks) and revised (sometimes in different mediums).

In one of the first staff meetings, we did a Reflection on the Word *writing*. This allowed teachers to consider and share the connotations that we associated with writing. As we went around sharing, teachers also saw the range of ways that our peers experienced writing. As I describe more below, this proved powerful. As someone who loved to write, I got to state my love and hear from colleagues who felt very differently.

Teachers then engaged in small inquiry groups (another component of PD requested the year before). For example, one group engaged in a writing workshop. My group focused on how we were approaching linguistic and cultural diversity with writing. We began by reading articles and sharing how group members' cultural backgrounds influenced our experience of school. At some point, the group documented what writing looked like in our classrooms over the course of many weeks. By doing this, I saw that writing occurred constantly throughout my day. Math, though, came up less frequently. In reading my colleagues' work, I had a better sense of what my students had experienced in previous years and would be doing going forward. I saw that where for me writing was so intuitive and easy to incorporate everywhere, for others other disciplines were better integrated. I was particularly struck by what writing looked like in the pre-K classroom since I had the least experience with this grade level.

As a school, the teachers looked at children's work samples, pre-K through 5th grade, in small groups. We implemented a schoolwide writing prompt and assessed what this looked like through the different grade levels. As talk of standards swirled in the national conversation, we began to identify what writing development looked like for us. A few years later,

really neat idea!

this was expanded on and formalized as teachers embarked on creating a continuum for each subject area. Looking at different grade levels and discussing expectations helped me to see my work as a small part within a whole-school commitment to writing. With this sensibility, I became less worried about covering everything and could focus more on skills and content appropriate to my grade span.

Additionally, as a whole school, we did Reviews of Written Work as well as artwork throughout the year. Through Descriptive Reviews of the Child, we also investigated how our writing curriculum affected individual children in our care. As part of this yearlong study, Alison asked me to do a Descriptive Review of the Child.

MY EXPERIENCE OF THE YEAR AND THE REVIEW

As noted, to launch the study of writing, we Reflected on the Word *writing* to unpack people's associations. Though this proved helpful, I was somewhat irreverent during this Reflection. I spent time I should have been writing about writing, passing notes with a grade-level colleague whom I knew didn't like to write. Reflecting now on this response, I see that I acted this way because I felt uncomfortable. Writing was something I treasured and felt confident about. I had studied creative writing in college and had taken all my electives in graduate school in literacy-related courses. Whenever possible, I pursued professional development related to literacy instruction. Though a few of my grade-level colleagues, including the one I passed notes with, treated me as a resource in this area, I felt that my strengths were largely invisible in the school.

At the time that we launched our schoolwide exploration of writing, I also felt like I was always pushing my colleagues and the school to take a more radical stance on curriculum, and I was uncomfortable in this role. Finally, my sense was that we were studying writing because it was an area of teaching where everyone needed help. This upset me because I had put a lot of time into my development as a writer and writing teacher, and into my curriculum. In full disclosure, I wanted recognition for my expertise.

The schoolwide study of writing continued with me feeling on the margins. I remember placing the children's writing samples on a continuum *how to make* across the grades and, again, feeling left out. I wanted my class's work sam-*sure teachers* ples to be part of the collection because I wanted people to see what my *feel validated* class was doing. I was proud of their writing and somewhat hurt when I *in the process* wasn't solicited for samples. I also felt initially frustrated by the continuum. It struck me as a way of solidifying norms instead of expanding what could be possible. I was confident my students were doing good work and yet, because I had deviated so much from the curriculum others were following, I didn't see on the continuum much work that represented my teaching.

Finally, I found it stressful to implement the schoolwide writing prompt. As with all formal assessments, this went against more typical collaborative practices in my classroom. One child's response stood out in particular. As described at the start of this chapter, without much passion, he had answered the prompt in the space provided. Then, on the back he had drawn an elaborate picture. I felt his true work was on the back—a metaphor of the degree to which the standard prompt and much of the curriculum didn't speak to his aptitudes.

I share these negative responses for a few reasons: first, to highlight, as we do throughout this book, that these were not perfect schools, nor did Descriptive Inquiry make me a perfect colleague. Collaborative cultures are thorny places with disagreement, and disagreement, no matter how necessary in a democracy, can be very uncomfortable. On the other hand, the processes gave me a place to air my feelings and, in doing so, held space for disagreement.

Second, if making one's words and deeds visible is part, as Arendt (1998) argues, of being human, going unnoticed can be dehumanizing. As I describe below, the chance to share a Descriptive Review of the Child was both beneficial to my teaching of writing but also exactly what I needed as a community member. In fact, when Alison asked if I would do a Review, I was secretly thrilled. Her asking itself felt like a recognition.

As noted, I was a confident and largely successful teacher of writing. Based on my own early experiences as a writer and an unusually strong methods class during my master's program (thank you, Stephanie Jones), I had a lot of ideas and methods to draw from. I had already grappled with my writing curriculum quite a bit. My first year, I had moved away from the citywide curriculum because of students' resistance (see Furman, 2017, for a detailed discussion of this), and I had developed practices I felt good about.

I chose William because I was somewhat concerned about his current writing abilities. William had a number of skills that lent themselves to writing, such as oral communication and spelling capacities (Ray & Cleveland, 2004; Ray & Glover, 2008) but didn't produce many products. What really concerned me was not William's capacity but that when he went to 3rd grade, in the context of high-stakes testing, his lack of productivity could lead the teacher to discount William as a student. I also worried that a low test score could hurt his prospects for his choice of middle school. Another teacher, Laryza Martell, had done a Review earlier that year in which she described how a child participated in literacy in unconventional ways. Laryza's Review had influenced and inspired me—expanding my understanding of capacity and literacy. In writing about William, I was interested in what he could do as a writer and how his capacity might further expand the conversation at the Earth School about literacy and ability. To prepare for my Review, I wrote extensively about William. Laryza had brought video into her Review for us to analyze. Alison suggested that because William produced very little on paper, video might give us more insights into his process than a work sample. I had found Laryza's use of video transformative, and Alison's recommendation that I use video proved to be an excellent suggestion.

I brought my writing and video to meet with Cecelia. Though Cecelia had worked with the Earth School for many years, this was the first time that we actually spoke together. During our meeting, Cecelia listened to my description and my concerns. From this meeting, we determined what data I would share and how I would share it. As discussed in Chapter 3, an Anecdotal Recollection is a process in which, typically, everyone shares a story related to the prompt and then the chair pulls common themes. Because my history as a writer was so central to my teaching and my relationship with William, we decided I would begin my Review in an unusual way. I would start with my own history as a writer—an Anecdotal Recollection of sorts.

Though we talk about Cecelia's role as chair in depth in Chapter 9, it is important to note here that Cecelia's deep understanding of the processes and confidence using them was what allowed us to diverge from the typical format of a Review. Fluent in the processes and the philosophical underpinnings, she could pull from them smoothly and adapt them, and with her there, others were willing to consider experimentation. Her experience supported both the unusual Recollection and the use of video.

The last piece of data was a Descriptive Review based on over a year of working with William. Writing and then later reading the Review of William was a pleasure. His charisma, humor, energy, and strengths made it highly enjoyable to visit him through this process. As Cecelia argues in Chapter 3, a power of Descriptive Inquiry is that it is framed around questions as opposed to problems. From the data and my concerns, Cecelia and I pulled together our focus questions:

- What other activities could be done to develop William's writing?
- How does one make space for a student like William, who so powerfully resists a classroom model that seems to be working for the majority?
- What constitutes being a writer? Can you be a writer without being able to "write" words on paper?

The questions speak to the range of concerns I had as a teacher. The first was practical. I had exhausted my wheelhouse of methods and needed some more activities to try out. The second was more philosophical: What does it mean when someone struggles with activities that work for almost everyone else? Within this question was perhaps another one: How as teachers do we sustain ourselves as we keep striving to include everyone? Finally, the third was epistemological. Inspired by Laryza's Review and William's abilities and challenges: What kind of thinker is a writer? What does it mean to write?

To think about these questions, Cecelia as chair led the participants through a series of processes. After each piece of data—my Recollection, videos, and Descriptive Review—participants were guided to reflect descriptively. We then turned to the focus questions. The entire Review took 2 hours.

The primary idea I took from my Review of William was to value children's process more. William was a great storyteller. It became clear that the permanence of words on paper didn't yet matter much to him. As I reflected on this, I suspected that many of my students felt this way. They seemed far more interested in the activity of writing than their products. I began to look for other ways to build on literacy development that put less emphasis on finished products. For example, my class began to do a lot more oral storytelling, which gave William an outlet in which he could be more successful to work on the composition of ideas. In fact, I now make oral storytelling central to my courses in early childhood literacy. I also have adult students practice telling stories orally to improve their written work. I have William and my Review to thank for teaching me the importance of this.

Responses to the third question of the Review—what does it mean to be a writer?—led me to think more deeply about the ways that people convey ideas. After the Review, I started taking other forms of communication more seriously—from block building, to math, to oral communication (see Furman, 2014, 2017). Again, considering what mediums helped William communicate and make sense of the world helped me think more deeply on this topic.

Jane attended my Review on Cecelia's invitation and made a comment that proved pivotal; she noted that writing is *isolating*. This made me think more deeply about writing itself and challenged some of my underlying assumptions. Specifically, writing is often depicted as social because through writing we ultimately communicate with others. Yet the act of writing tends to be isolating. Again, this shift in how I perceived writing informed my curriculum directly. I started to offer more opportunities for collaboration during writing. I also shared with William that I knew he was social and that writing might be isolating. I acknowledged he might find the task unpleasant. This didn't change the reality that he needed to learn to write, but it did affirm his frustration and provide a potentially helpful lens for thinking about his struggles. Years later, Jane's insight helped me to identify some of my own frustrations with writing when I started my doctoral program. It has also helped me work with my adult students as they grappled with some of their own frustrations with writing.

DESCRIPTIVE INQUIRY AND CURRICULUM:
THE PRINCIPALS' PERSPECTIVES

Cara's story provides one window into what it means to build curriculum through Descriptive Inquiry. As we've noted throughout this book, an individual story is both an important way in and incomplete. We turn to the interviews here to add layers of nuance and more perspective on the power of Descriptive Inquiry to influence curriculum.

Exploration of Content

An in-depth, long-term study of content aided by the processes, like the Earth School's study of writing, was a common feature of these schools. Michelle notes how often particular content areas were put forth for whole-year exploration ranging from math to writing to play to recess. Showcasing both the types of yearlong studies at Central Park East 1 (CPE 1) and the influence of individual teachers' questions, Jane spoke about an inquiry into dramatic play, saying

> two teachers were interested in dramatic play; they asked if we could describe a video of dramatic play and so they initiated that and we did that. And then, one of the children in that video was someone that eluded [one of the teachers] about writing, so we then looked at his writing and related to how we saw him developing story in dramatic play. That very much came from the teachers.

As with the Earth School's focus on writing, Jane emphasizes that the inquiry came from the teachers—in this case, two teachers leading the way.

Each school also used the Descriptive Processes to enrich work with outside facilitators. For example, a math consultant at the Earth School worked with teachers, analyzing and assessing children's math work, practices enhanced by teachers' close study of work through Descriptive Inquiry. Showcasing an overlap, Jane said, "We did PerDev [Perceptual Development], which obviously goes hand in hand with description. You do something and you describe with the person what you've done."

The processes also helped the teachers to think more deeply about the kind of work they were asking students to do. Michelle explained:

> It was important to me to help teachers learn to play. Let go of their sense of what they had to do in terms of being serious about school and about kids and about you know, what we had to accomplish, etc., and open it up to play. And I think that the Descriptive Reviews helped that, helped them do that. Later on it also helped create the sort of events for teachers where they would have to let go and do something artistic, or quote unquote artistic you know like you're going to draw a portrait of yourself or a portrait of your neighbor, and do something like that and let go of that tension and help them develop in a play environment.

Through the Reviews teachers got in the practice of frequently sharing their perspectives in a context where they knew they would be listened to without rebuttal. This led to increased comfort which, as Michelle illustrates, helped the teachers try activities about which they felt insecure.

When Alison was principal, teachers at the Earth School used the Descriptive Processes to study recess. This began with an Anecdotal Recollection on recess. Later, staff went out to the recess yard to "play." Many reported being self-conscious about playing but did it anyway. As with Michelle's description, a collaborative community had been established that allowed the teachers to take risks and play. After "playing," the teachers came back and shared their experiences in a go-round. Out of this came an awareness that some people like to play alone whereas others prefer groups. Prior to the teachers' recess play and Reflection, a number of teachers had been very concerned about a child who played alone during recess. After playing themselves, some, Cara included, reframed this child's independent play more positively.

Exploring Curricular Practice

Sometimes a particular teacher's practice around curriculum was explored more closely in a Review of Practice. The processes gave teachers a safe way to bring elements of both concern and pride forward to the group. A few years before the study of writing described earlier, the Earth School had a city mandate to use the Teachers College Reading and Writing Project curriculum. At that time, a long-term teacher at the Earth School, Jennifer Townsend, did a Review of Practice on how this curriculum overlapped with the more emergent integrated Core curriculum that the teachers developed. In this Review, Jennifer emerged as a strong writing teacher and curriculum developer. She found the Workshop Model helpful in her organization of mini-lessons but felt some of the curriculum was "contrived." She was also struggling to authentically integrate the workshop model with Core. Through her Review, she carefully described both curricula and found that the two could go together more smoothly than she had previously thought. A key theme that emerged from Jennifer's Review was that, in creating and implementing curricula, it is important, in Cecelia's words, to consider the "spirit" of the curricula and downplay the procedural rules and scripts.

The frequent practice of Descriptive Inquiry facilitated opportunities for teachers to share their practice more informally. Michelle describes how at the Earth School, "our teachers worked on curriculum usually in groups, grade level, often double grade levels." Again, Michelle emphasizes the collaborative community established, finding that "the Descriptive Reviews also gave them a basis for how to talk to each other and also how to deal with curriculum." Descriptive Inquiry helped the teachers structure the conversations. Further, the culture of Descriptive Inquiry that included frequent asset-oriented sharing, again in Michelle's words,

> also opened up the field so that everyone could bring in what it was they're good at because one of the things about Descriptive Review is that you do uncover what people are good at, what children are good at, what teachers are good at, and I think that it made it possible for them or easier for them to collaborate, and to accept ideas from others.

As an example of this, as a 1st- and 2nd-grade teacher, Cara's grade team met weekly to review what everyone was doing with curricula, to put together a homework packet, and to create a newsletter. For her first 2 years on this team, tasks were rotated. Some tasks were appealing whereas others were burdensome and stressful. For example, she was very nervous creating the math homework and often consulted more skilled teachers for advice, which essentially meant that whomever she consulted was doing two jobs that week.

Toward the end of Cara's second year, another grade team did a Review on their collaborations. A key theme that emerged from this Review was that there was flexibility in how teams function and structures for how teams operated could be changed.

After this Review, Cara's grade team decided that each teacher could specialize, contributing what they felt they were best at. Cara wrote the weekly newsletter, another teacher came up with the math assignments, and so on. The goal was no longer an equal distribution (in terms of number of tasks or time the tasks would take). Instead, they sought equity by having everyone do what they preferred. This change in task allotment made them happier and led to a higher-quality packet as they drew on their strengths and interests.

A number of elements of Descriptive Inquiry supported the move in this direction: (a) the focus is on individual strengths, (b) the emphasis is on what each person needs to be successful, (c) practices and curriculum can be flexible and change when they aren't working for individuals, (d) success is based on whether something is working for individuals as opposed to some predetermined practice, and (e) the alternative modeled through a Review gave the team ideas to work with.

Discussing Curricular Challenges

Descriptive Inquiry helps teachers have the difficult conversations needed to handle some curricular decisions. Through Reviews, Laryza, and then Cara, could challenge some assumptions about what it meant to be a writer. After the September 11th terrorist attacks, feelings in these Manhattan schools were understandably strong and raw. When one teacher at CPE 1 wanted to sing what he called "patriotic songs," Jane used the processes to talk about what people felt comfortable singing. Practiced in having difficult conversations with one another through Descriptive Inquiry, the teachers could draw on habituated ways of speaking in an extremely charged moment to have a difficult discussion. The processes also gave Jane as principal a way of facilitating the conversation itself.

For Judith, Descriptive Inquiry helped teachers at the Neighborhood School bring together the children's interests, responses to the 9/11 attacks, and the predetermined curriculum, a geography unit. She explains that

> when I was walking here from the subway, you know what popped into my mind about descriptive work? September 11th. The 1st/2nd grade [usually] studied tall buildings, but I think that was the year that they weren't studying tall buildings, thank goodness. But the 3rd grade [which usually studies colonial America] was doing a geography thing, and working with a consultant, and they were looking at the atlas like they do in the 3rd grade, and the kids were totally obsessed by the Middle East. They were so obsessed by that spot on the geography thing, the Middle East, and there were kids who were Muslim in the class, several. And kids had all kinds of feelings, so we decided to do a Silk Road curriculum. And that was totally based on observing the children, what their interests were, and what they needed, and I think a school that did a lot of descriptive work would do that and could turn the curriculum on a dime like that. And, I think it was really important for the children to forget about colonial America for that year. And, I think that's a way that descriptive work is important in the school. Although it wasn't doing a Descriptive Review, I think that the school had a descriptive bent to it that allowed it to respond to children.

That this idea popped into her mind shows the relevance that it had for Judith nearly 20 years after the attacks. As Judith explains, Descriptive Inquiry helped her teachers to "turn the curriculum on a dime." Again, the regular exercise of studying curriculum and children allowed the teachers to be responsive in an extremely difficult context. Because of this preestablished facility with creating responsive curriculum coupled with a method (Descriptive Inquiry) for analysis, the teachers drew on the diverse needs of students and teachers, all of whom were deeply affected by this event. In doing so, they rapidly and effectively moved from what was planned to a more responsive curriculum.

Using the Processes to Build Curriculum Around a Class

Teacher-researcher Karen Gallas (1998) describes the ecology of a class, noting that each group brings quite different needs and capacities. It is only through studying her students and her practice with colleagues that Gallas is able to find methods to support her students' work. Echoing this sentiment, Judith explains

> Okay, so different classes have different flavors and different clusters of children have different interests, so based on what those interests are, you have to know what those interests are and that's what we're going to base our project time curriculum or social studies curriculum or writing curriculum. These children are so interested in that, so let's do a writing unit on this. So if you don't do the descriptive work, then you don't know the children well enough, so I think it formed a way to get to know children and pull apart classroom dynamics.

Judith's comments draw the dynamic connection between the child, the group, and the curriculum. All three influence and inform one another. If teachers are to adapt curriculum meaningfully, they must know their students well. Additionally, as discussed earlier in this chapter, Descriptive Inquiry helps teachers study content together, know their students, and have in-depth discussions. In doing this work, they can "pull apart classroom dynamics" effectively to construct curriculum.

COMING TO KNOW A SCHOOL'S CURRICULAR CULTURE

As discussed in depth in Chapter 1, practical wisdom is values-laden work. Practically wise pedagogy and curriculum development must therefore be informed by and inform one's values. Coming to make explicit personal values and the values embedded in a school's culture is an ongoing process, one we argue that can be supported through the regular practice of Descriptive Inquiry. The following is a brief story of a school's beginning efforts to improve the curricular enactment of their values around social justice.

In Chapter 4, Rachel describes how staff at City-as-School learned to use Descriptive Inquiry as the default mode of working together on major pedagogical and school culture questions and issues. Over the last 2 years, that work has raised important questions about the school's culture and its curricular responsiveness to their students. The faculty organized into inquiry groups to work on varying facets of curriculum viewed through the lens of culturally responsive practice (CRP). CRP provided the lens needed to enable the kind of study of curricular culture needed for the focus on social justice. Defining the inquiry topics began with a close study of the notes from a student focus group that a faculty member organized. The ideas that resulted from that descriptive study went through a back-and-forth process between the full faculty and the faculty Professional Development Committee (PDC) until the following topics were fully framed through the lens of CRP: Understanding Individual Students; School Values and Expectations; Curriculum; Working with Off-Site Internship Mentors; and a book group focusing on readings about race and racial justice.

Over the 2-year inquiry, teachers and school counselors have worked collaboratively in the structural frame of Descriptive Inquiry. Each group has raised its questions, ranging from "How does this apply to me?" and "When will we be done?" to "What are the best artifacts to collect to study our topic?" and "How do we best include students in the study?" The inquiry processes have then facilitated their response.

Cecelia worked periodically with the PDC to help group leaders find ways for their groups to think through knotty problems. For the telling of this story, we focus on the unearthing of two ideas that were key to the school's efforts to know itself more fully: culture and value/s. The members of the PDC used the language of school culture freely, and given the study they were doing, Cecelia thought some work on that idea would be helpful. The PDC did a Reflection on the Word *culture* and then put their ideas alongside a number of definitions of culture coming from various sources and having varied emphases—for example, anthropological, white institutional. The Reflection helped the group see the complexity of the idea of culture and that there were multiple perspectives on its definition. As the school was in the beginning stages of their work with CRP, the PDC decided to do the same activity in their groups to ground everyone's thinking in an idea basic to CRP.

The idea of value/s also arose from the discussions of the inquiry groups' efforts in the PDC. Cecelia was trying to be attentive to the ideas the inquiry groups were grappling with and to the fact that the faculty had not explored the interplay of values running through the large curricular work they were undertaking. For example, what are the values underlying CRP? What are the values implicit in the Faculty Community Agreements that the school had developed to support their work with CRP? What values about schooling and issues of race and culture do individual staff members bring to their work? The importance of helping the school and its staff make their value stances more explicit grew over time.

The inquiry into the idea of value/s began with a Reflection on the Word and then moved to looking closely at the Faculty Community Agreements, using these questions:

- Which of these agreements are we best upholding with our work?
- Which one of these do we most need to work on?
- Of the agreements that received the most attention, what are the values embedded in them?
- What do these values reveal about our core values as a community?

In the discussion of the Faculty Community Agreements with the PDC, a few of the statements raised an important issue for the group regarding the tension between valuing the good of the group over personal needs:

- Acknowledge the difference between intent and impact—Even if our intentions are well meaning, our actions can still harm others.
- Oppression exists and is real—Many are experiencing it. Be aware of the language and behavior that you use to address and/ or connect with people. Many words and actions have been used historically to oppress.
- Speak from your experience—Use "I" instead of generalizing.

Wishing that all faculty colleagues shared the belief of the rightness of these commitments, this tension was a source of frustration for some members of the PDC. However, it became a thread to hold on to and revisit as the work with CRP continued. For example, in the second year of the school's work on CRP, at an early meeting of the study group facilitators, they responded to this Recollection: "Think back to a time in your study group or teaching team that felt like a meaningful or critical moment in which you and/or colleagues enacted important values. Tell the story of the experience. Close by reflecting on the values that were present in your actions and the actions of colleagues. What does this experience reveal about your values as an educator, our shared values, and possible tensions between different values?" In grounding their inquiry in times when their values came through, the teachers had a foundation from which to build their pedagogy and curriculum.

TO BE KNOWN THROUGH ONE'S WORK: THE POWER OF SHARING CURRICULUM AND GRAPPLING WITH WORDS AND DEEDS

In this chapter, we have described multiple levels of being known through one's work: children through their art and writing; teachers through their building of curriculum; schools through their efforts to clarify their value stances. And we have described the multiple ways Descriptive Inquiry can support school people in developing this needed ongoing knowing: Descriptions of Children's Work, Reviews of Teachers' Practice, Recollections, and descriptions of school documents.

We began this chapter with a query into how one develops a curriculum that is responsive to individual students. From that base, the chapter explored how teachers can develop curriculum that responds to their and students' needs, strengths, and cultural values and so supports their ongoing growth. And the chapter clarifies how the value context of the school matters and needs careful attention if it is going to support the important and difficult work of building responsive and truly educative curricula. Throughout, we have shown how through the Descriptive Processes communities come together to support the students, teachers, and their schools in this endeavor.

We opened this chapter by drawing attention to the child's work product. This chapter has also been about the work products of teachers. Just as we seek a classroom curriculum that encourages and supports children in doing their best work and lets them base their inquiry on questions that matter, so we call for a schoolwide curriculum, implemented through PD, that supports teachers as they follow their own leading edge. As demonstrated in this chapter, the questions teachers bring to their practice vary greatly and cover the broad swath of human experience. These inquiries range from how to respond to national tragedy, to how to teach to one's values, to what it means to write or play with others. In engaging in inquiry, teachers with the support of their colleagues found their way through thorny challenges. Yet knowing what to do is not the whole story. Just as it matters that the child is known through their works, it also matters that the teacher feels both supported and known.

The culture of a school is also a work product, a work that shapes and supports curriculum. As described here, that work product needs constant attention if it is to be what the educators and families in a school need and want it to be. For the schools described here, examples of the values they wanted to shape their practice focused on: (a) seeing/knowing the capacities the students and teachers brought to their work, (b) teacher input into collaborative exploration and building, and (c) the importance of a willingness to change and a willingness to make space for nondominant cultures. Descriptive Inquiry was the mode of work they found to be compatible with these value commitments.

CHAPTER 6

Using Descriptive Process to Rebuild and Sustain a Democratic School Community

Jane Andrias[1]

> It's quiet again when the children finish speaking, until the woman breaks into the silence. "Finally," she says, "I trust you now. I trust you with the bird that is not in your hands because you have truly caught it. Look. How lovely it is, this thing, we have done—together."
>
> —Toni Morrison, Nobel Lecture, December 7, 1993

Please take 3 minutes to write down all your associations with the word *intention*. You may consider different forms such as *intent, intended, intentional, intentionally,* and *intend.* You may try to generate a definition. You may consider ways *intention* is used in popular culture: Are there any song lyrics that mention it? You may consider the etymological origins. If possible, do this exercise with a few colleagues and then share what you came up with. Don't worry if some of your comments overlap. As you consider what you came up with (alone or with others), you will get a sense of what this word means to you. You will likely firm up what you already thought you knew as well as discover some new elements. Now take this word and its rich meaning forward as you think about what it means to compose a school with intention.

Much like an artistic creation, a school is an expression of its makers. It is composed of their ideas, beliefs, passions, and vision for children. With direction, the finely tuned sensibilities, expertise, and devotion of each contributor working in concert with the others can yield a whole that is greater than its parts. Yet each part is integral to what is created. No one aspect or person is more important than another, but each one matters for the work. A school is like a painting, a sculpture, a dance, an opera, a musical performance, or an oral legend, its story carried and retold by many.

The following is an account of a school as a work in progress. As with the making of any work, the process is not even, easy, linear, or transparent and is often messy. The making of a school involves looking closely at what is there, revisiting what has been, attending to a particular piece to understand the whole, and daring to do what has not been done before. And always, the work bears the imprint of its makers as they create and re-create a space that embraces change in the social/educational order, revising what is there, drawing on new materials and recognizing that one small change can impact the whole. Education, when thought of in this way, is a creative process of leading out, an opportunity for those involved to be transformed and to transform how others see what is possible for people to do together.

THE SCHOOL

Central Park East 1 (CPE 1) is a small public elementary school in District 4 in East Harlem, New York. It was founded in 1974 by a group of teachers in an effort to offer educational alternatives and choice to local children and families. The school was conceived as an intentional community where humanness and democracy in all its disarray would serve as context for decisions about policy, curriculum, and practice—decisions made collectively by those working most closely to the children—the school's teachers. At the core was a belief in the capacity of every child and adult to be educated, to exercise choice and to take authority over their learning and life. All members of the community would be heard and known through their ideas and through their work. Teachers would have the most influence on how the school was shaped and run. Families would receive a weekly schoolwide newsletter, bringing them into the staff's thinking about CPE 1's approach to teaching and learning and offering them opportunities to join with us in the work.

By the end of the school's first year, to protect CPE 1's educational vision, handle daily business, and negotiate school district matters, staff selected Deborah Meier, one of its teachers, to serve as director. CPE 1's founders recognized that their ideals could not be mandated. In order to build the school's coherence and strengthen its integrity, the very people who shared these beliefs had to develop the knowledge needed to realize these ideas. The collective activities of conversation, discussion, disagreement, questioning, and resolution would be key, as was the possibility of continually transforming and refining the enactment of those ideas.

REVISITING WHAT WAS THERE

Any institution shaped by ideals has to periodically revisit its underlying values and examine how they are being enacted as it continues to move forward. I had been the art teacher at CPE 1 for 14 years when I became the school's third director in 1995. The school was committed to progressive teaching and learning. Every day, every child pursued a self-chosen project, classes were multi-age and multi-grade, and curriculum was generated from the teacher and the child. But in the years prior to my becoming director there was less focus on enacting democratic values and practices around decision making. Decisions that had an impact on everyone were being made by a few and not by the whole body. Many people felt excluded, silenced, undervalued.

Holding to strong ideals is particularly difficult in the course of changing demands and pressures from a centralized school system. As a staff, I saw us losing sight of the very principles that made us a viable community for all children and adults. We were becoming more reactive and less proactive, more reflexive and less reflective, relying on habitual practice rather than taking the time as a community to examine our teaching and how we knew children. Our focus was problems rather than possibilities; we were more inclined to yield to the voices of the few than to come to agreement as a whole.

The challenge was to identify and regenerate what we felt important in our founding ideas and to do that in a way faithful to our core beliefs about democratic governance. We needed to better understand and change how we conducted ourselves as a collective decision-making body, and we needed to continue to broaden our knowledge about teaching children; we needed to reestablish a process for talking together. We had also isolated ourselves as though we were not part of a larger school system. We had to bring some visibility to the school as a participating member of the school district that had encouraged its beginnings.

DESCRIPTIVE PROCESS: A PALETTE OF POSSIBILITIES

In addition to myself, many staff members had for several years been participating in Summer Institutes. Staff recognized the knowledge to be gained about a child through a Descriptive Review and Reviews of Children's Work, but we found ourselves unable to conduct Reviews on a regular basis. School-related issues perceived as urgent would take precedence. The values and ideas inherent in the Descriptive Processes go beyond addressing the needs of particular children. I believed that the processes could be used to explore schoolwide issues, policies, and programs; they could be used to rebuild a shared vision of the school.

The August Retreat

Cecelia, then co-director of the Prospect Summer Institute, had done some work with the CPE 1 staff on decision making in the spring of 1995. That summer I met with her to talk through my concerns as the school's new director, and we planned the staff 2-day summer retreat together.

At the opening of the retreat, I told everyone that we were going to draw on the Descriptive Inquiry Processes at all staff meetings. Descriptive Reviews, whether we were talking about a child, a piece of work, our practice, curriculum, an issue, or doing a Reflection on a Word or a Recollection, are inherently democratic in that they make room for, honor, and protect every voice.

The morning of the retreat we began with a Reflection on the Word *process*. We listed words that captured aspects of process: proceed, evolve, develop, digest, do, create, shape, transform. We recognized process as how a task is shaped and created, and that the "how" is value based. We wanted to entertain possibilities, balancing independence and interdependence, attending to how difference is dealt with.

We came away from the Reflection understanding that the process we would use for arriving at decisions was as important as the decisions we would be making. We agreed that we needed to be conscious about the values and standards we chose to enact in our processes, and that we would discipline ourselves and one another to hold to the ethic and conduct of Descriptive Process.

Our conversation that afternoon focused on what we knew about the structure of Descriptive Process and how that structure might serve us as a teaching and learning community. We would draw on the Processes to explore the foundation of our thinking. This meant working with and through something over time, slowing time down, and not necessarily moving in a linear trajectory or having an end result in mind. Since we understood that the Descriptive Processes are not intended to provide immediate answers or solutions to problems, but to direct attention to possibilities and other ways of thinking, we realized that our work would probably open up even more questions.

The next piece of work we did was to articulate what each person believed the school to be. The focusing question for that Review was "What is Central Park East 1?" Each staff member (there were 20 of us, including teachers, paraprofessionals, and school aides) shared an issue that was important to them that seemed to conflict with the core ideas of the school. The following themes emerged:

- We define ourselves as a child-centered school. What does that mean?
- We define ourselves as inclusive of all children. What does that mean in terms of "special education"?
- How do we balance teacher-selected, thematic curriculum with curriculum that emerges from children's interests? (Ideas around work, authorship, and authority)

- How can we extend and refine our observation and description practices and use them productively as guides for teaching? (Ideas around knowing children, standards, and assessment)
- How can we get a better understanding of what colleagues do in their classrooms and share our teaching practices with one another? (Ideas around visibility, respect)
- How do we make decisions? (Ideas around democratic governance)

Descriptive Process as a Regularity

During the school year, staff met weekly every Monday. Cecelia prepared and chaired a Review one Monday a month, and she and I decided on the focus of these Reviews. We used Descriptive Process at all of the other Monday meetings—sometimes to address an issue, describe practice, or describe curriculum or an activity or a child. In the beginning I chaired most of the Reviews at these meetings, but the content grew out of my weekly conversations with teachers, current matters, and the issues and questions raised at the retreat. By focusing on particular aspects, we hoped to get a better grasp on the wholeness of the school.

A few folks volunteered to set the agendas for these meetings and a 6-week calendar of our weekly Reviews was presented to staff and posted in a central location for staff's approval. The calendar was subject to change if something more pressing came up or if a meeting sent us in a different direction from what was planned for the next week.

Areas we explored included (a) the relationship of independence and interdependence among staff, (b) how to make our questions about teaching and learning public and discussable within the school community, and (c) the role of reflective process in the school. We shared stories about the idea of knowledge and about the process of collaboration. From our stories we began to explore shared work for the staff and for the classroom.

Uppermost for me was finding a place for valuing every teacher's perspective and finding a way to bring that into our descriptive studies. Three teachers of upper-grade children, for example, felt they needed to know more about the project work that was so central to their classrooms. They observed and documented the work of several children and made a presentation to the rest of the staff, using the Review of Practice process. Their colleagues listened, responded, raised questions, and made recommendations. In the course of doing this, staff addressed the question of what we value in all children's works.

As a counterpoint, a pre-K/K teacher described project work in her classroom. The two Reviews helped us identify elements of continuity across grades in relation to the specifics of teaching practice, provisioning and planning, and child-centeredness during project time. The knowledge that resulted helped the staff get a clearer picture of how individual classroom practices reflected our shared beliefs of teaching and learning.

The upper-grade teachers had been exploring the idea of a portfolio project through which a child could demonstrate growing expertise in an area of interest. The Review allowed them to articulate their ideas and get feedback from the staff. The portfolio they created included a journal of the development of the inquiry, research connected to the topic, and a piece of visual work that would be presented to the class and adults connected to the student.

We also did two Reviews on the value and influence of the arts in the school. We talked about standards and ways of making space for all kinds of learners, not just in the arts but in all subject areas.

A more experienced teacher who valued the use of LEGO in her upper-grade classroom was concerned about how she could communicate to parents the value of children working with the material. The staff suggested that we do a Descriptive Review of a large LEGO construction that was built jointly by three children in her room. Another teacher volunteered to chair the Review. The notes of the Review helped the teacher and all of us construct a written piece on the various aspects of math, narrative, physics, social learning, and the ethic of hard work that the activity yielded. So, although the teacher had been incorporating LEGO in her room for many years and intuitively knew its value for children, she and we needed to return to the material and the process to articulate what we knew.

After doing several Reviews of drawings by children for whom drawing was a central mode of expression, I suggested that in order for us to understand this better, we dedicate a meeting time to actually draw from observation and from imagination. At the Monday meeting, this suggestion met with some resistance at first but folks did settle into the work. When we stopped to reflect on the experience, people talked about how they became immersed in the work, noticed the silence and concentration, and talked about how they tried to solve problems of perspective, exactness, and expressiveness. They also spoke about the pleasure of physically guiding the tool and creating marks on the page. We agreed that more classroom time would be devoted to drawing, giving it the same value as writing. We began to talk about drawing as a legitimate and important form of expression for a child and as a window into a child's thinking and understanding. This study was co-chaired by me and a staff member.

Although I often helped prepare and chair Reviews not chaired by Cecelia, teachers began to take responsibility for preparing and chairing for each other. Note taking and dissemination of notes were done on a rotating basis by each staff member. For example, two of the newer teachers—the movement/drama teacher and a K/1 teacher—had been talking about a particular child and asked me if they could present a video of a 1st-grade child playing in the dramatic play area. The classroom teacher's question was how she could draw on the child's strong narrative sense that came through in the dramatic play area to encourage and support his writing. We had never done a review of a video, but both the question and the challenge were interesting and held a lot of possibility. The three of us did some preparatory work on how to guide the group through the description. The teachers planned and presented the Review for all of us to engage in.

Reviews done this first year were very much grounded in the work of our circumscribed community. The Descriptive Processes made it possible for us to address "difficult" issues not only about one another's practice and children's works but also about where we held common beliefs and the varied ways we enacted these. As we were becoming reacquainted with our beliefs and practices through the use of Descriptive Process, we had also found a way to bring teachers new to our staff into the thinking of the school.

Description and the Wider Community

An important aspect of our school was the writing of narrative reports that went home to parents. Teachers wrote a full narrative about each child in their class twice a year. No matter how much experience a teacher had with writing reports, we always felt the need to revisit the format and the content before we began the writing process. We also wanted to support the newer teachers. We gathered some reports from the past, divided into smaller groups, and did close descriptions of the reports. We were interested in how descriptive the report was, how well the child was captured, and whether the child was kept whole and not reduced to labels or categories. Some children were hard for some teachers to describe from a strength-based point of view. When this happened, other staff and I worked with the teachers to help them see and write about the child honestly with the parent as the audience in mind.

We used description to look at narrative reports every year—often revising the format and trying to be clear so that the parent could see their child as they were at school. I also met with parents on a few occasions to read old anonymous reports. Their comments, questions, and concerns about what they learned about the children from these reports helped guide the writing and the family conferences that followed the reports.

The work we were doing in our study at staff meetings was often the subject of my weekly schoolwide CPE Notes to families. The CPE Notes gave parents a window into how we thought about the many facets of teaching and learning at the school. It also provided a way to inform the newer parents and reacquaint our older parents with our beliefs and practices. We often dedicated part of the Parent Association meetings to topics that we were studying as a staff to get parent feedback and use their questions to inform us. In these instances we used Descriptive Process at parent meetings to do Recollections, for instance, of a time we were read to as children, a description of a video of a child reading with their teacher, a parent's Descriptive Review of their child, Descriptive Reviews of a child's spanning work collection folder, close readings of narrative reports.

For all that we were accomplishing, I was concerned about what we were not yet considering—our school in the context of the growing demands of the city's educational landscape. For years we had been able to avoid bumping into the system's expectations that were often in conflict with the values and standards we held at the school. These came in many forms: minutely and categorically articulated standards for curriculum, assessment, and promotion as well as rigidly designed programs for instruction, remediation, and special education. But this was no longer possible. If we were going to maintain our integrity and credibility as an educational community for all our children and families, we had to be clear about what we thought and were doing in response to this climate.

By my second year as director, staff agreed to develop policy statements that reflected our stance and approach to standards, promotion, assessment, and curriculum and present them to the district. The content of the statements was drawn predominantly from the Descriptive Inquiry work we were already doing. Although acceptance by the district for these policies required much evidence and convincing, because we had that evidence and more from the descriptive work, the policies were accepted with some minor conciliations on our part.

An Issue: Special Education

By fall 1996 staff was more committed to and comfortable with Descriptive Inquiry. The processes were making it possible for us to address who we were as a school and who we wanted to be. Although our inquiries revealed a range of perspectives among us, we generally shared the same value base, making it possible to have discourse that was honest and respectful and that ultimately brought us together in decision making. However, there was one issue we were avoiding, or at least circumventing. The issue that had been with us for several years was special education, how it came to live in our school and how we were living with it. No issue divided staff more.

The prevailing policy in the city was that children who were evaluated and identified as having "extreme" special needs be placed in small self-contained classrooms. From CPE 1's early days, we had been teaching children who may have qualified for such designations in all of our classrooms with the support of resource room teachers. All children were admitted to our school through the lottery process, which involved parent visitation and parent choice and no screening of children. Somehow the parents of children who may have qualified for special designations found or were guided to our school and applied through the same process as a parent of a general education child. Either the family had rejected the categorial designation and placement of their child or they had never been involved with the special education system. We thought we could serve the children without separating them from the larger student body.

However, by 1990, without the full staff being consulted or informed in advance, we found ourselves with a Modified Instructional Services (MIS) 4 early childhood class comprised of 12 children spanning grades Kindergarten through 2nd with one special education teacher and a paraprofessional. The children were assigned to the school by the Special Education office. Their parents and caregivers knew nothing about the particular nature of the education we offered. And unlike all the other children in our school who remained with us until the end of 6th grade, children in the MIS 4 class would have to leave after 2nd grade because we did not have a special class for them at the 3rd- and 4th-grade levels. The teacher of the MIS 4 class, who was not familiar with our educational approach and philosophy, had been hired by the director and a few selected staff, unlike our practice of hiring collectively.

We had many children with individualized education plans (IEPs) in our school who had designated time with special education resource room teachers. Were the MIS 4 children so distinctly different from children whom we had with us all these years? After teaching the MIS 4 children as the art teacher for 5 years, I still wasn't clear on how to distinguish between children having particularly unique learning styles and other children being challenged beyond what we were able to support in our general education classes.

From its beginning there was considerable disparity among staff regarding the separate class. Some folks considered it a violation of our core beliefs about how we educated all children who came to us. Others accepted it as being in a diplomatic compliance with the district, and some seemed to ignore its existence as though the MIS 4 class was "renting space" from us, just occupying a room and not an integral part of the school. Regardless of one's stance about the presence of the MIS 4 class at CPE 1, what was being overlooked was how children, their families, their teacher, and their paraprofessional were accepted into and treated as members of the community.

As a school community, the coherence we were working to restore in looking closely at our beliefs and practice with Descriptive Process did not include how the special education class fit into the fabric of the school. We were not opening up our thinking and learning about the special education system and, more significantly, about the children and adults in the class. We were becoming more uncomfortable with one another about this issue but did not address that discomfort openly. Small, silent alliances formed. As CPE 1's director, I saw this division as a threat to the very existence of our school as we knew and valued it. We had to address the discomfort.

My own feelings on this matter were strong. I did not think I could continue to be the leader of a school that had separate classes for some children who came to us directly through the procedure of the District 4 Committee on Special Education and whose parents had little or no information about our school. However, my feelings about democratic decision making were as strong. I knew that imposing my beliefs would be counter to the professional community we were building through descriptive work, no less to the values of the school and would erode the trust we were rebuilding.

At my request, the staff agreed to embark on a 1-year study of special education. Our intention was to use Descriptive Inquiry to think together and deepen our understandings about special education, its structure, and more importantly, about the children who were already in our school. It was my hope that we could bring CPE 1 to special education rather than bring special education to CPE 1.

I wondered if we were the right school for the special education children. I knew the work before us would include exploring our attitudes about special education, addressing our confidence about teaching some children, and expanding our educational environment to accommodate more kinds of learners. We had to learn about the ideas and techniques driving the instruction of the children. We also had to encourage the families of the special education students to become part of the larger parent body. We had to return our focus of coming to know all the children in our school in a way that we said we valued.

The map of our study of the special education system was somewhat more linear and clearly set out than our exploration of the school's values and practices. Staff had to become more familiar with the system at large and all the facets of special education so that we could yield the best results and services for our children. We had to learn about the particular characteristics of the children that deemed them in need of a special class. This inquiry would have to include acquiring information about conditions such as severe visual impairment, hearing impairment, traumatic brain injury, seizure disorder, mild cerebral palsy, and medications.

I am certain that we did not anticipate how complex and challenging this inquiry would be. It took the courage and good intentions of every person and the collective body to pursue this work. Not surprisingly, this 1-year commitment turned into a study that lasted 5 years and had an impact on our school and our work that reached far beyond the original intention.

Inquiry on Special Education: An 8-Year Exploration

After a conversation with Cecelia about staff agreement to pursue an inquiry on special education, she suggested we frame the overarching inquiry around longitudinal studies of six children, three from the special education group and three from general education. We would use Cecelia's one Monday meeting a month for these child studies and Cecelia would prepare with the presenters, chair the Reviews, and write up and distribute the notes from each Review. The sources for these child studies were the Teacher's Descriptive Review of the Child, Descriptive Reviews of Children's Work, Reviews of the spanning collection of the child's work, teachers' narrative reports, the child's reflections on their work, descriptions of videos of the child in different settings, and parent Reviews and comments that they felt comfortable sharing.

Before we could begin the actual child studies, it felt important to explore staff's worries, doubts, and concerns about the question of special education. We understood that our starting place and how we framed the entire study would have an impact on the shape of the inquiry and decided to pay attention to the language we used in our formal meetings and casual talk about children.

The Question of Success

We began by asking ourselves what we were worried about in terms of teaching children who came to us with special education designations. An overwhelming concern was the idea of what it means to be "successful" in school. It seemed to all of us that this was an important starting place.

Once we looked at the ways success was linked to external rewards, standards, and expectation, we thought about success as being more about process than product—the process of striving, struggling, trying, fighting for, or having a purpose, of having to do with courage and risk. We realized that success could be something determined by and felt from within the person. We wondered what our students' own standards of success might be and how they were related to what the child knows about their own strengths.

We then talked about the implications of success in terms of our perception of ourselves as teachers and of our school. We thought about the pressures we put on ourselves to be successful with all children and wondered if saying that a child needs more support is a reflection of our having failed that child. Did we think about success more than we would like to admit? How did we and could we measure our success? We wondered why outside criteria rather than our knowledge of the child was what counted as evidence of the child's success.

At the end of our reflection, we had the frame for our study on special education: If we can be successful teaching children designated as special education, then we can be successful teaching all children.

Being Part of the School Community

What CPE 1 considered to be important for all children's education conflicted with the special education system. These differences underscored the divergent assumptions we held about the capacity of all persons. Should some children only be taught to master skills and content? Did they only need training to function adequately and not an education that would give them access to possibilities—to forms of expression, interpretation, thinking, and exploration that allow the creation and manipulation of knowledge that we provided for all our other children?

An underlying assumption in the realm of special education is that there are deficits to be identified and remediated. The MIS 4 classroom reflected this difference in its approach to many aspects of classroom life. For example, very little time was allotted for learning through hands-on projects, play, and engagement with materials. CPE 1's philosophy, in sharp contrast, is that we begin to educate children from their interests and strengths. Our experience had taught us that there is a great deal to be learned about a child's thinking, style of learning, interests, and strengths, through careful observation of their interaction with materials. In all our classrooms, learning with materials and ideas was structured so that children gain authority over their education and learn about themselves as thinkers and makers in partnership with the adults in their life. The children in all the general education classes were expected to make decisions for themselves as they extended their understanding of the world.

Although the tone in the MIS 4 classroom was calm and kind and the children felt safe and protected by the teacher's clarity and devotion to them, most of the children's time was spent in prescriptive and direct instruction determined by the teacher. The teacher of the MIS 4 class worked in a dual reality. She was expected to attend all our meetings and retreats but also received training in all instructional areas and was supervised by the division of special education. How was she to negotiate this binary experience?

Not surprisingly the MIS 4 teacher and paraprofessional felt like outsiders. When the teacher participated at the Monday meetings, she was tentative in her responses and shared with me that she was insecure about how she was received by other members of the staff. The structure of the Descriptive Processes brought her into the conversation, but she still was cautious about sharing her ideas and perspectives. She was learning about us, but we were not coming to know her.

We were also noticing difficulties between special and regular education students, staff members, and the special education teacher. Children in the special education classroom played among themselves at recess as though they were separate and were perceived and treated as separate by the rest of the student body. Though we made efforts to "integrate" the students into all the schoolwide programs (art, chorus, dance), we did not succeed in breaking down barriers.

We talked about how to bring them more fully into the fabric of our daily life in school. How could we integrate all of the children during the course of the week? The art classes had already been grouped to have the children in the self-contained classroom join with the other early childhood classes. The choruses and other voluntary activities were open to all the children. The lunchroom procedures were modified to give the older children the option of sitting wherever and with whomever they chose. The parent association was making an effort to encourage the parents of the children in the MIS 4 class to attend meetings and have a presence and voice.

This led us to think about the public places in the school. We did a Review with Cecelia of how the MIS 4 children used the school's common areas. The general education children enjoyed freedom of mobility around the school and had access to common spaces; this was not the experience of MIS 4 children. We questioned how inclusive we really were as a community. Was being inclusive more like tolerance than pluralism? How did we arc toward difference and other ways of thinking? How democratic were we? Just as we agreed that we needed to know more about the system that was growing around us and insinuating itself into our school, we needed to know more about the children in the MIS 4 class and their teacher who were already part of our school.

In contrast to the idea of inclusion was the idea of exclusion. What did it feel like to be the children and the adults in that classroom? What did it mean to be excluded? A teacher suggested that, rather than doing a Reflection on a Word, we do a Recollection on a time we were or felt excluded from a group or a community using these guiding questions: What were the circumstances? How did you respond? How did that experience shape you? Though our stories were vastly different, what they held in common when we were marginalized were feelings of humiliation, confusion, anger, self-doubt, and being misunderstood. We also wondered how we were spoken about by those inside. It was as though we didn't matter. The Recollection made public how many of us were attracted to teaching at CPE 1 because we saw it as a place where we could fit in. Yet in many ways, perhaps unwittingly, we had been excluding some adults and a whole group of children from being equal members of our school.

The Recollection did highlight the discomfort many of us had with the word *inclusion*. It seemed to hold the idea of people being asked to, invited to, or allowed to join a community by those who held more privilege inside that community. This word remained important to us throughout our inquiry.

The Idea of Special

We continued to look at language to uncover the ideas embedded in the words we used. We planned that our next Reflection would be on the word *special* to see what it held for us.

Rather than leading us to the idea of deficiency, the word took on a surprisingly positive case. A rich collection of associations to the word *special* and anecdotes about specific children yielded what we valued about childhood, that each child was special in a particular way and that it was our responsibility to notice and nurture that specialness. We began to see the common ground from which we had been and could continue to educate all children.

Longitudinal Child Studies: Looking Closely at the Particular

With the understandings we gained through the Reflections on *success* and *special* and the Recollection on *exclusion*, we started our child studies. Reviews of the six children were presented at one staff meeting a month throughout the next several years.

In order to bring Rita, the MIS 4 teacher, into our midst, Cecelia and I asked her to select a child from her class and do the first Descriptive Review. She chose a child, Earl, who was particularly elusive to her, a child she could never quite grasp. Her reason became the standard for teachers choosing the five other study children—a child somewhat beyond their grasp.

As with all Descriptive Reviews of the Child, the teacher (as presenter) was as much the subject of the Review as the child was. It is through her eyes and her words that the child appeared in front of us. Rita described Earl's imagination and the role it played in his work. As Rita prepared the Review, she became more aware of who he was, noting his humor and storytelling abilities, his attention to pattern, and his interest in how things work and how to make things work. Earl was now among us and belonged to all of us. At the same time we were seeing Rita in ways that most staff did not know her. Most apparent was her love for the child, her sense of humor, and her willingness to learn from her peers. I think this first Review was when she became fully part of our school.

And so began the unfolding of the school lives of six children and their teachers in all their complexity and wonder, four of whom I mention here: (a) Earl, the contemplative child with penetrating concentration and contrasting whimsical humor; (b) Judy, a delicate person with a keen sense of justice who was a child we would learn about as though we were reading a poem; (c) Simon, who had a strong aesthetic, a sense of beauty and elegance with an intense interest in the internal structure and workings of rules or guidelines to help him solve problems; and (d) Janice, who hid from conventional school tasks of reading and writing and came alive during our schoolwide study of East Harlem; when given the choice of her inquiry, she pursued her passion about braiding hair.

Weaving of Our Work

The Reviews were compelling portraits. We became more attuned to seeing children through description and devoted many of our other Monday meetings to describing children not directly connected to the longitudinal child studies. Often there would be two concurrent Descriptive Reviews presented, prepared, and chaired by teachers. Our minds were infused with mental images of the children accompanied by the words and voices of staff. The work had taken on a life of its own. Every Review, whether from the six child studies or of other children, a teachers' practice, or a child's work, led us to new questions, new places to explore.

The Backdrop: Moving into the Classroom

It was time to look at the setting or backdrop of the places that children spent most of their time. We did a Review to document the ways in which individual children used the resources of a particular classroom to support their learning. This opened up new areas for description—a room where a new teacher was struggling with order/disorder became the stage for looking at how classroom arrangement suggests certain ways of being for children. With the teacher's invitation and trust, we gathered in his room to describe what we saw and then spent time with him rearranging furniture and materials until he achieved the kind of order that gave him a sense of equanimity. It also gave him a new lens through which to see the children in the course of the day. The MIS 4 teacher asked a few of us to help her redesign the room so that a child whose balance was compromised could move from place to place by holding onto a surface or edge. The idea behind our work was that if the room were safe for this child, it would be safe for every child. We considered how the hall spaces could be extensions of the classroom for children and adults who needed more mental or physical room.

Collection Folders: Looking at Our Artifacts

From its beginnings, CPE 1 had the practice of collecting student work in a folder for each child from the time the child entered until the child left the school. At various points during the school year, the teacher and child selected pieces of work that reflected the child as a thinker, learner, and maker to go into the folder in addition to the child's journals and record of books read that year. These collection folders were stored in a room and were accessible to the child, the teacher, and the family at any time. Our newer teachers, however, were not clear about the purpose of the collections. We revisited the original purpose of collecting children's work by first describing the collections of two study children. In addition, three teachers chose a folder from a child in each of their classes and in small groups we described the spanning work from these folders. In each instance, we determined which of the child's interests were sustained over time and noticed how and when these themes reappeared in the student's work. From this we resolved to make it a practice that every child look through and reflect on their folder with an adult at least once a year.

We did not lose sight of each child's particular needs for support and used that understanding to create classroom spaces and learning opportunities that could accommodate the "specialness" of each child. We began to think of the word *special* to coincide with the headings, Ways of Thinking and Learning and Abiding Interests, in the Descriptive Review of the Child. For example, in Luigi's collection, we noticed how he organized the imagery in his drawings. He often created a grid-like structure on the page in which he drew miniature and detailed elements of the larger subject matter of the drawing. In one instance, he created an elaborate and detailed drawing of the interior of a house. Teachers who had Luigi in their class recalled that his block work was also highly structured and differentiated within the structure. Others recalled that he loved cooking and that, although he followed recipes when he cooked, he always added an interesting ingredient to enhance the flavor of his dish. And yet, he struggled with detail, description, and elaboration in his writing. We talked about how to help him draw on the "special" way he constructed visual work to improve the construction of his written work by helping him put verbal language to his visual work—labeling, annotating, adding captions, and then finally joining them into a narrative. His organizational style also led us to wonder about him as a math thinker and worker.

Teaching and Learning: Moving From the Particular to the Larger

Looking at the particular children opened the door to larger questions about our approaches to literacy and math learning and teaching. We were moving from looking at the particular to the whole to get a different perspective on our school as a coherent work.

The Reviews of the collection folders taught us about the individual child and always brought to mind other children. They were also a source for seeing teaching, learning, and curriculum across the grades. We began to pay attention to examples of reading and writing in the collections, and this resulted in a long-term study of what literacy looked like from pre-K through 6th grade. Over several months of Monday meetings, every teacher presented descriptions of three very different readers and spoke to the teacher's way of working with each child. This work included the teachers' assessments, documentation, and instruction, as well as a suggested collection of children's literature for each child. We began to develop a more descriptive stance around coming to know a child as a reader as well as coming to know one another's practice and concerns.

As we studied the folders we noticed an absence of examples of math work. That led us to wonder about the kinds of written math assignments we were giving children. What math activities and thinking were we providing on a daily basis? And how often were we noticing and documenting the math thinking in children's work and activities that was not intentionally designed as a math activity? We set aside time to do a study of math as a subject matter, and also as incidental to other areas. We agreed, when asked, to visit others' classrooms with an eye toward seeing math thinking in the children's work at different times of the day. This led to our describing math assignments and other classroom work to see where the child came through as a math thinker, after which we decided to pursue a longer study of math teaching and learning at the school.

The question of how to study difficult topics such as slavery, the Holocaust, and people doing "bad things" was raised by the upper-grade teachers. These topics were generated by questions the children were asking, casual conversations children were having, and issues that the teachers felt were important to study in the context of history and social justice. At an upper-grade meeting, teachers talked about their concerns for children when exploring these issues. Their conversation led to a Monday Review of planning for a study on race by one teacher and of Columbus by another. How decisions about curriculum and from where curriculum is generated became an outgrowth of both of these Reviews. It was an area where staff had great differences. Our questions were: How do we balance designing curriculum that teachers feel is important with curriculum that emerges from a child's interest or a growing interest among the children in the class? Is there room for both?

The relationship between emergent and teacher-generated curriculum in our classrooms had surfaced as a pressing issue and ultimately led us to the idea of a schoolwide curriculum as shared territory for staff, children, and families. Our collective study of East Harlem allowed us to see one another as teachers in the planning process and for the MIS 4 class to be even more a part of the school. Doing the study together gave us the opportunity to see how a preplanned curriculum could be shaped to provide space for each classroom and/or for individual children's interests and questions as they emerged.

Process and Practice

We were learning a lot from the Reviews, Recollections, and Reflections within the structure of the processes. But the descriptive work is only as strong and useful as it impacts on our daily work, language, behaviors, and consciousness. As with any learning process for children and adults, there is dissonance, unevenness, wandering; there are departures. Sometimes we found ourselves working on two levels at the same time. On the one hand was what we were able to do within the intentional frame of the Descriptive Processes, and on the other was what happened to this stance on a daily basis within the challenges of our classrooms. The realization of this duality by staff was a turning point for us. We knew we had to hold ourselves and one another more accountable for how we used language when we spoke about children and families. We had to be more vigilant about our more casual talk with one another. We had to be more honest about our reactions, our ways of seeking help, and our vulnerabilities.

Even as we were developing a more descriptive way of talking about and understanding children, we became more enmeshed in the world of special education. We were tempted by the services special education could provide. As we were moving more into the realm of special education, we found ourselves falling into the habit of using the vocabulary and imagery of deficits. Teachers were also more inclined to ask for evaluations of children who had been in our regular classes since early childhood. There did not seem to be a space between feelings of concern, feelings of inadequacy, and a sense of urgency.

A Review of Practice: A Place to Stop and Look More Closely

A year into our study of special education, our school psychologist, Roberta Roper, expressed concern about the number of requests teachers were making for referrals of children. She wanted to share her insights about children beyond testing. We felt that it would be helpful if staff understood the referral process from beginning to end, the role Roberta played in the process, and how she could support children and classrooms that might mitigate the need for an evaluation.

Cecelia worked with Roberta to prepare the review. The focus questions they shaped were: How can the insights Roberta has into children become useful for teachers? How can her insights be translated into forms that teachers can use in their work with children?

In her Review Roberta spoke about the theoretical ways through which she learned to see and interpret children's behavior and how through descriptive work she shifted from a theoretical lens to building a collection of ways to see, expanding her actual experience with children and including in her ken a fuller range of childhood. This more inclusive view of children's development added to her ability to understand.

Among the ideas that teachers took away from the Review was that evidence of a child's understandings can be seen in many forms and expressions. Although some evidence may be through verbal communication, we also come to know and appreciate a child's understanding by paying attention to the child's physical person, spatial organization, and relationships with others.

Following the Review, staff recognized what Roberta could offer beyond official referrals. The resource room teachers understood that they could draw on Roberta's evaluation reports in writing a child's IEP so that the plan would be more consistent with what the child really needed. Teachers requested that her insights from testing be included in Descriptive Reviews of the Child to enhance and broaden their perspective. And finally, teachers wondered how reliable their perceptions of a child were and wanted an opportunity to talk to Roberta about that. We agreed after this Review that we would ask Roberta to spend more time in classrooms and to work with individual children and suspend referral requests for a while. We were slowing down and taking more time to consider how to work with children.

In her Review, Roberta talked about her work with perceptual development (PerDev). The descriptive and perceptual work enhance each other. In the same way the headings of the Descriptive Review emphasize a particular aspect of the person's physical presence and gesture, the perceptual lens informs us about how to differentiate the components of a child's movement and how that may be related to the child's ways of negotiating formal and informal learning. As with the Descriptive Review, the aim of the PerDev approach is to relate this information to the whole, working toward full integration of the person. The approaches complement each other and broaden the frame through which we come to know and support a child.

As an outcome of her Review of Practice, Roberta extended her work with PerDev at the school. We received a considerable grant from the district for an afterschool program using the perceptual development approach with nine children selected by the whole staff and run by three teachers, our school psychologist, and me. Each of the teachers met with the same three students for a 40-minute period after school twice a week. A third meeting took place where we made decisions about how to proceed with the child based on descriptions of our work with each child and descriptions of the children's work. This work was shared with the staff through Descriptions of Videos of us working with the children and through Reviews of our documentation of some sessions and some meeting notes. The perceptual lens was enriching our work with Descriptive Inquiry and having an indelible impact on daily practice—on how we saw, spoke about, understood, and were with children and with one another.

Creating Support Systems

We thought about how to make use of the district's requirement that all schools have a Pupil Personnel Committee to keep track of concerns about and interventions for particular children. We named our support group the Children's Consultation Committee. The group provided time and space for drawing on possibilities inside and resources outside of the school. Consistent members included the director, educational evaluator, social worker, and psychologist from the School-Based Support Team and the family therapist whom we paid to work with us once a week. Any staff member was welcome at meetings to be part of the conversation or bring concerns about a particular child. Each of us (except for the family therapist) was assigned to two classrooms to meet with teachers about a child or concerns the teacher wanted to have addressed at our meetings. The support person visited the classroom and observed the child.

Based on these visits and conversations, the committee developed plans to support the child. These plans often included a Descriptive Process as a way of gaining a broader perspective on the child within their classroom. Most of the time, we were able to avoid a special education referral. We were also reaching beyond the information we had access to at school and drawing on experts in psychopharmacology, trauma, vision, audiology, brain injury and seizures, asthma, food allergies, foster care, adoption, and social workers in community-based organizations. These gave us new perspectives and insights into children and outside support systems, broadening our understandings, compassion, and empathy. These qualities supported decisions and choices we would make about children in the school context.

Just as we had written policy statements for other areas, we did for our referral process as well. The statement was largely for our own use, but we did make it available to officials during the mandatory State's Special Education Quality Reviews. When we did proceed with a referral, we expanded it to include materials that represented the fullest possible picture of the child, making it possible to choose the most appropriate support services and placement possibilities. This was a new experience for the special education committees. The child became more knowable to them as a person and more difficult to reduce to a label or category. And interestingly, we were then more likely to receive the supports that we thought were helpful to the child and the school.

Self-Contained Classes: Thinking, Rethinking, Revising

When it was time for our self-contained group of 2nd-graders to leave us because we did not have a 3rd/4th-grade self-contained class, the dilemma was whether to create an older class grouping to keep the children who were now a part of our community or let them go to another school and eventually phase out our MIS 4 self-contained class. Phasing out the class meant saying goodbye to children who had been with us for 3 years. But creating a class for them was antithetical to my deep beliefs about having any self-contained classes. We also had the children's families to consider. Parents of the MIS 4 students were appealing to us about how we might maintain their children in our school. Staff and I struggled over the choice and the risk.

After much deliberation I asked staff to consider forming a self-contained class that would accommodate the children as they moved to 3rd grade. To meet the required enrollment for a for a 3rd- and 4th-grade MIS 1 class, I proposed including some of our Special Education Teacher Support Services (SETSS) children rather than bringing in new special education children. The risk we would be taking was relegating our SETSS children to a more restrictive environment within our school.

We chose to move ahead with the second class after teachers carefully and tirelessly presented brief descriptions of children in evidence of why they felt the smaller class would benefit the child. We selected the children as a whole staff and with the parents' involvement and consent. We convinced the district's Committee on Special Education of our plan, and they consented. Although we were further into the special education system, we felt we had some control over our class groupings and student longevity at our school. We knew we would have to be even more vigilant about our attitudes and our language. For us, the decision was daring and spoke to our resilience as a community.

The staff hired a teacher who seemed to understand what our school valued, and we began the next school year with two self-contained special education classes, the MIS 4 and MIS 1 classes. By midyear, it was clear that the MIS 1 grouping was problematic. The image the children had of themselves as different and isolated was exacerbated. The SETSS children who had been in the general education classes were now in a very different setting. We had taken a chance, and it was not working. We had to rethink what we were doing and imagine what could be possible.

We explored special education configurations in other schools and programs and, after presenting many possibilities to staff, decided that for the next school year we would create a 4th/5th-grade Collaborative Team Teaching (CTT) class. This class had two teachers, a general education and a special education teacher, along with with eight children from the self-contained class and 18 children from the general education population. Even with the considerable dedication and effort of the teachers and the support staff, the class never cohered into a unified group.

To help us understand the difficulties, the two teachers of the CTT class did a Review of Practice, focusing on how they could work to unify the class. They described how the children used the room and the ways they worked together. Our intention was to build on what was positive. Yet as much as the teachers intended to draw on recommendations from the Review, the group remained as two classes within one room. The Review revealed that we had not prepared the teachers or the two groups of children to meet the challenges of this new configuration. We had considered neither the strong historical bonds of the MIS 4 children who had been together since early childhood nor the very different sensibilities of the two teachers. We knew that we had to find another way.

So with a leap of faith in our growing capacity as teachers of all children, we disbanded the MIS 4 and CTT classes and created "inclusion" classrooms with the special education students and general education students in classrooms throughout the school. Having educated ourselves about how to traverse the terrain of the special education system, we were able to secure additional special education teachers and paraprofessionals to support the children and work in partnership with classroom teachers.

Since staff knew children across the school through Descriptive Reviews and Descriptions of Work, we were all able to participate in the class configuration process in an informed way, putting the children at the center of our placement decisions. Every classroom, special education, music and arts teachers, paraprofessional, and school aide contributed what they knew about the individual child in order to make the best possible assignment. We created class groupings based on the needs and strengths of children and on the teaching style of the adults of that class. We did not concern ourselves with traditional grouping models and sometimes created groupings that spanned three grades. In making placements, we attempted to maintain diversity, support friendships, stimulate interests, and create working classroom communities.

When we were less sure about a child's placement, teachers shared brief descriptions of that child. We were drawing on our growing capacity to be daring, to disagree and still trust in ourselves and one another, to question our choices, and to make mistakes and learn from them. What progressive meant for us was that we had to move forward while holding on to values that mattered.

We were talking about a child—not a special education child but a whole, unlabeled person. This person, like all other persons, had their own ways of appearing, of being with others; they had their own interests, their own style of learning and thinking, their own capacities, and their own ways of making sense of the world.

Our Public Face

We had cultivated a stronger presence with the District Committee on Special Education. Our child studies and descriptive work were written into our annual school plan. When it was time for district special education reevaluations and annual reviews of children, we went to the meetings with the child's parent and with a folder of the child's work and descriptive evidence to argue for supports and class placement so that the child would remain at CPE 1. In this way we "brought the child with us," making them present. District administrators were impressed with how well our teachers knew the children and how well we were accommodating and educating them.

We had achieved district recognition, received permission to move to full inclusion, and could decide on our own (with parental input) which children we could educate in a least restrictive environment. We also received agreement that parents of children in special education as well as regular education would have the same entrance application and admissions process. When I wrote about this in the CPE notes, we were surprised by the positive response from our parent body, many of whom expressed relief that we were returning to what they thought the school stood for at its beginnings.

Descriptive Inquiry: Balance and Pace

One of the challenges of our descriptive work was how to balance and pace the child-centered descriptions with studies of schoolwide matters. To protect the child studies, we needed to develop a rhythm for keeping children at the center, rendering them as present as possible. Teachers asked to have follow-up conversations about children who were the subjects of Descriptive Reviews. They proposed that we reserve a staff meeting every 6 weeks with 15 minutes allotted to each teacher who had done a Review of a Child to talk about how the teacher drew on and formed working knowledge from the Review—how what they learned from the Review impacted on daily work with the child and their practice and what new insights they now had about the child.

The focus of the Descriptive Reviews of Children and their work did not distract us from our ongoing inquiry of who we were as a school. The child Reviews became points of departure and provided direction for that work. We went more deeply into looking at documentation and assessment, social development, the arts, perceptual development, project/work time, narrative reports, schoolwide curriculum studies, and what it means to be a graduate of CPE 1, which eventually developed into the articulation of graduation requirements. There were also the long-term studies of reading and math. We found ourselves going back as we were moving forward to relook, reconsider, and re-create.

We also began to focus more on the adults in our community. We began a yearly practice of doing a reflection on ourselves as teachers. We paid particular attention to the locations in the classroom/school where each of us spent more of our time, which children we spent more time near, what areas of curriculum and which activities we planned more carefully, and what we were more interested in observing and documenting. This stood as an interesting companion piece to what we were learning about how children used space.

In another Review we looked at the ways a general education teacher, a special education teacher, a paraprofessional, and an aide worked together in a K/1/2 classroom. We were most interested in how they made decisions about teaching and caring for the children in the classroom and the ways they worked interdependently. We saw the potential of each adult as a trusted individual and as part of the whole of this classroom. The four people in the Review could not have been more different from one another, yet by drawing on one another's knowledge, experience, and humanity they were totally accessible to one another and to the children. The Review made us conscious of respecting what each person brought to their work. We were becoming less judgmental of one another and addressing our differences more directly; sharing our doubts as teachers; and talking and listening to one another about children, practice, curriculum, questions, doubt, and joy.

We had grown as a professional community interested in and reliant on one another's thinking, perspectives, and questions, which allowed us to share in the public space of a full staff meeting our teaching vulnerabilities. I could now ask staff to bring a brief description of a child who challenged their teaching practice. The meeting was structured so that the teachers could give voice to and make public their struggle and the ways they were learning to work with the child. It was not about getting advice. Each staff member described the child and how they worked with the child. The music teacher talked about a child who remained separate from the group during music class and how he learned to draw on the other children to accept the way the child was present with the group. A teacher talked about a child who had compromised physical mobility and how she learned to redesign the physical space of her classroom to support her movement around the room. Another teacher spoke about a child who was not able to do an assignment. She was rethinking her presentation of the work, considering how different children might receive and process that information.

The work around these individual children led us to focus on specific issues. A teacher asked that we devote a session to addressing how children sat and attended during class meeting times. At the meeting, while folks described a particular child or incident, I took note of what our bodies were doing and shared my observations midway in our meeting. Some folks stood up frequently and stretched; others drew or doodled in their notebooks; others did some kind of work with their hands; some chewed gum. And yet we were all attending to and participating in the content of the meeting. In other words, most of us had particular behaviors that we depended on to get us through. Could we draw on this awareness to extend our latitude with children and help them understand how to regulate their body and gain more control? As a follow-up, we did a session with our movement teacher to help us understand the ways we each used our bodies to help us attend to the content of what was taking place. We became more aware of the physical and sensory space in our classrooms and the more public areas of the school with the most challenged child in mind.

Two of the newer teachers who taught the 5th/6th-grade students presented us with the question "What does it mean to be a CPE 1 graduate?" They had been playing with this question and wanted to flesh out a set of graduation requirements that each 6th-grader would present to a committee. We met as a staff to listen to their ideas, divided into smaller units, each group addressing the scope and details of a particular area of the recommended requirements. Requirements included evidence of their thinking in math, literature, science, social studies, physical education, and their independent search projects. The children would also address what they were bringing about themselves as learners, thinkers, and makers, and as members of a community to draw on to support themselves in their next school. What grew from this was a practice that continued for several years.

Each child selected as their adviser an adult from the school with whom they were comfortable. It was the adviser's responsibility to support the student's preparation and presentation of the graduation requirements.

The presentations were in addition to the graduates' close looking at the spanning content of their collection folders with their adviser and a family member. Each child wrote a reflective piece for the yearbook using some of the headings from the Descriptive Review. The piece was based on how they were seeing themselves as thinkers and learners, what abiding interests seemed consistent over time, and what new passions arose.[2] Looking at a span of work done over several years helped us see the child "unfold" over time. It gave the child a sense of history, of the present, and of the possibilities for the future.

As a staff we did some close readings of the 6th-graders' reflections on their collections. We had uncovered another way to think about the idea of *success* as we looked at children over time. A child who became very anxious about conventional math work for a very long time had mastered loom beading. This work required elaborate graph patterns and accurate estimations of numbers of beads necessary for the piece of jewelry. She was able to work through her difficulties to do the arithmetic calculations not only for her creations but in more abstract problem solving. Another child who had an amazing capacity to bring my plants back to life as though she breathed life into them would not document her process. She resisted any research and writing. Through her drawings and with her teacher at her side she pursued a study on plants that resulted in a detailed, well-researched book with illustrations. A boy had difficulty remaining within the classroom. He loved cooking and eating Italian food, and his teacher encouraged him to focus his search study on Italy. He created a large map of Italy working in the hallway and wrote a travel guide accompanied by his favorite Italian recipes. For as many children as there were, no matter how they entered the school or whether they received special services, there are stories that speak to their interest, knowledge, and drive to demonstrate what they are learning. The stories also speak to how teaching from a person's loved work arcs toward education as an integrative act. They did this in the company of the adults who were interested in how they thought and learned and who came to believe in their capacities.

We saw that success had to do with how a person takes authority and shapes their life as they move through school and their adult years. The descriptive work made visible that all the children had interesting ideas, a sense of who they were, awareness of what mattered to them and of how to draw on their strengths, engage with others, and imagine themselves as people who can affect the world they live in. We had spiraled forward from our question about being successful as a school to what it means to be a CPE 1 graduate, a CPE 1 staff member, a member of the CPE 1 community. We could measure our success as an educational institution by what our children carried with them, by how they transformed over the years as thinkers and shapers of their world.

CONCLUSION

Our work began as a set of sketches of a school from memory and legend. We started from what we found there in those sketches to see what mattered to us and what we wanted to develop. The respect for time, questioning, reflection, and inquiry embedded in Descriptive Processes allowed us to explore new ways of knowing and working together. We gained new knowledge and skills through our close looking within and beyond us. We challenged the status quo and sought change we had never imagined before. From there came our successive collective iterations as we continued our process of revision toward coherence and integration of the whole.

The ethic underlying descriptive practice as intellectual, democratic, and humanistic became integrated in our daily habits of thinking about and working with children, families, and one another. Any Descriptive Process requires an integrated statement of themes, threads, ideas, and perspectives that emerged to render the person, the work, the issue, and the activity whole again, making it larger than the sum of all its pieces. That is what we were continually doing to make our school.

Perhaps, though, this would not have become our work if it weren't for the 12 children in the MIS 4 class whose presence demanded that we open our eyes and minds to see and to learn together. Maybe the measure of our work and our success to become who we thought we were was how we did this together.

POSTSCRIPT

Jory captured our attention and imagination the very moment he arrived for 1st grade in Donna's K/1 class. He entered our school after we had moved to fully inclusive classrooms and while we were well into our inquiry. The descriptive work and the PerDev work were firmly established as ways of seeing and knowing and were infused into our practice and sensibilities. We were paying closer attention to the person in all his physical and sensory aspects as well as to his emotional, psychological, and intellectual/academic ways of being. The descriptive work grounded us particularly at times when we strayed or were uncertain about our choices and challenges. It was a thinking space that stabilized us and opened us up to discovery.

Jory became one of the children I referred to as belonging to all of us, touching all our lives and with whom we were as much in love as we were baffled and concerned. In many ways, Jory embodied the evidence of our progress as a school even as his person and presence periodically brought forth our doubts and questions. In fact, the school that Jory entered was not the same school in which we began our work on special education. He entered a school that immediately noticed him as a person, not as a problem.

Jory was a small child with a furrowed brow and a wide smile who held his head tilted upward and slightly to one side. His movements were floppy and undirected, and he sometimes waved his outstretched arms from side to side, trying to find his way and his balance. He stumbled and tripped even when there were no apparent physical impediments. Jory had to have physical contact with something sturdy or stable to maintain his balance, his body positioning. So he touched what was nearby, held someone's hand, gathered an adult's face in his hands while they were speaking, and positioned himself near a wall or table or adult body or nook in the classroom or closet where he could lean his body. His language was undifferentiated when it came to naming objects or shapes but fairly nuanced when expressing his feelings or making a humorous or even ironic comment about a situation or person's actions. However, his intonation and cadence were more like a younger child's. At various times during the day he had vocal and physical outbursts that were fairly contained in space but dramatic. These could be mediated by an adult's gentle touch and quiet talking into his ear. When he would collapse onto the floor in the hallway and roll his body around, it was helpful for an adult to stand nearby until he felt the boundary provided by the adult, settled himself, and regained his balance.

We did not know anything about Jory before he entered the school. He was not connected to the special education system. He came to us through the lottery through cousins who were already at CPE 1. At the end of the first day of school, his teacher told me with incredulity that he wasn't able to identify or recall the words for apples, pears, and oranges from looking at brightly colored pictures of them in a book. She wondered if he had a strong language discrepancy and handed me the book as she handed me Jory, who was to be picked up by his grandmother in the lobby.

I sat with him and together we looked at the book. As I turned the pages, he named every fruit an apple. There was something about the way he positioned his head in relation to the book and the light that made me wonder about how he was seeing. It occurred to me that his undifferentiated vocabulary may have had more to do with his vision than his language retrieval or processing.

As his teacher and I talked about him over the next few weeks, we wondered if how he used his hands and body were strategies for seeing around him and finding boundaries. We needed to learn more about Jory. A few years earlier this would have been code for requesting an evaluation. But now it meant drawing on our experience with the Descriptive Processes and the PerDev work, our growing knowledge about teaching many kinds of learners and the wealth of information that we gathered over the years about resources and supports available to us as a school and to individual children and families.

We presented Jory to the Children's Consultation Committee and created a plan. Our first action was to meet with his family to gather more information about his early history. We were particularly interested in his vision. His family agreed to have a full pediatric exam, including audiological, visual, and neurological. The most outstanding discrepancy was with his vision. He was given glasses, which he resisted wearing. He actually hid them in the back of the coat closet until he told us that he hated them. We finally realized that they were not comfortable for him, and his family had a new pair made that he wore without complaint. We were learning how to take cues from his behavior about how his body was responding to changes. Many of his large physical movements seemed mediated by his renewed vision as did his ability to verbally identify objects and pictures. But we were still not getting a very full picture of him.

Donna prepared a Descriptive Review with Cecelia that was a more detailed account of what we were already seeing. Before the Review, several staff made time to observe him in a variety of settings. Donna's Review was rich and participants' perspectives were insightful, but more questions than possibilities emerged for her and for all of us. In the end, we decided to consider an evaluation. We then spoke with the family about referring him for an evaluation. They were enthusiastic about the possibility of being able to get more support for him and for us.

The evaluation made clear that Jory would benefit from receiving special education services, adaptive physical education, and occupational therapy. All would be provided during the school day. He became of interest to our occupational therapist (OT), and his teacher, Donna, who had become adept with the PerDev work and began working with Jory under Roberta's supervision. In addition, Jory was one of the children who was included in our PerDev after-school program.

At the end of his first year, we realized that he would benefit from a second year with Donna and we created a K/1/2 class with a general education and a special education teacher, a paraprofessional, and an aide.

With all these supports in place, Jory began to adapt more easily to classroom and school routines, learn how to read, develop strong interests in construction, and participate in school performances. He became more confident about moving about the school independently and working with other children. He was becoming calmer in all settings and more resilient at times that used to cause him anxiety. He replaced holding a face in his hands with a penetrating gaze that made one feel seen and known. His eyesight did not interfere with his vision. He seemed to know a person at their core and used that as an opening to a long-lasting relationship.

Jory was far more responsive and connected to a few adults than to any children. We wondered about this and met with some family members, learning about their family structure and living situation and early history. Jory was very protected by his mom, dad, and extended family. The family worked with us and we with them at every step.

As Jory became more visible to us, he also remained mysterious. He was the child the music teacher brought to the storytelling we did at one meeting about a challenging child. Jory had developed a fear of the music room. The music teacher, drawing on what we had learned about Jory's visual challenges and imagination, showed Jory several items in the room that he suspected might be the cause. With Jory's input, he figured out that it was a green monster in a *Sesame Street* video. With Jory, the teacher discarded the video in a large trash can, promising to never return it to the room. He took his hand and led him back into the room to join his class.

Jory remained at CPE 1 through 4th grade. Although he continued to grow in many ways, we realized that our ability to educate him to his full potential was limited. Our OT specialist had become a full-time staff person at a funded special education school. Roberta and I spent a half-day at the school and were impressed with the caring atmosphere and opportunities available to children. We encouraged Jory's mother to visit to consider it a possible placement for Jory. It was difficult for all of us to part with one another. But we knew that Jory had many strengths and abilities to take with him to his new school.

Jory came to us as a puzzle—an individual whose pieces did not seem to fit together. Whatever age he was at one moment, he wasn't at another moment. Over his time with us, the pieces began to come together and we could see a more integrated person.

Although he was not one of our original study children, he became emblematic of what we were capable of doing as teachers and as a school. He tested our stamina, our search for understanding, our know-how, our willingness to stretch and shape our practice, our spirit, and our commitment to draw on the values that defined us. He held up a mirror that reflected the difficult work we had done together for more than 6 years—the work of holding onto what matters as we moved through a process of revision and transformation.

NOTES

1. With appreciation to Elaine Avidon for reading and helping to edit the chapter.
2. We extended this practice to every child in each classroom at the end of every school year.

Part III

SEEING AND ACTING WITH OTHERS

HOW DESCRIPTIVE INQUIRY SUPPORTS PRACTICAL WISDOM

CHAPTER 7

Changing a Perspective
No Easy Task

Cara E. Furman

> In every case, if a teacher couldn't see something, see a child in a certain way, he or she would always ask someone to come in or to have a spontaneous meeting about it or [ask] do I do a Descriptive Review or can you [Jane] come in?
>
> —Jane

The Common Core teacher standards require that the teacher use "understanding of individual learners and diverse cultures to ensure" that "each learner . . . meets high standards" (Council of Chief State School Officers, 2011, p. 17). Embedded within this standard is the assumption that teachers will take an empathic and understanding approach to all learners. As we have demonstrated, working to develop an "inclusive learning environment" that meets the needs of "each learner" (p. 17) is necessary and extremely challenging (Himley & Carini, 2000; Ruitenberg, 2016; Smith, 2007).

As you reflect on this challenge, consider any people whom you perpetually find frustrating, perplexing, or simply opaque. Are there people with whom you could never shift a negative dynamic? Now bring to mind anyone you currently find or recently found challenging to engage with in some way. Throughout this book we have introduced you to many such children. In Chapter 1, Cara wrote about Thomas, who seemed to resist the rules teachers laid out. In Chapter 3, Cecelia described Dajay, who challenged her classroom expectations of stillness with constant movement, and Chris, who perceived (accurately) that he was invisible to his teachers. In Chapter 5, Cara shared her confusion over William, who would not write despite all his gifts with language. In Chapter 6, Jane wrote about Jory—a child who many in her school found compelling and mysterious. In other cases, the challenges occurred between adults. In the introduction, Meredith was frustrated by some of her students and her colleague's way of responding. In

Chapter 4, Rachel inherited a school culture rife with interpersonal tensions among staff. Note the differences among what different teachers found challenging and the different kinds of challenges. Now again consider someone you find challenging to engage with. Settle your mind on one person.

Write a question you have about your work with this person. Then, using the headings of the Descriptive Review, describe this person in some detail: Physical Presence and Gesture, Disposition and Temperament, Connections With Other People, Strong Interests and Preferences, and Modes of Thinking and Learning. After you have written in some depth, try to rearticulate the question you have about your work with this person. Then share your writing and your question with a few others—a small group is ideal.

Perspective. Your frame. The lenses through which you see. Your vantage point and what that vantage point allows you to see. In each of our examples, changing how we worked with the people required changing how we perceived them. For example, Cecelia describes how she initially saw Dajay's actions as in opposition to her teaching goals. She recounts regularly asking him to sit down and how this request often went "unheeded." Reflecting on her experience, Cecelia comments, "He was a source of frustration." Yet Cecelia spoke in the past tense. After juxtaposing Dajay's movement indoors with his tree dance, Cecelia came to feel quite differently. Therefore, the question of this chapter is how we can continue to expand our scope of seeing, maybe even moving to a new place from which to see "from another angle."

A MOST NOBLE DEED

In a folktale attributed to Mexico, a dying mother tells her three sons that whoever performs the "most noble deed" will receive her inheritance (Baltuck, 1995, p. 19). The first son gives half of his possessions to the poor. Despite being a weak swimmer, the second dives into a powerful river to save a child. The third finds a man who had vowed to kill him sleeping at the edge of a cliff. After some quick consideration, the third son takes "his enemy" in his arms and moves him to safety. This act of kindness turns enmity to friendship. After hearing about each act, the mother concludes that giving to the poor and saving a child are "the right way to behave" (p. 20). By "risk[ing] your life to save one who had sworn to kill you," it is the third son who has acted extraordinarily. He has, in the words of the mother, "with one act of kindness . . . transformed hatred to love and made the world a better place" (p. 21). Remaining open to others and reforming a troubled relationship is, according to the mother, a "most noble deed."

Where the act of rescue and the transformation of a damaged relationship is the focus of the folktale, I am most intrigued by the son's ability to shift his perspective of the man in a critical moment and then to quickly act in a way that not only saved the man but also restored their relationship. As a teacher invested in helping others see and act differently, I am most intrigued by a key detail left out of the folktale: What happened as he considered the man at the edge of the cliff? We hear about his action, but we cannot see his internal workings. We do not know what mental process led to the third son being able to act over and above the "right way to behave." Specifically, what were the previous experiences and relationships that resulted in the deep-down knowledge of what must be done so that, despite his first instinct, he rescued the man?

Our colleague, long-term early childhood educator and regular summer participant at the Institute on Descriptive Inquiry Charles Ragland, in a session on mentoring likened the experienced teacher to a swan. He explained that the new teacher simply sees the elegant form gliding above the water, not the awkward legs frantically paddling beneath the surface. In Chapter 2, we used the word *exercises* to describe some of the preparatory work that teachers engage in prior to acting so that their actions appear smooth in the moment. These inner workings are often and unfortunately left out of the conversation about teaching, yet they are crucial.

Alisa Algava, another participant of the Institute on Descriptive Inquiry with extensive experience as both a teacher and a school leader, commented

> I used to think that few and far between teachers had the "magic" of truly seeing, respecting, loving, guiding kids in the way each child needs and deserves. (Of course this is totally compounded—if not caused —by the screwed-up educational systems and sociopolitical economy of racial capitalism we learn and live in.) It was only after being introduced to Descriptive Inquiry that I realized this "magic" can indeed be shared, learned, and grown.

As must be infinitely clear at this point, in Cecelia's case with Dajay, her "pumping legs" beneath the surface were strengthened by a long-term engagement in Descriptive Inquiry. It was that work that supported Cecelia in noticing Dajay's dance and bringing that noticing back to her work with him in the classroom. As she let her new interpretation help her rework her approach to him, the vantage points from which she saw him expanded and opened up new possibilities. As described, I too consistently turn to Descriptive Inquiry whenever puzzled by a student, as I did when working with Thomas. I find that because of this regular practice, I, like the third son, assume now that I will find a peaceable way (Furman, 2018). We are in good company. In addition to the school leaders and teachers quoted throughout this book, Descriptive Inquiry has helped many shift their perspectives as well (Abu El-Haj, 2003; Carini, 2001; Carini & Himley, 2010; Gasoi et al., 2016; Himley & Carini, 2000; Knoester, 2008; Rodgers, 2011a, b). So how has it done so? In this chapter, I analyze some of the components.

THE POWER OF PERSPECTIVE

I start with a story. I am on Facebook looking at an image of a friend's two children leaning against a wall of the Colosseum staring at what appears to be smartphones with intent. Soon a comment appears, something to the effect of "Wow, even at the Colosseum, children are more interested in their phones." Seen from that lens, the picture is a perfect capture of technological ennui. The mother, though, steps in by responding, reframing, "Yes. It could look like that, but they are following a children's guidebook that they found very interesting." I am struck, watching this mini-narrative unfold at how much changes with just a tiny bit of information. In hearing the mother's account, not only do we better understand what the children are doing, but our perception of them has shifted too. No longer are they examples of a generation lost in their phones but instead they are two young people learning complex history in a rather sophisticated way. Same picture. Same children. A world of difference in the interpretations.

This example illustrates both the power of perspective and what can begin to shift it—more information, new ideas generated by a group, reimagining. In this case, the shift was made easily. Someone who paid attention and cared for the children quickly corrected any misconceptions by placing the action in context. Put differently, the children had what Foucault (2001, 2012) refers to as a truth teller, someone who is willing to speak the truth frankly, even when doing so is risky. The mother was willing to risk upsetting and even possibly losing the corrected friend, for the sake of providing the context, and a truth, about her children. In doing so, she helped everyone see them through a capacity lens. The original commenter acknowledged she was wrong and shared her updated perception. In schools, more often than not, that truth teller must be the child's teacher. And to be able to see each child through a capacity lens, the teacher must often alter their own initial impressions.

In this chapter, I will describe how shifting perspective is achieved through attending; taking in the context; juxtaposition; and finally, care.

ATTENDING

Dewey writes, "A moving blur catches our eye in the distance; we ask ourselves: 'What is it? Is it a cloud of whirling dust? a tree waving its branches? a man signaling to us?'" (1910/1997, p. 102). I offer a classroom blur. A child. I come at the request of his teacher to observe and find him literally spinning during her lesson. I do an anecdotal of him during a meeting in which I transcribe every action for a short stretch and, in doing so, capture a child pivoting round and round and round on his bottom. I watch him outside playing tag—shifting his body constantly to relocate the child he is chasing. I work with him and notice that he can turn his head when asked to but otherwise tracks objects by shifting his whole body.

It is in pausing with a situation that we can make sense, determine better what might be occurring. Yet, as any teacher knows, this pausing in the classroom is not so easy. Try taking a picture of a child. More often than not, you find yourself with a blur. That said, there are many actions that can help a teacher look more closely such as video or audio taping, studying work samples, and taking notes. In Descriptive Review, though any of these approaches might be taken, a key element of the methodology is describing. As Carini (2001) writes, "describing, I pause, and pausing, attend. Describing requires that I stand back and consider" (p. 163).

Returning to the child, describing I paused and describing I was able to see and see again the spinning child as he moved through space. The child who had seemed to be a blur of movement is suddenly brought into focus through description. Returning to the classroom, I see that he is not simply spinning aimlessly but instead turning to follow the conversation. Every time a classmate speaks, he swivels. Then swivels back to the teacher. When the meeting ends, he collapses on the floor. Yet what I have done is not simply describing. It is taking what I have seen, looking more closely, and, as I explain in the next section, placing one idea alongside another.

CONTEXT

Dewey writes, "If a person comes suddenly into your room and calls out 'Paper,' various alternatives are possible" (1910/1997, p. 116). For example,

> If the cry is the usual accompaniment of the delivery of the morning paper, the sound will have meaning, intellectual content; you will understand it. Or if you are eagerly awaiting the receipt of some important document, you may assume that cry means an announcement of its arrival. If (in the third place) you understand the English language, but no context suggests itself from your habits and expectations, the *word* has meaning, but not the whole event. (p. 117)

In Descriptive Inquiry, context is often achieved by taking the holistic approach of a Descriptive Review of the Child. By describing the child in this way, particular actions can be contextualized. Carini writes,

> Another boy, age 10, a student at Prospect School, when asked about a vial of water he had taken to carrying around, responded that he was trying to start life in a bottle. Further conversation revealed that the basis of his quest was knowledge of the origins of life gleaned from a documentary. The same boy's

persistent and absorbed interest in dissecting roadkill found and brought to school took on a somewhat different meaning when viewed from the angle of a search for life—as did his fascination with Mary Shelley's *Frankenstein*. (Himley, 1991, pp. 22–25, quoted in Carini & Himley, 2010, p. 155)

First, I highlight that the teacher began by attending. They noticed the child's actions, carrying a vial of water, and followed up with this noticing with questions and gleaned "his quest was knowledge of the origins of life." As such, the teacher has determined meaning from an act that could be dismissed as eccentric or neurotic by putting it in the context of its meaning to the child. I was doing the same with the spinning child. When I witnessed him struggle to turn his head when playing tag, I began to wonder about his ease with this movement. When I visited him in class, his meeting area spinning made sense. I saw him spin to face one speaker and then the next. No longer was he aimlessly spinning or restless but a person trying to follow the conversation. When he collapsed at the end of the meeting, where I previously saw silliness, I now see exhaustion.

JUXTAPOSITION

In her interview, featured in Chapter 9, Cecelia describes juxtaposition as a way of knowing—a capacity to frequently place one characteristic, concept, perspective alongside another. In the Descriptive Review of the Child, one feature about a child is placed alongside another often seemingly very different characteristic. In the previous example, Carini illustrates this idea in action. Her story shows the ways an interest that might seem troubling and morbid, dissecting road kill, could be seen as inquisitive and life-affirming, when juxtaposed with an interest in *Frankenstein* and the child's expressed interest in life's origins. Here context, made richer through juxtaposition, and ascertained by attention and ideas about meaning, matters quite a bit.

Another child I once worked with was frequently removed from class for acts classified as aggressive such as pushing blocks into the backs of classmates. After observing this child, I was struck by the way he moved in the hallway, head facing upward, not forward. I tried this myself and found this made balance difficult. I frequently saw the same child leaning against walls as he walked, lying on the floor, and turning the pages of a book by pushing with his palms. These noticings, taken alongside one another, made me see his block-pushing differently. Perhaps, I wondered, he was not intending to hurt classmates with the blocks. Perhaps he was trying to determine boundaries. Or maybe cause and effect. (Both difficult to perceive when your head is tilted toward the sky.)

CARE

Returning to Dewey and the shout of "Paper," he argues that without context, you cannot readily make meaning, but you can (and should) assume meaning is there. As he explains,

> You are then perplexed and incited to think out, to hunt for, some explanation of the apparently meaningless occurrence. If you find something that accounts for the performance, it gets meaning; you come to understand it. As intelligent beings, we presume the existence of meaning, and its absence as anomaly. (1910/1997, p. 117)

Read through this lens, the children looking at their phones leaning against the Colosseum are presumed to have purpose. The child collecting road kill is assumed to have purpose. The child spinning is assumed to have purpose. I will go a step further. Teachers should not only presume meaning but make these presumptions through the lens of care. As Carini writes, observing is "an attitude or way of looking that I prefer to think of as *attending to children with care*" (Himley & Carini, 2000, p. 56). Carini goes on to describe the Descriptive Review of the Child as "an exercise that is meant to do just that: to value and recognize your [teachers' and parents'] interest, caring, and knowledge and to build upon it for the benefit of children" (p. 56). To do so would mean not simply looking at the children on their phones and assuming they had a purpose but also looking and assuming something positive about the children. The child pushing blocks into his classmate is given the benefit of the doubt that his purpose was not to harm his peers but was perhaps an exploration of physical boundaries.

Whether the lens through which we look focuses us on the positive or the negative matters quite a bit. When I stopped labeling the child pushing blocks into his peers as aggressive and began to see him as someone struggling to orient himself in the world, I had a more positive entry point. The block-pushing still had to stop, but I now had a way to frame my redirection from a place of gentle care. Our relationship improved, and more importantly, so did the ways I treated him.

As another example, my 3-year-old can be rough with his 10-month old brother. As much as I love my older child, watching him squeeze his brother, yell in his face, and pinch his cheeks is maddening. Usually I crankily and firmly say, "Leave your brother alone." Desperate to offer the benefit of the doubt, I once asked, "Is he just so cute that all you want to do is touch his face and squeeze him?" "Yes," my older son said soberly. And with this query and confession, we had a way forward. Instead of saying, "Stop bothering your brother!" I could say, "Are you just loving him so much you want to squeeze him?" The former comment got defensiveness and rebellion; with the latter, the result was, more often than not, a pause from the activity and a gentler touch with the baby.

CHANGING PERSPECTIVE

At the beginning of this chapter, I asked you to write about a person you found frustrating. Put differently, you wrote about a person you needed to see from another angle. After writing and sharing, has your perspective shifted? Has this changed how you feel about the person? Did your question change after you had described the person using the headings? Did it alter again after you got feedback? Finally and crucially, has this exercise given you some ideas about how to engage differently with this person?

In this chapter I have identified some ways that Descriptive Inquiry helps people to attend to someone else's perspective and, in doing so, think about and act differently with others. Finally, I close by emphasizing that, ideally, attending, taking in the context, juxtaposing, and finally finding ways to care is done in the company of others—true friends, like the mother at the beginning of this piece, willing to speak truths about what they see that might expand your vision. In the following chapters, we examine this collaboration more closely. In Chapter 8, we look at a school-based structure in which teachers were supported by peers in changing perspective and identifying new ways of acting with children. Then, in Chapter 9, we zoom in on Cecelia's work, looking specifically at what it means to support schools not as a consultant but instead, as a true friend, an interlocutor who listens and speaks frankly.

Supporting and Being Supported

Cara E. Furman and Alison Hazut

Think of a student who struggled to be successful in a particular class. Success is broadly defined. Perhaps this was a student who frequently fought with the teacher. Perhaps they had conflicts regularly with fellow students. Perhaps pacing was a challenge; they liked to work slowly and couldn't keep up. Perhaps difficulties with working memory made completing math work very challenging. This could be a student you taught, observed, or was in school with as a peer. The student could be you or your own child. Take some notes on this student using the headings of the Descriptive Review of the Child: Physical Presence and Gesture, Disposition and Temperament, Connections with Others, Strong Interests and Preferences, and Modes of Thinking and Learning. Also describe the context. Focus on the elements of the environment that the student struggled with. If you know of any, consider environments where this child did well. For example, in Chapter 3, Cecelia described how Dajay blossomed when he was outside dancing as a leaf falling from a tree but struggled in her classroom.

Consider how you would tell this as a story. Seek out colleagues and share. What themes emerge? Specifically, focus on what you knew going into this situation that positively informed your response. Who or what helped you to respond with care? As you read this chapter, keep your student in mind as you work to understand how teachers at the Earth School support students who struggle in their classes.

In Chapter 5, Cara shared how Descriptive Inquiry helped her as a teacher at the Earth School be more inclusive of a child and feel more included herself. In Chapter 6, Jane explores a range of ways in which Descriptive Inquiry built a more democratic and inclusive community at CPE 1. In both cases, using the processes during regular faculty meetings with the full teaching body achieved those goals. In this chapter, we add another layer, that is, looking at how, in addition to the regular whole-school practice of Descriptive Inquiry, the processes of Descriptive Inquiry were modified and compacted somewhat into a structure called the *Support Team* to meet a particular need and accommodate the busy pace of a school. We share this to show how, in the context of a well-developed schoolwide descriptive stance and the practical wisdom about children that resulted from the practice of Descriptive Inquiry, a principal and teachers can modify the Descriptive Processes to supplement other ongoing work. Namely, we describe the Support Team, a practice that grew out of Descriptive Inquiry.

To describe the Support Team from multiple angles, this chapter is narrated by two voices. First, Alison, the principal who developed this process with the support of colleagues and Cecelia, will speak to how ongoing practice of Descriptive Inquiry led to the desire to create the Support Team, the ways in which the processes influenced the structure itself, and some of the influences the Support Team had on the school. Cara will then share how she drew on Descriptive Inquiry as Support Team Coordinator.

ADJUSTING OUR VISION OF CHILDREN: ALISON'S NARRATIVE

Teachers working collaboratively in support of children's growth and their own practice makes good sense. As showcased in previous chapters, true collaboration where educators feel safe, seen, and understood among their colleagues is hard to build. It takes a culture of empowerment, voice, and a sense of freedom to be creative. It also takes democratic leadership, what Cecelia refers to as authority. Developing this kind of teaching and learning culture has been a focus of mine as a school leader. In fact, in a Review of Practice with the full staff, I shared my belief in and efforts to enact democratic leadership. In that Review I described the kinds of decisions I made as principal and named when I had tried to be inclusive about whom I consulted and when I made the decisions myself. I also described how I worked to communicate my decisions with the school community. For me, and I think for the staff, the Review was an opportunity to publicly sort through my efforts to enact democratic decision making and assess those efforts in the context of the school and its needs.

Keeping children at the heart of all of my decisions has been paramount and a key part of my leadership. As I will describe below, the need to put children's holistic needs at the forefront of our work presented a moment where I took the lead and drew on my authority—making a change that I then worked with the staff to enact.

Identifying an Area for the School's Growth:
The Need for an Alternative Way of Seeing

At the Earth School we began to notice a steady rise in the number of children being referred to special education. This trend was concerning in a school where, not so long ago, we consciously did not identify any child for fear that labels would lead to isolation of some children and go against our deep belief in the capacity of every child. One of our guiding principles was to know each child through their unique experience and use their strengths to guide us in supporting areas for growth. Regular practice of Descriptive Inquiry helped us to keep this principle alive, keeping us close to our values and invigorating our methods.

Yet, slowly over time, we began to acknowledge that there are circumstances when specialized services are needed to support children. Despite our commitment to knowing and treasuring each child, something had happened. We found ourselves in a place of thinking that we should and could "fix" children, rather than consider the circumstances that caused their fragility, such as poverty, trauma, and the very short supply of mental health supports in schools. The change had occurred in our school, reflecting what seems like a more pervasive focus in our culture on modifying the individual. It was also the result of No Child Left Behind legislation, high-stakes testing, the implementation of the New Teacher Evaluation: Annual Professional Performance Review (APPR),[1] and the Common Core.

As often happens with cultural shifts, we weren't aware of this shift in mindset in our day-to-day work and so we didn't speak about it; it's one of those things that becomes unearthed when you take the time to step back, reflect, and look closely. During one of our monthly Descriptive Reviews of Children, while we were in our last round of the process, it was clear that we had a plethora of *outside-of-the-box* thoughts about how best to support the child. I felt that some teachers could take that thinking and truly implement it to shift practice in support of the child. A few, though, would leave the Review seemingly inspired and then go back to doing the same thing they had done before. As we left the Review that day, I began to think that somehow we needed to bridge this formal work with our more informal structures in order to ensure that all of us were trying out innovative methods with our most vulnerable children.

In New York City, when children struggle in the classroom, a first step in getting services is a referral to the Pupil Personnel Team (PPT). At the time, PPT was a mixed group of educators, including our guidance counselor, social worker, psychologist, special educators, and myself. This team's primary purpose was to work in support of children who had been diagnosed with learning disabilities. Together we reviewed IEPs, assessing progress as well as revising services to best support each child. In addition, the team would meet with teachers who had concerns about children who were labeled "at risk"—a term given to us by the, New York State Education Department (NYSED). Often, the PPT would develop a plan of support that included some form of remediation and/or a typical special education service. It made sense that the PPT would draw on its members' experiences and expertise in order to support children. This practice, though, had some negative consequences. Inadvertently a reliance on external expertise meant that we were lumping together "at risk" children with those who had been evaluated and diagnosed, and who were working on specifically targeted plans. Discussing children both with and without IEPs, the conversation sometimes veered toward how the child might be modified as opposed to a closer look at how classroom conditions could shift so that the child would thrive. Because the IEP process often results in medical labels in order for a child to receive services, we were generalizing too much of the time with some blanket terms like "attention deficit disorder" and no longer coming at the work through a descriptive stance. This labeling had significant implications. For example, a child who needs constant movement and has trouble settling into an activity and a child who has trouble transitioning from one activity to another in class because they focus on the current task so intently could both be labeled as having attention deficit disorder. What these children would need both from an expert and in class is very different. Additionally, following the national trend, most of the children diagnosed were Black and Latinx even though our school was unusually mixed racially. As a school that actively sought to combat racism and teach for equity, this was very disturbing.

Although we had been doing Descriptive Reviews and Reviews of Practice during our regular professional development, we weren't applying those practices in one of the most vital school structures: PPT. It was a startling revelation. As a school leader, I began to realize that we needed to reflect about professional development and share ways that we were growing and learning beyond our monthly Inquiry sessions. In essence, how were we taking what we learned from Descriptive Inquiry and applying that understanding to our daily work with children?

Developing the Support Team Collaboratively

I approached a teacher on the PPT, Vanessa Keller, to help me imagine a new structure to look more closely at children and find creative ways to support them. I turned to Vanessa for a number of reasons. First, she was general and special education certified. She looked at children holistically and not from a deficit stance. Further, she was creative in her approaches to children and able to use Reviews to inform her practice. I thought these qualities were needed in order to shift our focus back to environmental supports as opposed to fixing the child. I hoped that together we could find ways to help classroom teachers support children as she did—that is, more holistically and in an asset-oriented way.

Our first step was to engage in reflective writing over the course of several summer days when our minds were open and we had the time. In this writing, Vanessa and I reviewed our meeting notes from PPT discussions over the past few years. We focused on specific children about whom we were wondering in terms of how their IEPs were working or not working in support of their growth. We reflected about our process and also reviewed the children's work to deepen our understandings about their strengths and some of the gaps the PPT was concerned about. Through this writing, we began to see why and how these gaps had happened at least from a systemic point of view. For example, with the emphasis on high-stakes testing all of us were capable of making fear-based decisions, as the school was evaluated on the scores of such exams. Classroom teachers were and still are under extreme pressure even in a school that has always placed these exams in their right place—one piece of information about a child that was of less importance to our work with the child than our ongoing assessments of the child's work.

Vanessa and I envisioned a new group: the *Support Team*. I recall it taking us quite a while to come up with that name. As the group was developed to help teachers and do better by students, we wanted something that resonated with teachers. Therefore, we asked the full staff to weigh in once we articulated the role the team would play at our school. At this juncture it seemed important that I move from taking the lead with Vanessa's collaboration to involving the staff more democratically.

Nevertheless, I was committed to some details. Of utmost importance was who made up the team. As a school, we believed that a dynamic group of committed educators, who were looking for more meaningful connections with colleagues, would do this work well and be eager to take on this extra task. When I consulted the staff, we decided that we needed teachers who had the long view of children—those who teach special classes like art, science, and cooking for all children, PreK\K–5 grade. As an added plus, the teachers who held those positions were veterans of the school and especially committed to Descriptive Inquiry. I therefore suspected they would bring descriptive language and a holistic approach to the table. Out-of-classroom teachers know children for several years and see them outside of the general class context; they also are less concerned with standardized testing. I had already observed that our out-of-classroom teachers often felt on the outside of professional work in the building as in staff meetings we tended to work on content and grade-specific matters. Bringing them into this team was a way of honoring their work, maximizing the use of their expertise as well as their robust understanding of children. As I had hoped, they all eagerly accepted the offer to serve on the team. We also wanted our guidance counselor, a general educator, a special educator, and myself on the team. I wanted a teacher, in the role of Support Team Coordinator, to lead this effort for two reasons: to develop teacher leadership and to make it more possible for me to be an active part of the group while the coordinator would lead the meetings.

Through some trial and error, we came to a process. The group met weekly for 30 minutes. The coordinator was responsible for a rotating schedule of presenting teachers, one or two each session. Teachers presented a child to our Support Team through a set of guiding questions that condensed what we used to reflect about children through the formal

Descriptive Review process and allowed the teacher to describe concerns. *What are the child's interests and strengths? How does the child approach choice-based work versus teacher-directed tasks? What concerns do you have about the child's development?* The coordinator reviewed work samples ahead of the meeting, helped the teacher frame a focus question, and met with the teacher to flesh out the description. She would also take notes to help bridge these pre-discussions with our formal sessions and serve as important documentation as we tracked progress over time. At the meeting, after hearing the description and sometimes the teacher's frustration and doing a go-round of responses to the focus question, a Support Team member buddied up with the presenting teacher to work with the teacher and/or the child. The Support Team met in the middle and at the end of each cycle to reflect on how things were going for the children and teachers they had reviewed/worked with over the last period. The documentation that the coordinator kept was critical in tracking progress. It provided a follow-up trail. In the school, we had often engaged in deep verbal and mindful debates and discussions, but we had not kept written records other than the notes from the monthly Descriptive Review sessions. The Support Team documentation and our follow-up meeting became integral to our reporting outside of the school about children's progress. And this ongoing documentation provided us with rich qualitative data, which helped us to be specific about the growth of children and teachers' practice. It also helped us to celebrate success and feel the rewards of our work—something educators often don't find the time to do.

Supporting Children and Teachers Symbiotically

Over time I noticed that the Support Team was as important for teachers' growth as it was for children's growth. This benefit was unexpected. Often, teachers shared intimate details about their perceived failures in their work with children. It seemed they appreciated the chance to vent and express worries and doubts about a child's learning in their care. They needed to reflect in a safe space. Using the Descriptive Processes in the context of the Support Team provided this environment.

One teacher in particular comes to mind. Mindy brought a child forward, Jenny, who was thriving during open work (a time when children experimented with materials and developed projects of their choosing), lunch, and recess but who would avoid almost all teacher-directed work. Mindy's assessments showed that Jenny's skills did not meet her expectations for her age,[2] whereas her conceptual understandings were strong. Jenny engaged in a lot of negative self-talk, seemed unwilling to take risks in learning, and avoided the academic work of the class by doing open-work or self-directed activities all day. To us, these were signs of a lack of confidence. In addition, Jenny behaved in ways that challenged Mindy's authority in the classroom. This combination of factors meant that we were concerned about Jenny's overall happiness in school. At the Support Team meeting, Mindy revealed her frustrations with Jenny and her guilty feelings about not yet figuring out how to reach her. These revelations also made us concerned about Mindy. The teacher's happiness too was at stake. We wondered how we could help both of them in a relationship that seemed mutually fraught.

Each member of the Support Team had a few flexible periods in their weekly schedule that allowed them to partner with teachers through co-teaching and intervisitations, and to work in small groups or even one-to-one with a child. The kind of support was thoughtfully planned by the team, and we agreed that plans needed to be short and intense, ideally, daily over a period of 6 to 8 weeks,[3] and sometimes longer.

Another integral part of the process was bringing the parents into this work. The Support Team Coordinator and the child's teacher would meet with parents to share the plan and gather input. Children being served through the Support Team were also conferred with to ensure buy-in. The coordinator did an informal interview with the child before a plan was developed, and the coordinator and the teacher met with the child to discuss the plan. At the close of a cycle, the child reflected with the coordinator about how the plan had worked.

Ultimately, one of our teachers on the Support Team partnered with Mindy in a unique way. She offered to teach her class once a week while Mindy spent one-on-one time with Jenny in her classroom. In Chapter 7, Cara argued that sometimes people need to find new ways of seeing students to work with them. Our plan was to give both Mindy and Jenny a new way of seeing each other by providing a different learning space with engaging materials. This strategy would help them both move past their frustrations and start to heal a relationship that hadn't been particularly smooth.

Mindy, for her part, felt strongly that she needed to connect with Jenny and also that she could reach her through interesting activities. She also wanted to help develop Jenny's skills, primarily in basic mathematics, and while she saw the need for relationship building, she didn't want to lose sight of that endgame. All teachers like to see children make progress and can create their own internal pressures. Mindy felt pressure to move quickly to reach her academic goals for Jenny. In addition, even though our school sought to honor the child, we operated in a context with tremendous pressure for children to succeed quickly. The pressure of high-stakes testing gave us little wiggle room around promotion. Though I worked hard to protect children and teachers from this pressure, it still seeped in. It was actually possible for Mindy to make more space and time for this child to grow than she thought she could. As such, the Support Team aimed to slow her down by helping her to see that she was no longer alone in this work and that we all agreed it would take time to do this well.

Having a team acknowledge Mindy and provide her with space, time, and permission to focus first on the relationship and Mindy's strength proved huge. As principal, I knew that my staff, like Mindy, were all incredibly hard on themselves. Even though I know that teaching is emotional, personal work, I had found it difficult to regularly carve out opportunities to acknowledge the complexities. Schools are incredibly busy places, and we are all entrenched in the work. The Support Team structure was a natural opportunity to describe growth in teachers and children, and to listen to the frustrations and successes. The Support Team gave me as principal the space to take care of my teachers in ways that I had previously found difficult to find time for.

Mindy and Jenny began by making a marble run together out of recycled materials. Mindy's documentation of the work showed that Jenny was taking responsibility and working with skilled perseverance. She particularly thrived with a clear yet flexible structure about how their time would be spent. For example, Mindy wrote, "Jenny would often check the timer to see how much time was left before they needed to clean up. She even alerted me when there were only 3 minutes left yesterday." After 3 weeks they'd co-constructed a marble run made primarily out of carefully cut-up paper towel rolls and tape. Mindy shared the process with the Support Team at the mid-review meeting.

With a much-improved relationship and a deeper knowledge of Jenny's abilities, Mindy and Jenny were ready to take on some academic goals. But, as noted at the start of this chapter, finding creative ways to use what we know about a child to support more traditional skill building is not always clear, and Mindy still needed help. She now used the team to plan how to build on the work already done with Jenny and start on the mathematical skills that Jenny needed to solidify.

Together, through descriptive rounds, we reviewed a few projects that would require Jenny's depth of understanding and simultaneously support her basic computation. We decided that a budgeting project would strike the balance we were looking for. In a traditional Descriptive Review, a project like this might be posed as an idea but not a plan. Many of my teachers can run with this whereas many others need logistical support putting the plan in action. Typically, that support might come from a colleague the teacher is close to, a coach, or me. For example, in Cara's Review of William, the need for authentic writing opportunities emerged. Responding to this need, the pre-K teacher, Shonelle Cooper-Kaplan, offered to have her class write letters with Cara's class to support William. Cara's and Shonelle's students already met weekly as "reading buddies." Shonelle therefore built on a previously established relationship with Cara as well as a connection that already existed between their students. Yet sometimes, without a structure in place, changes don't come and the teacher continues to struggle with the same student.

Although Mindy had an important influence on what was ultimately done, she was one teacher who benefited from additional support. Our

Support Team Coordinator offered \$75 from her budget to help Jenny consider how to plan a party for her class. I then agreed to match that amount so that they had larger numbers to work with and to show my support. Mindy thought it made sense to have Jenny bring the project into the classroom and allowed her to choose a few friends to work with. The Support Team teacher who had been teaching the class while Mindy was working one on one with Jenny continued to be present during these times. She worked with other children while Mindy focused her facilitation on Jenny and her small group.

Jenny too ultimately influenced the plan. She decided to conduct surveys among her classmates to see what they wanted to do and eat during the party. Each member of her small group gathered the data and then shared it with Mindy, who guided them through moving from tallies to addition and then to analysis of what they should purchase. The children continued to research where to buy the food, plates, and utensils in order to pay the cheapest price. The project was a huge success from the planning to the event. In her final interview, Jenny was able to see that the party had succeeded because of her thorough planning and solid math skills.

The Support Team Intervention was also a huge success. Jenny made progress in terms of her mathematical skills. Yet, perhaps more important was the reciprocal trust that was built between Jenny and Mindy. Having worked closely together, they now trusted each other. This allowed both Jenny and Mindy to be happier in the classroom. It helped Jenny learn more smoothly with her teacher.

At the culminating Support Team meeting, Mindy began by sharing that though she still had concerns about Jenny, she was pleased with how far she had come. Mindy spent most of her reflection time recognizing how her pedagogy had changed over the two-month period and that the behavioral concerns had almost completely dissipated. Mindy seemed to recognize the importance of bridging open work and teacher-directed curricula. She talked about tweaking her schedule somewhat to provide more time for open work and ways that she could extend and weave classroom curricula through the open work structure where Jenny thrived. It was clear that she felt gratitude for the Support Team as she was no longer alone in what was a very difficult situation. During the end of the cycle session, Jenny reported increased confidence in terms of her mathematical skills, but she also felt that the time spent one on one with Mindy was the best part. She even pitched another project idea as she also enjoyed working closely with her peers on something that was meaningful to her.

Concluding Thoughts

The Support Team is a prime example of how a school can grow practices without outside resources. Public schools are always charged with meeting the needs of our "at risk" populations, but there is never enough money to get external help to think creatively about how to accomplish this, nor is there money to support the kind of internally developed work we were doing. As a principal, I had very little discretionary funds to work with. This challenged my ability to apply practical wisdom. I had to think very creatively about how to hire the Support Team Coordinator and to justify why our specials teachers would have some flexible time built into their schedules. Outside administrators and policy makers would regularly suggest using certain packaged, prescribed programs to work with our most puzzling children. This option would bleed an already very tight budget and, frankly, would not help personalize learning experiences for the children. It was also rare that these programs fit with the values already in place at the Earth School. Similarly, many popular staff developers and professional development packages felt out of place with what my teachers needed and valued. Budgeting for the Support Team meant committing money to the kind of personalized and contextualized problem solving about teaching that I believed so deeply was best for children.

Though we didn't seek traditional external avenues, we did not confine support to the walls of the school. For some of our kids coming through the Support Team, we believed that life experiences outside of school was what was most needed and would best level the playing field. We envisioned a plan for family field trips on the weekends and looked for grant opportunities so that we could fund them. Because mental health was in many cases connected to our concerns regarding children, I began to research how to integrate on-site mental health providers and ultimately hired an additional psychologist for the school.

The Support Team was built from a shared belief in the school that we educators have the needed tools and ideas and that, with the concentration of our time and focus, we could accomplish almost anything. Once teachers began to see the value of our Support Team, our calendar filled up and we began to notice that small groups of teachers were meeting during off periods and having similar discussions about children and their work.

Descriptive Inquiry laid the foundation for the Support Team, but I found some teachers needed even more. Coupling our monthly Descriptive Inquiry work with this more weekly and daily approach, I felt our roots went deeper. As an administrator I've found that faddish new approaches or top-down administrative directives rarely lead to meaningful change. Instead, when a new approach is rooted in a school, that's when we begin to see cultural shifts. Before I left the Earth School, we saw a slow decrease in children referred for special education evaluation. Committing to our meeting times to do Reviews of Practice, Work, and Children yielded the richest ideas to help us move forward in our craft and for us to continue honoring the children we served. Time, the Descriptive Processes, our belief in ourselves and our children, and the pedagogical and emotional supports that the Support Team facilitated allowed all of us to grow in this work.

BEING SEEN AS A TEACHER AND A LEARNER: CARA'S NARRATIVE

I (Cara) have worked at the Earth School in a variety of capacities and over a stretch of time. My initial exposure was as a substitute teacher. I had found the school online and, from my reading, believed it was in sync with my values. When I substituted, I was thrilled that not only was the curriculum progressive and the children kind and engaged academically, but that the teachers were unusually welcoming. My first time substituting, I was in a class that was known to be difficult. That day, teachers made a point of making sure I felt welcomed. When I returned, I was greeted warmly and heralded for doing well with a class tough on substitutes. I knew when I applied for a position that spring that this was a place I very much wanted to work.

I took a job as a 1st- and 2nd-grade teacher and again felt welcomed. Teachers met with me over the summer, and the principal, then Michelle, was enthusiastic about my ideas. Teachers were accepting of my limitations as a new teacher and generally supportive of my successes. I had colleagues who shared their ideas with me and leadership who gave me helpful advice. I can still remember each meeting I had with Michelle and Alison (first as assistant principal and then as principal) because they always offered key insights.

Leaving after 3 years for graduate school was very difficult. I loved teaching, the children and families, and my colleagues. I had lots of freedom and support in the school. That said, I missed time for writing and reading. I missed the regular adult conversation that a life in academia affords. Graduate school had always been in my plans, and I felt that as I moved into my late twenties, it would be wise to get started.

Yet, after I left, I missed the school tremendously, and as I will describe, I was thrilled when an opportunity arose that allowed me to return on a part-time basis for 3 more years. Ultimately, it was a move to Maine that led to my exit from the school. Even so, I continue to email Earth School colleagues for ideas to share with teachers I work with. When I'm in the city, I try to visit as well. I also still work closely with staff through the Summer Institute on Descriptive Inquiry, and I treasure this opportunity to stay engaged with the school.

Striving Toward Improvement

As described in Chapter 2, Aristotle (1999) argues that a true friend sometimes offers their critique, and as someone who loved the Earth School dearly, I found myself playing this role. We have emphasized throughout that though each school we feature is strong, none is perfect. Jane writes in Chapter 6 that "what progressive meant for us was that we had to move forward while holding on to values that mattered." Similarly, I was once grilled by a state reviewer who was evaluating the Earth School. She had located a weakness of the school and was trying to get me to speak to it. I can't recall the weakness, but whatever it was, the data clearly identified a problem. I remember trying to explain to her our approach to this challenge by saying, yes, this is a challenge, and yes, it's one we are working on in these ways. In that moment, I then articulated something that I immediately knew to be a deep belief: What makes this school so great is not our perfection—it is the constant, thoughtful, and proactive work toward steady improvement and, as with CPE 1, the ongoing attempt to live in accordance wi.h our values.

This claim goes against the dominant strain in education where schools are assessed and then typically given very little time and support to improve. A challenge too is that sometimes schools, administrators, and teachers are better at identifying problems than figuring out how to address them. One of the things that draws me to Descriptive Inquiry is that through the questioning, sharing, and collaborative problem solving that it supports, Descriptive Inquiry is one of the rare schoolwide structures that consistently helps schools identify and work through challenges.

In the rest of this chapter, I will focus on two problems and the ways in which Descriptive Inquiry helped me address these as Support Team Coordinator. When I left the Earth School to pursue my doctorate, I had two primary critiques. The first was that I had experienced some intellectual isolation at the Earth School and the second was that too many Black and Latinx students were getting diagnoses and that these diagnoses were not really helping the kids.

The Polis

When I speak of isolation, let me emphasize that the Earth School was not an unkind, cruel, or even cold place. Far from that, the Earth School was very social and caring. There was minimal infighting. We liked one another as colleagues, and we showed it. The halls were busy and friendly; classroom doors tended to be open and people came through them regularly. In fact, we went beyond simply sharing space together; we shared space in friendly ways. New babies were always celebrated and losses mourned together. Staff meetings involved food, and many of us would gather before the meeting, eating and chatting. Birthdays were highlighted. A steady group regularly went to happy hours together on Fridays. People were always willing to help one another, whether to cover class so someone could use the bathroom, to work together on curriculum, or to contribute to a collection after the birth of a new baby. My colleagues were generous, kind, and full of good ideas. In other words, we consistently demonstrated comfortable collaboration (Fullan & Hargreaves, 1996) as introduced in Chapter 4.

Yet, despite all this goodwill, some teachers, including me, felt isolated. Arendt (1998) defines the political as a space in which people come together as equals to engage in a shared pursuit. As introduced in Chapter 2, Arendt says that the political provides a table around which everyone is gathered together, but everyone also has their separate place. Through one's place at the table, an essential human need is met; we are seen and see others.

There were many moments in which this sense of politics did occur at the Earth School. For example, as noted in Chapter 5, I learned a lot about teaching from my Review, but probably more importantly, I felt really seen for the first time through my strengths as a teacher. In each Review, I also came to know my colleagues more intimately because in hearing their feedback, I saw their strengths as teachers too. When I returned to the Earth School to facilitate the Support Team, one of my goals was to build on these areas of shared work and make them more constant. Luckily, Alison was a big step ahead of me, having already created a structure that facilitated this.

Labeling

Alison and I felt that we were over-diagnosing students with learning disabilities. For me, this was a source of anger and pain. As a classroom teacher, I had students I believed were misdiagnosed with IEPs. As Alison highlights in her section, factors aside from learning disabilities were driving these children's challenges in school. For example, the family in one case was experiencing a series of traumas. It angered me that children were saddled with labels when the deficit, in my view, was in the environment we had created for the child.

I was also frustrated with the kind of support some of my students were receiving. The issue here was twofold. First, because of staffing logistics, much of the instruction students received with an IEP involved them being pulled out of their classrooms. For children who needed social connections with their class and context, this was sometimes jarring. Second, sometimes the supports worked in ways counter to their strengths. For example, one year children receiving support services participated in a relatively didactic skill-based phonics program. This program was definitely helping some students read and write. It wasn't, though, the right service for some of my students. Yet because of the way this program needed to be executed, it was very hard for our limited number of special education teachers to develop alternatives for the children for whom it did not work.

Entrance Into the Support Team

My introduction to the Support Team was informal and fortuitous. While in graduate school, I had come to visit some teachers and students. Running into Alison in the hallway, I told her that I was very much missing both teaching and the school. She immediately jumped into gear, telling me she had the perfect job for me if I wanted it and if she could get the money to fund it. The conversation was entirely unexpected, and I left surprised and thrilled. The Support Team had already been in operation for 2 years but was currently in need of a new coordinator because the current coordinator was moving into a new role in the school.

When we talked more formally about the Support Team, I was even more excited. Alison had created a structure that addressed my two deepest concerns. As she has described, the Support Team combated the isolation teachers were experiencing while helping them to work better with children who were struggling. That Alison and I both identified the same issues is no coincidence. In fact, I credit our Descriptive Work indirectly with this. Because we were a school where we talked monthly with each other in very intimate ways, it makes sense that we could come to some shared understandings. Further, as Michelle highlights in Chapter 5, because of the Reviews, we were also a school where we knew how to have hard conversations with one another. Finally, because of the democratic nature of the Review, people could speak honestly with authority. I had learned from working with Alison over time that she took in feedback (even when it was likely hard to hear) and made changes.

Becoming Support Team Coordinator

Despite my enthusiasm for the role, I also brought a few reservations based on my prior concerns. First, how could I help teachers by supporting them alongside their students? This was a nuanced challenge. As a teacher, not only did I find it frustrating to have kids with IEPs disappearing for long stretches from my class but, often more so, I rarely knew what happened when they left until much later on, if ever. As a result, I couldn't improve my own instruction for the children based on what the specialist was doing, and I couldn't help the child ease back into our work by building on what had just come before. I didn't want to duplicate this problem.

Another reservation was that the teachers might feel undermined by my work with them. I wanted the teachers to feel that someone cared about their concerns. As Mindy's story highlights, it can hurt quite a bit when a child struggles in your class. It can lead to feelings of loss, despair, and anger. How could I let the teachers have those feelings and then help them with the child? How might I introduce new instructional practices without taking over or undermining? Alison assured me teachers were receptive to the Support Team, but I was nervous. In addition, I would be an outsider to some who had never known me as a teacher. I wondered if people would question my credentials now that I was becoming an academic and had been out of the classroom for a few years.

Third, though I was committed to honoring my colleagues, I also came to the position because I believed that we as a school needed to do better by children, especially Black and Latinx children. I needed to push for changes without shutting down my colleagues. Ultimately, I turned to Descriptive Inquiry to pave the way, a process that was facilitated both by informal conversations with Alison, Jane, Cecelia, and a number of official inquiries conducted in the inquiry group (see Chapter 1), in the spring at the school, and a year later at the Summer Institute.

Based on these conversations and my graduate studies, I brought one addition to the Support Team model. Every time I worked with children or visited a class, I wrote the teacher a letter (Furman, 2016a). I wanted teachers to know what I was doing with their students. I also wanted a way to communicate that might offer some ideas in a non-didactic way. Descriptive Inquiry guided these letters. Most were written similarly to a Review of the Child in that they were filled with descriptions and anecdotes about my work with the child. Then, mirroring the conclusion of the Review, I focused on wonderings. In this area, I never suggested next steps for the teacher, though I did describe next steps I would try myself. I offered questions I was left grappling with, materials I might use, activities and assessments I would try. I also shared my feelings here sometimes—showing enthusiasm when something went well but also expressing frustration at times. Unlike the Reviews that bring in others' feedback, in this case the letters were singly authored. Both descriptions and ideas came from me. The teachers would respond to them at times in writing, at times by meeting with me, and at times I would simply see changes in the classroom that seemed related to a given idea in a letter. I sometimes, but not always, brought these letters to Support Team meetings when I felt they would help us think through a more difficult conundrum or help us stay descriptive when a child brought up strong emotions.

To assess and improve my work, I, as noted earlier, did two Reviews of Practice. The first in the school was framed around sharing my work and seeing how it did or didn't support teachers. Over the summer, the purpose of the second Review was to determine how I would leave the position since I'd be taking a faculty job. As Support Team Coordinator, I was also teaching a course on Descriptive Inquiry at a local university. I often shared my notes in that course and my students in go-rounds gave feedback on the notes and suggestions for next steps. This helped me write more descriptively and bring back fresh ideas to my colleagues. For one especially loaded, and I felt racially charged, discussion of a child, I wrote up a Review on this child, believing that this format would allow me to advocate for the child's needs more effectively than a more direct confrontation. Before sharing the Review with the Support Team, I shared it at the inquiry group Cecelia and I co-led and got a number of great ideas. The Support Team meeting itself was very difficult, but I felt that showcasing the child in this way led to people knowing him better and, ultimately, to some improved practices. I also implemented ideas from the inquiry group in my subsequent work with the child.

A further help was our collective experience conducting Descriptive Inquiry. When I asked teachers what they wanted help with, they built on a school culture that rewarded inquiry and were confident expressing questions and challenges related to their practice. When I sent my colleagues pages of description, they didn't balk but generally expressed gratitude that I could offer descriptions that they wanted to do but didn't have time to write up. Again, a culture where teachers were already committed to describing meant that my colleagues appreciated the descriptions instead of finding them strange or even intrusive. Finally, a culture where teachers collaborated regularly, and sometimes around difficult topics, meant that almost all of the teachers smiled when I walked in the door. They were used to seeing others and being seen (even if it didn't happen as much as I wanted), and they saw an outsider presence as friendly and helpful, not judgmental and hurtful.

Effect of My Work as Support Team Coordinator

Tracking my work with students over time, I was pleased to see (as Alison notes earlier) fewer students being referred. With the opportunity to very closely describe and study children (a luxury the classroom teachers rarely had the time to do), and some additional professional development with PerDev (described in depth in Chapter 6), I could really fine-tune my own assessments so we could better decide when a child needed extra supports in class, when the child needed help but didn't need testing for a disability, and when a child could benefit from the official services of a special educator.

Just as Alison had found that the teachers were grateful to talk with others about their practice, I was struck by the degree to which teachers described the sense of companionship that the meetings and the letters I wrote brought them. Although teachers are sometimes characterized as wanting only specific strategies or techniques, the practical help provided through the Support Team was acknowledged but seemed secondary. In a Review of Practice of the Support Team, one teacher used the phrase "friend of the school," and others commented that what really mattered about the work was the chance to think about teaching with someone else. This resonates with what I know of Descriptive Inquiry. Yes, it helps teachers teach better. I leave every Review I present, chair, or attend with an idea I can try the next day. Yet, I also leave each Review feeling known, and this matters sometimes as much as any practical shifts.

IMPLICATIONS

We have emphasized that Descriptive Inquiry provides a solid foundation for developing practical wisdom. Frequent exercises apart from daily challenges of life prepare us for living. The regular practice of Descriptive Inquiry gave the Earth School a solid foundation to build upon as the Support Team developed to address some challenges. We close by highlighting the interconnection between Descriptive Inquiry and the Support Team in promoting practical wisdom.

First, we want to emphasize the democratic habits of Descriptive Inquiry. When Alison found that some teachers were labeling students and not being particularly creative in their responses, many principals might have sent in a professional developer, gone in themselves to fix the situation, asked a coach to improve the teacher's practice, or even reprimanded the teacher. Instead, drawing on habits developed through Descriptive Inquiry, Alison established a democratic structure that brought a broad community in to address the challenges.

Further, where many principals could have approached teachers from a deficit model, building on the commitment in Descriptive Inquiry to see people as capable, Alison sought a way to "support" her teachers. As with Descriptive Inquiry, she practiced this by building on the teachers' questions, insights, and needs in addition to the needs of the child. This was crucial for me as well. In starting from the teacher's questions, I could enter as a true friend, offering collaboration instead of imposing my goals on the teacher. When I borrowed from the Review by offering ideas to think about instead of suggestions, I had a way to showcase alternative practices as a peer.

Alison developed a structure that pivoted on description. With a staff used to hearing and writing Reviews, Alison could trust that people could come to the meetings able to describe. Even if there was some desire to label, her teachers had a facility with descriptive discourse. I then drew on this capacity for description and receptiveness to it in the letters that I wrote. This allowed me to balance my desire to honor the teachers and the children dually as the descriptions of the children gave the teachers and me a place from which to begin our problem solving. Further, in learning about the teachers from hearing their questions and witnessing their practice, I had insights into how to help them realize their teaching values. Finally, where I initially worried my support would be undermining, in knowing my colleagues well through this process I could celebrate what they were doing well and, at times, even advocate on their behalf.

The Support Team supported the teachers and the children by building on what was working, not replacing it. Similarly, the Support Team and the more formal practice of Descriptive Inquiry mutually supported each other. Moving between the work in the Support Team and the inquiry done after school, students, teachers, and administrators were all, in Alison's words, better able to "grow." Part of true friendship is having the capacity to disagree and offer criticism. Descriptive Inquiry proved particularly relevant in moments of critique. I turned to Descriptive Inquiry when I needed a way forward with Thomas in Chapter 1, feeling like we as a school needed more insights for working with him. When I was upset with how another child was being treated, I elected to make him more visible by writing up a Review and sharing it at the Support Team meetings—an action that I believe helped change the tenor of the conversation about this child to be more capacity oriented.

Finally, it is important to note that the challenges Alison and I identified in the school—seeing children and helping teachers to feel seen as well— were not unique to the Earth School. In her interview, Jane comments that

> teaching in a classroom in elementary school, I am convinced is
> the hardest job in the entire world. I don't care what else you do in
> terms of teaching to be in a room with 25 children . . . you're lonely,
> intellectually . . . although it may be very interesting, there is no other
> adult and even if there is another adult, there isn't the time to say "We
> need to stand here and talk about Jessica."

As such, Alison's Support Team addressed two challenges perhaps endemic to teaching: (a) teaching is lonely, and (b) much of that loneliness is the feeling the teacher gets when faced with a perplexing child. It stems from that feeling of "we need to stand here and talk about Jessica" and the sense that no one is there to stand with you. The Support Team provided regular opportunities to stand there and talk about the student and therefore proved ultimately supportive of both the child and the teacher. We continue discussing this power of the "we" in Descriptive Inquiry in the next chapter as we discuss Cecelia's collaboration with schools.

NOTES

1. The New York State–mandated evaluation system for teachers and principals in which teachers are rated using the Danielson frameworks.

2. Teachers had developed Continuums of Learning for Literacy, Math, and Social & Emotional Learning through a process of reviewing children's work and studying developmental theory as well as a variety of standards. They use these continuums as guides for curriculum planning and assessing children's progress.

3. This timing fit loosely with new external mandates that interventions be attempted for 6 weeks before referral for an IEP. We were more flexible than the guidelines, believing that 6 weeks was not always enough time.

CHAPTER 9

Listening So as to Attend

Descriptions of Cecelia's Role in Schools

Cara E. Furman, with Cecelia E. Traugh and Laurie Engle

In this book we have focused on schools with much in common. They are all in Manhattan. They all define themselves as progressive. Each developed as part of the movement toward small schools, and each developed with a mission. Each school came to Descriptive Inquiry during tumultuous periods, and each principal made Descriptive Inquiry a central part of the development of teachers and their schools.

Another common feature is key. Each principal worked closely with Cecelia. Throughout, we have argued on behalf of democratic communities in the promotion of practical wisdom. In Chapter 4, Rachel explained that simply bringing people into a shared space is not inherently productive. Similarly, in Chapter 6 Jane comments multiple times on the importance of the person chairing in Descriptive Inquiry. For example, when using Descriptive Inquiry to solve problems between staff members she notes, "I must say I had to be at the helm or Cecelia had to be at the helm for these."

In this chapter, I highlight some qualities that Cecelia brought to the helm by describing her work at schools. As we have done throughout this book, I will depict her work in its particularity and then restate themes that could be useful to others. A description of Cecelia's ways of working with inquiry is a necessary component of the story of these schools and school leaders. It also brings insights into how someone outside a school community might play a key role in attending to the school and to developing its practical wisdom.

Cecelia and I grappled quite a bit with form and authorship. For Cecelia, describing herself in depth was awkward. On the other hand, I simply couldn't describe her practice in much detail. I had been present for only a very small part of this story. I didn't know the nuances of Cecelia's work nor her intentions. For both practical and philosophical reasons, we therefore have sought coauthorship throughout this text. Drawing explicit attention to collaboration, in this chapter we adapt a different format: that of the interview.[1] Below is a slightly modified and edited version of a conversation between Cecelia and me after we had written much of this book.

Finally, as her interview reveals, a key part of chairing is listening, describing back, and pulling themes. Alongside the two restatements included at the end of this chapter, we invite readers to also consider the themes they hear.

SETTING

It is summer in Bennington, Vermont. Cecelia and I sit in the cramped dorm room in between sessions at the Summer Institute on Descriptive Inquiry. A floor fan rotates and buzzes, but the room is hot. The wooden chairs are stiff. This is a room for living and working. Towels hang on the back of the beds, books that Cecelia has brought to the Institute fill the shelves, a computer sits on the desk, and papers abound. In other words, as the principals and the teachers in this book do, Cecelia and I make do in a cramped, multi-purposed, lived-in physical setting to talk practice at length.

LISTENING TO CECELIA

Cara: I wanted to start with asking how you would describe what you do in schools. Thinking about that broadly, but also logistically, what are actual things that you do in and with schools?

Cecelia: What do I do in schools? Well, first of all, I'm invited in. I don't go on my own. So that's the first thing.

Cara: Ever?

Cecelia: Not to do this work. When people understand what I do and are intrigued, they invite me in. Then I go in with the expectation that there'll probably be some kind of long-term work. I typically go in because they're interested in having people in the school learn how to do the Descriptive Review of the Child. Why this process in particular, I don't know other than it is the best known of the Descriptive Processes. Then a big part of what I do is sitting with the principals and talking about what they're interested in and how they want to pursue those interests.

I mostly settle on the structure of being in the school about once a month because I know that schools have other business to do. So I go in with that structure.

Cara: Do you go in to meet with the principal or the staff or both?

Cecelia: Usually with the principal. At first, I talk about how the work might look. And then I start working with teachers. When I work with a teacher on a Descriptive Review, a big part of my role is to sit with them and help them know what's descriptive and what's not descriptive, to consider what kind of evidence they want to draw on, to determine what is going to be a useful question.

As time goes by, my work is a combination of working with individual teachers, being part of their Reviews, and getting acquainted with the full staff from the Reviews. The work evolves from there. New inquiry processes are introduced as my relationship with the school develops.

Cara: Would you say that it is rare that you would have long-term conversations with other people who are on staff, such as the teachers?

Cecelia: Yeah. It's really with the principal. Sometimes I spend time in a teacher's classroom, but not regularly. Like with one teacher at the Earth School. He was doing a Review of Practice, and he felt beleaguered. So he thought that it would be helpful if I visited his classroom. And it was, you know. It was interesting to see him in an actual operation. But I was still relying on his description of his work, not on my description of what I saw.

Cara: Just a really brief clarification. I think you made a point of saying that even if you were in his classroom you were relying on his description? Would you say that that's the same thing with the principals, that even though you saw them with their staff you would primarily rely on their description?

Cecelia: Yeah, because the principal often has a reason for a particular person doing a Review or reason why they want a person to engage in this work in a particular way. And I will know that, but that doesn't enter into how I engage with that person. Instead, any time I work with someone, I build our work around *that* person's description.

Cara: This seems important. Like if Jane as principal is saying I read this this way you're not the kind of observer who comes in and says, "Actually Jane, I saw this situation with your staff differently." So you are relying on her depiction of her review of her practice.

Cecelia: Yeah. After a Review, if a principal says, "da, da, da, da" I will sometimes say, "No, I didn't hear that. I didn't hear it that way at all." The teacher's perspectives must sit equally alongside the principal's. I do rely on a person's description of their own work.

Cara: What can you say about why you take this approach?

Cecelia: My short answer is that I'm interested in the person's thinking, in the person's ideas. I don't want to implant my ideas into another person's thought. I want us together to explore the implications and possibilities of their ideas and ways of seeing. I can plant seeds with questions, but it is their plant growing in their soil.

Cara: I'm interested in hearing what you would say your role is. How you would name it, if you would name your role? Does it ever change across settings? I'll admit I tried to name it and I couldn't so . . .

Cecelia: Well, it doesn't exactly start out this way, but it tends to evolve
into an outside adviser. That's not wholly what it is. But that is an
aspect of it. To do so, I develop a relationship with people and a school.
I listen carefully and over time get to know the school and get a sense
of how they respond to various things because each school responds
differently, has different kinds of issues that can be of interest or at
times of concern. Over time, principals will start asking me, "Well,
what do you think I ought to do?" Or, "What would you do?" So
that's, that's part of what I mean by *adviser*. I rarely tell a principal
what I think she should do. I do try to help her lay out options, expand
her array of possibilities. For example, in Chapter 4, Rachel describes a
moment when I described the tension between instructional and socioemotional development as a false dichotomy. I didn't tell her what to do
here, but I did reframe in a way that helped her feel some "relief."

    Adviser in a little larger way too, I think. Not just in giving advice in
a particular circumstance, as I did with Rachel there. I will go back to
that idea about being in a long-term conversation, some of which go on
for years. I don't like this language so much as *thought-partner*, but I
guess that describes my work to some degree.

    I am somebody with whom people can talk and not feel they have
to perform or have an answer. Teachers and principals both see me
as someone they can go to and not be judged. This means they can
really talk through things that are bothering them in their work. No
matter what the source might be. For example, the sources of issues for
principals are not always the teachers or children at all. It might be the
district.

    I can be an advocate too. Like when one of the schools had an
external evaluation, and they didn't agree with how it came out, I
attended the meeting with the superintendent with whom they had the
problem. I was there as a listener and as a support for the school. The
principal and I "debriefed" the conversation afterward as she wanted to
know how I had heard the discussion and the issues raised. So over time
that can become a part of my role.

    It's interesting actually to think about advocacy because when I do
the work with parents (and to some degree teachers), it's not in direct
advocacy of any one thing, but it is using Descriptive Processes to
advocate for a way of looking at kids. I use a particular way of looking
or asking people to practice that particular way of looking. It's an
indirect advocacy for having a more expansive, humanizing view of kids
and their work.

    It's a funny role. I'm not a coach although in some ways I coach.
Like at City-as-School, I help them think through learning the process,
but again, I don't see myself as a coach at all in the sense of teaching a
particular thing. It's an unusual role.

Cara: And it's different from what many professional developers do, which has more content attached to it, often an agenda with benchmarks for success or failure.

Cecelia: That's right. What I try to offer is a lens for looking and listening with greater nuance and care and then acting with a greater sense of possibility.

Cara: I guess that speaks to this question: Where did this role come from? How has this evolved? What's influenced your way of being with the schools?

Cecelia: Well, I guess my work stems from my experience of being a school leader. When I moved to New York, I had been a director of a middle school where I used the Descriptive Processes as a way of building a coherent set of ideas and practices. I was invited to bring this work to New York schools. I didn't invite myself. For example, the principal at Central Park East 1 was having trouble with decision making in the school. As Jane notes in Chapter 6, being a staff-run school was challenging and the school was struggling to figure out how to use the Descriptive Process. It was kind of a mess, and the principal needed help thinking about those things. So she invited me in. I started working and as I worked I drew on what I knew from my experience in Philadelphia. And, through a November conference on Descriptive Inquiry, a principal at the Earth School said she would like to have me come and do descriptive work. So I started doing that. Well, then Judith saw what was happening at the Earth School and got excited about it, so I started doing it there. I didn't insert myself. I didn't have a thing I was advertising. Do you know what I mean?

Cara: I do know exactly what you mean.

Cecelia: I should add, I don't know if this is attached to the role and I don't have a name for it except that I am a really careful listener. And that is essential to what I do. Now I put that listening alongside a whole set of ideas I have. This practice helps me recognize the possible meanings of what a person is saying. This recognition is a kind of interpretation, allowing me to ask questions aiming to draw out more of that person's thinking, to help them elaborate on an idea. Over time I can provide multiple interpretations of what I hear. And that people find useful. But I'm not going in with a particular thing. You know? I don't, for example, offer a particular thing to do with a kid. It is different from what I know some of my colleagues do. They are less patient with how people do certain things. They will go in in a more hands-on way. This is really strong for a lot of the folks. Really, that way of working is important. But it's not what I do.

Cara: Can you speak more about your role in schools and its relationship to Descriptive Inquiry?

Cecelia: My doctoral dissertation was on inquiry, and I was interested in that because of Edwin Fenton's [1967] work in inquiry in social studies. That's what I had been working on as a high school teacher. So, the idea of asking questions was a big piece of that and the democratic stuff too. Descriptive Inquiry for me is a vehicle for school people to really engage in whatever questions they've got about their work, about the things they work with. That's what they count on me to help them do. They don't ask me to come and teach them about social studies or even inquiry in social studies, which I do know about.

For example, when people find out that I've done a lot of work in exploring race using Descriptive Inquiry, people are interested in doing that. They're not interested in having me, this old white lady for God's sake, come and talk about race. But they know I have a vehicle that's reasonably effective to safely raise some issues that are important and that relate to the persons in the immediate group, not the theoretical reading stuff. Like there are some very fine organizations that focus on the theoretical, but what they often don't do is carry what teachers are learning into the particular of the things that teachers are doing in classrooms, into how they carry ideas into particular teaching actions. And that's what Descriptive Inquiry helps with. How do these ideas play out? What issues do they raise? How are you thinking about the description of kids? Having studied this topic, what are you doing with it?

Cara: In this book we talk about democracy and authority. I wonder how these concepts fit with your work?

Cecelia: Well, you know, it's interesting and it's different depending on context. I have two different pieces of work. I continue to have the work of being a school leader now in higher education. And, I have the work of sitting alongside school leaders. And, while related, they are different.

That said, one thing in both roles that is key is the whole business about having voice. I count on the processes and the go-round. That is a democratic thrust I write about in Chapter 3. I think that creating that, hearing voices the best you can, trying to see the other person for who they are, not who you think they are, those little bits are key to democratic interactions. Practicing this, the go-rounds and processes become the care-of-the-self exercises you write about in Chapter 2, you know, like the wrestling moves. They become habits. They are then part of the way the day-to-day work is done. They become part of how relationships are built. There's confidence in the other person so that you know that that person's thinking comes from some kind of understanding and knowing, whether you agree with them or not. This becomes part of the way the staff sees each other. I think that's part of democratic work. Those three parts are important to me. Over time the descriptive work builds those qualities that are necessary for a school to operate democratically.

Cara: Would you say as chair, it's almost like you're protecting the rules of the democracy in a way? Like the processes, they're not laws, but they are structures that you follow, but they need a human person to be enacted.

Cecelia: Yeah, I like that. When you wrote about practicing the moves so that they become habits. I think that those structures are moves of a kind. When Michelle talks in Chapter 5 about how the descriptive work changed the way teachers treated each other when it was brought to the Earth School, that's what she's talking about. She's talking about a place where people became ingrained in those moves, and whether they think about them as democratic or not, they are still part of the fabric of the place. I think that that creates a more democratic school than it would be otherwise. Whether it's fully democratic or not is a whole other question. I don't think I can guarantee all that.

Cara: How has being a school leader and working with school leaders interacted with each other? What is the significance of your having experience with both of these different worlds?

Cecelia: They do feed each other. The school work always keeps the higher education work in some kind of balance. It helps with perspective. So that, that's one thing.

And it really gives me insight into how teachers think about their work. What they've learned someplace, how they actually use it. When you're in teacher education and you're teaching students those things, you wonder what actually happens to it all in the classroom. It's hard to sometimes know. Not that I taught all the teachers I work with, but I certainly recognize some of what they've learned through their teacher education programs, and so I see how it all kind of gels, meshes with what they're learning from work with children, and what the whole system is making them learn. You see how kids in their classrooms do or don't interact with all that they've learned. I see the sense they make of their experience, and that's a really useful body of understanding that a lot of teacher educators don't have because they don't have that access to teachers' thinking in those classrooms. So that's one really important thing.

One of the things that the leader's inquiry group[2] has shown me is that, whether you're working with elementary school teachers or you're working with high school teachers or you're working with faculty in a college setting, some of the very same issues around leadership come forward. I can tell my stories, which come out of my work right now with college faculty, and they sit right alongside the stories of the principals from high schools and elementary schools. They're not qualitatively different in terms of what the essence of those stories are. So, it feeds both ways. By that, I mean there is a learning value for the principals, but also I bring it back as a leader to my own work.

Cara: How do you see your work relating to practical wisdom?

Cecelia: When I read *Practical Wisdom: The Right Way to Do the Right Thing* [Schwartz & Sharpe, 2010] and I saw that passage, "In order for individuals to remain, to develop and remain practically wise, they need our context that's also practically wise," I thought, "You know? That is what I see happening in these schools." I'm thinking of City-as-School right now because that's the newest example. When I'm working with the teacher leaders there, I see them asking different questions than they asked at the beginning. In the beginning they were asking much more sort of "prove it to me" practical kind of questions. But now with some experience in working together, they're asking questions that cut a little deeper into purpose, the idea behind how something connects to the values of the place. They're very different questions. They're more of a collective than they were before. Their retreats are qualitatively different in terms of how they talk with each other. People would be exploding at each other, etc. etc. They don't do that anymore. Now they engage in a shared thing every time they practice a Review. And because of it they have a different understanding of each other than they had before. And that to me is a kind of wisdom. They can listen to each other and not fight. I think that's a big deal. So does Rachel. The work builds that collective understanding, which is different than expecting agreement. The work makes people braver and better able to dig more deeply because the idea of disagreement is not so difficult or upsetting. Disagreement is not conflict. It can lead there, but it need not.

Cara: No one ever labels themselves this way, so let's pretend that you are practically wise. How do you cultivate that?

Cecelia: I said this already in a prior answer, but now I'm feeling like this is more and more important. One of the ways I cultivate my practical wisdom is by working to continually enlarge the set of ideas that I can put alongside and expand the meaning of what people describe. As I said earlier, I don't often provide answers, but I do try to expand people's thinking about possibilities. I think of this as a kind of philosophical stance. An idea I find myself frequently drawing on, for example, is that of Isaiah Berlin [1991] when he talks about competing values. So many times, when I'm in a conversation with a principal or a faculty member about a conflict they are trying to sort out, it is helpful to locate the values in the various forces and to begin to recognize that there is value on multiple sides but that priorities must be set given the context. Having a body of ideas that you can use and keep drawing on matters a lot. At the Summer Institute this year, we are reading *Reuben's Fall* [Leafgren, 2009]. I read this book a long, long time ago. The reason I wanted to come this year was because I wanted to sit with people and actually think about and hear how people were reading it. Reading together is the kind of thing that helps me expand ideas, keep old ideas fresh, put different ideas alongside each other. When possible I also do this with colleagues. For example, I hired a psychologist as my associate dean. There is a difference between taking a psychological stance and taking a philosophical stance. Each one shines a different light on issues. For example, the philosophical stance seems more open ended than the psychological. Philosophy asks about the nature of childhood; psychology has developed stages of development. A bit too generalized, I know, but useful, I think. Philosophy takes on issues that cannot be measured, the spiritual side of being human, for example; this is not a central concern of psychology. Having these two vantage points available to me has been invaluable as I work to make sense of issues in my work in schools or as a leader.

Cara: In education we talk a lot about community building. Often, educational communities are defined as those who are like us. For example, elementary school teachers study with other elementary school teachers. You have the leader group, then there's the teacher group, then there are the groups you work with at your university. But there's not really someone just like you doing this exact work in any other place. So obviously you're not getting community through the other ones of you roaming around the country. How would you think of community in terms of supporting your own work in schools? What kind of community helps you? What is the democracy that helps you develop practical wisdom?

Cecelia: Well, again, I think the community that's here [at the Summer Institute] does that. One of the things that I learned early on coming to the Summer Institute was that I had a lot to learn from teachers. Listen, when a university colleague of mine and I first came to the Summer Institute, we were the first teacher educators here, and we were not that welcome to be honest with you. Lots of suspicion around us. But I learned a tremendous amount from the teachers using the Descriptive Process.

For me the kind of community that I need is a community that includes people doing work and interested and willing to raise questions related to it, using some kind of process that's related to description. Description has got to be the core of it.

Community definitely grows me. Like the group that Abbe and I worked with over this last year with the parents. I didn't have anything in common with those folks in terms of our roles. Nothing. I'm not a parent. But I got a tremendous amount from that, and I did feel part of that particular community. And, I hope the group gained a tremendous amount from the practice of an antiracist stance we were exploring every month with each other.

Cara: As you're talking, I'm thinking of something you said with my dissertation when my readers asked where I was getting my books from.

I tried to explain how I was stumbling upon them in different places and looking from different fields and trying to find connections across them. You said that I was reading like a teacher. As I'm thinking now, that is a form of reading and engaging that I see you doing both as a reader, but also as a person. And it's profoundly democratic in that it's a pulling from many different sources. It's not only that going to the Summer Institute for the first time you were learning that it was important to learn from teachers, but I think also that, to put words in your mouth, that it is important to learn from others. It seems significant that you've made the person closest to you at work, your associate dean, someone who is very much different from you—from her field to her personality to her race. That just seemed important somehow. It's very democratic.

Cecelia: I think that's true. I think that that feels true to me in many dimensions. I get Mike Rose's blog [mikerosebooks.blogspot.com], and I sent his last one out to the graduate faculty and I got a note back from one of the faculty members, who says, "So, what do you find so interesting about Mike Rose's books?" I said, "Well, you know, I'm really pointing out this blog, but I'll tell you. One of the things that I find very interesting about Mike Rose's books is that he's talking about hairdressers or shop teachers and what they know. He's thinking about knowing from different professional perspectives and very different ways of making sense of the world. Well, that feels really important. That, that's really important."

INTEGRATED RESTATEMENT

As described, in Descriptive Inquiry, an Integrated Restatement is the chair's drawing together of the different strands that emerge typically after a go-round. Occasionally, as demonstrated here, multiple people will provide a restatement to add another layer of nuance.

Laurie Engle's Integrated Restatement

Cecelia asked a teacher recently retired from the Neighborhood School (TNS), Laurie Engle, to read the interview and comment on the description of Cecelia's work. As Laurie has worked with Cecelia over many years doing Reviews of Children and Reviews of Practice and has been part of the over 20 years of Cecelia's work with TNS's faculty and principal, Cecelia thought Laurie could offer insights and nuance into the description of her work, from the teacher's vantage point. Laurie's thoughts are offered here as a first take on a pulling together of ideas:

I find the fact that principals ask Cecelia to introduce the Descriptive Review of the Child as a starting point so interesting—that the entry point for descriptive practices for schools is the Review of a Child. This makes me wonder: What are the schools looking to do? What is the problem they are trying to address or solve that the Descriptive Review gives them a window into? Where do their dissatisfactions lie? I think one of the reasons this stands out to me is that doing Reviews of Children offered me a focused but broad way of looking deeply and specifically at a child and expanded my lens as a teacher. Once I had those categories of ways of looking at a child, I could see so much more in the actions and thinking of children and respond in a more nuanced way. The description of how Cecelia works with teachers on a Descriptive Review is crucial. I can speak from experience in saying that the questions she asks are important: What is the evidence you are drawing on? In what ways is it limited or expansive? What are the questions that are raised? And then: What is the framing question or questions? There is a real dialogue and shaping of how to collect information and shape the presentation. I have heard so many teachers say that gathering and thinking about the "evidence" changed their view of a child and what they would do next. In several places in the interview, Cecelia suggests a more passive role than she actually played. Yes, she does not have a programmatic agenda such as the Teachers College Reading and Writing Project, but she actively responds, not in a judgmental way but in a listening and questioning way. At the root of the questions Cecelia asks are the validity and meaning-making capacity of the child. The way she asks is deeply respectful of the teacher and the child and helps the teacher to construct a broader view and understanding of the child and their practice. One more thing about "What is going to be a useful question?" is Cecelia's idea that it has to be a real question, something the teacher really wants to know and that will enrich the relationships of student, teacher, and class community or school community.

I found Cecelia's description of relying on the teachers' descriptions of their work so interesting and so different from what most people do in a school. It is also such a different perspective on how change happens. Cecelia enters the teacher's reality and perception of the child and of the teacher's own practice. However, as I said earlier in relation to Cecelia's role in helping a teacher prepare for the Review, she relies on the teacher's description but responds to it in a rich and active way. To me, this is the best kind of teaching—to hold several issues in mind but respond to the person as they present themselves. It is important that Cecelia bases her reaction on evidence, not competing interpretations about how someone and their practice is viewed. The fact that Cecelia's work is "in relationship," not the vacuum of absolutes and hierarchy, is important too. Expansiveness of possibilities and array are recurring threads in Cecelia's approach to teachers and children.

Another crucial idea is that the work is done over time. As Cecelia would often remind us at TNS, development stretches out over a long time, and we should not look for immediate answers and resolutions. We should be looking for progress toward deeper understanding and capacity—for individuals—kids, adults—and also for schools. I remember seeing notes from early TNS meetings and realizing how much our thinking and language had developed over time. And, it is over time that Cecelia can provide multiple interpretations of what she hears. This is at the heart of the expansiveness Cecelia provides.

Cecelia often talks about tensions between two poles within a community—democracy could contrast with efficiency or accountability, etc., but the role she plays and the Descriptive Processes help the community to lean more toward democracy, in my experience, lean substantially more than it would without them and without her.

One last point, and a return to where she begins in the interview: Cecelia's experience and expertise focuses on a process that builds coherence. She is not asking teachers to replicate a model. And the idea of invitation is so important. She is not imposing what she offers.

Cara's Integrative Restatement

Listening to Cecelia's interview, I heard a number of themes that I will restate. To do so, I return to the care of the self. Here, Foucault's (2012) work on Socrates and the cultivation of leaders is helpful. In one of Plato's dialogues, *Laches*, Socrates's interlocutors query how leaders develop. The first and relatively obvious reply is that leaders develop skills in leadership from a good teacher. By this account, the key to good leadership might be traced to learning to write effective memos, give motivational speeches, and impart skills like balanced literacy to teachers. Yet, according to the dialogue, something more emerges as central to leadership—the development of an ethos. This development cannot be transferred like skills but instead is cultivated through a type of dialogue referred to as *parrhesia* (free speech). Many elements of this concept resonate with Cecelia's work.

Invitation. Foucault emphasizes that free speech involves a kind of game in language that everyone has decided to participate in. A key element of Cecelia's work is that of being *invited in*. In this way, though an outsider, she is careful not to be an intruder. The same is true of her work once within the school. She doesn't enter a classroom unless asked in. When teachers reach out to her, she works with them but, again, waits for the invitation. The person she works with always chooses the content and the question. Cecelia cites Rukeyser in Chapter 3 to make the point that questions "make a meeting place" (1996, p. 162). This is true for those participating in the

Review as well as for Cecelia and the presenter as they plan together. In this way, she is being invited into their concerns, not imposing her own.

Listening With Care. Accomplishing her goal demands that Cecelia be able to listen, and she highlights this as a strength. A key to parrhesia is the belief that frank and honest speech is necessary to cultivate the ethos of the leader. Parrhesia describes an interaction; to speak the truth demands a certain kind of listener. The role of listener came through in a variety of ways. Cecelia asks the principal to set the parameters and determine the content of the work they do together. Cecelia describes getting to know the staff through Reviews. In this way, she meets the staff almost entirely by hearing them speak in the public forum of go-rounds. As in Chapter 7, listening is in the spirit of finding meaning and capacity. Again, relying on listening, Cecelia draws on the principal's depictions of events. She lets the principal determine what needs to be worked on and builds her support around what she hears as the principal's concerns. A similar attitude of listening is brought to her work with teachers. As she described, her support hinges on how the teacher perceives a situation.

Frankness and Truth. According to Foucault (2001), two of the critical and interrelated features of free speech are *frankness* (that the speech is forthright, straightforward, and plain) and *truth* (the ideas are derived through reason, one's personal experience, or the uncovering of additional facts). Along these lines, when Cecelia speaks, it is largely to repeat back what she has heard, to ask questions, even to juxtapose new ideas. She pulls together ideas, seeking areas of commonality as well as divergent themes. What she does not do is offer specific suggestions of what a teacher might do.

Cecelia responds in many forms. Chairing reviews, she provides the restatements. Sometimes, when talking to a principal, she tells the principal how she heard comments made during a meeting—what she, Cecelia, heard being said by staff. Sometimes these conversations happen in the large group, sometimes more informally one-on-one. For example, in Chapter 5, Cecelia explains how after listening to Rachel and her staff, she heard a challenge in the school related to tensions in values. Cecelia also shows an appreciation and aptitude for listening by making sure to hear a diversity of voices, in person and in texts.

Content. Typically in schools, consultants offer methods or information. For example, I was able to work with a wonderful math specialist who led teachers in experiential workshops that highlighted ways of doing and assessing math. Many of the teachers I work with deal with consultants who tell them exactly how to implement a curriculum.

In contrast, as Rachel emphasized when reading an earlier draft of this chapter, Cecelia shares the processes, helping principals and teachers to use the processes to better inform their instruction. This is powerful work. Socrates suggests that a good leader knows themselves from an ethical perspective. A focus on what one does is shifted to how one approaches the world. Cecelia helps teachers and their schools learn a way of being, rather than technical know-how that can be directly imparted. She helps people cultivate a form of inquiring, describing, talking, and listening developed through the processes of Descriptive Inquiry.

Community. Throughout this book, we have argued that practical wisdom develops in democratic community. In a Socratic version of the care of the self, one develops through engagement with interlocutors. As highlighted by Foucault, Socrates intentionally draws from a diversity of perspectives, including those who are definitively unlike him. Similarly, Socrates seeks out as many sources as possible, finding interlocutors from different social classes, ages, and professions. Cecelia too highlights the need for diverse interlocutors. She promotes this way of being in schools by bringing in the Descriptive Processes, which she argues supports democracy. Throughout the interview she emphasized the value of doing this work in schools because, as she says, "community definitely grows me." Her commitment to different voices is modeled throughout the interview as she names and quotes both colleagues and texts. As highlighted in her answers, Cecelia models careful listening and growing with others; she is able to take in questions and comments and develop her thinking as she goes.

Finally, in frequently offering restatements and juxtaposing ideas, Cecelia weaves ideas together—providing teachers and principals with a fabric that captures their thinking on a question.

POSTSCRIPT

Cecelia: After reading this chapter several times, I became concerned that the ways I work might seem too idiosyncratic. I offer here two different methods of thinking about work with adults that might help provide some context for my way of working. They are not ideas that have shaped my work, but I recognize in them compatible thinking.

First an idea describing a characteristic of the schools in Reggio Emilia. In their structures, they include "wise healers," *pedagogista*, or pedagogical advisers and philosophers. I have not seen these people in action, but their title feels comfortable. A second idea is Paulo Freire's (Freire & Macedo, 1996) "cultural circle." His description fits aspects of the work I do with teachers:

The cultural circles were spaces where teaching and learning took place in a dialogic fashion. They were spaces for knowledge, for knowing, not for knowledge transference; places where knowledge was produced, not simply presented to or imposed on the learner. They were spaces where new hypotheses for reading the world were created. (p. 121)

This passage helps me see the circle of teachers and leaders engaged in an inquiry process as a kind of "cultural circle." In that circle, I help the group create a space for knowledge-making, a space where new possibilities for thinking and acting are generated. I'll return to these ideas as they connect with building practically wise school cultures in the penultimate and final chapters.

NOTES

1. Although the framing and summarizing is largely mine, the deep thinking is Cecelia's. I am grateful to Doris Santoro for suggesting the interview format as well as to Andy Doan, Rachel Seher, and Laurie Engle for their insights regarding Cecelia's work.

2. A group of principals and leaders from other educational settings that meets once a month to use various inquiry processes to explore a range of issues and questions that arise through their work.

Part IV

WHAT DOES IT MEAN TO LEAD SCHOOLS FOR HUMAN DIGNITY?

CHAPTER 10

The Authority of Values Within Collaborative School Communities

Cecelia E. Traugh, with Rachel Seher and Abbe Futterman

Along with exploring how Descriptive Inquiry has been a means for school principals to build school and teacher practice, this chapter is an adventure in descriptive knowledge-making. I highlight three aspects of leadership that emerged from the principals' stories about the ways their work with Descriptive Inquiry supported their work in schools and that are important to being a democratic school leader within a collaborative culture. I find they help us think about authority in fresh ways. These aspects of leadership are (a) building school culture, (b) negotiating competing values, and (c) working with difficult and divisive issues. It is important to emphasize that these three facets of leadership work are related to one another. For example, working with competing values is often a part of a felt need to work on a difficult issue. The decision to take on these facets, or to ignore them, is critical to shaping a school culture. However, I have discussed them separately so that they can be seen in some depth. In my discussions, I rely on principals to tell their own stories and, thus, I hope, draw on the link between authorship and authority. To do so, I draw heavily on interviews with them. I also include two narratives from school leaders, Rachel Seher and Abbe Futterman.

LISTENING FOR MEANING

Throughout this book, we have invited you to participate in various processes. In this chapter, alongside the ideas about leadership, I also describe my process of finding meaning in the narratives and invite you to participate. Faced with long, in-depth interviews of four elementary school principals, my task was to find the threads of thinking running through them. I share how I did so in some detail as I followed the same mental process I use when pulling threads after listening to Anecdotal Recollections. My first step was to name the idea I found in each story, to name what I thought each story was about, and then to cluster the stories around the ideas. For example, the stories about decision points made a cluster; the stories about parents' relationships to school went in another. I follow the same process with each cluster, this time finding what are usually more general themes, such as language use and change over time. It is through this process that the central frame for this section and the subtopics emerged. During an Anecdotal Recollection, I handwrite my notes and rapidly start to sort themes as I listen to people share orally. After everyone has spoken, I take about a minute to process my notes.

What is key to this way of thinking is that I do *not* begin with the ideas that I then look for in the stories as illustrations of my preconceptions. I begin with the stories and work to let the ideas emerge from them. This is the way I learn from experience—others' and my own. I have confidence in the understandings I develop through this Descriptive Process, and I work to help teachers and leaders to have confidence in the knowledge they create and the questions they raise through a solid and careful Descriptive Inquiry process. It is always useful to put this descriptive knowledge alongside others' work and thinking to find whether or not the ideas speak to each other in agreement. Through this process new questions can be raised, and understandings and perspectives can grow.

That said, though I let themes emerge from the interviews and subsequent narratives, the perspectives I (as author and also as chair) bring to this way of working matter. So, I begin this chapter with a brief description of some of my thinking about Descriptive Inquiry and its supportive role in the work of leaders. I start with the idea that building practical wisdom in schools through Descriptive Inquiry clearly has implications for leadership. Teachers are frequently the educators who first learn about this mode of inquiry, but it is very difficult to make it a schoolwide practice when only individual classroom teachers form the base. Interest from leadership, if not required, is extremely valuable. In my own work as a school leader or a dean of schools of education, this fact has been obvious. Taking on a new position as the leader always requires some decision making about how to enter the place and learn the people and their ways of working. Because I have confidence in Descriptive Inquiry as a way to develop a school and its faculty as a learning community, whenever I entered a new place I explored how to best weave Descriptive Inquiry into its fabric. I either found the individuals who were interested in Descriptive Inquiry and built on their capacities to bring inquiry to the full group or found individuals who were interested in learning about Descriptive Inquiry and sent them to a Summer Institute so that they could serve as supports as I introduced the work to the full staff. In contrast, Cara has experienced this from the point of view of a faculty member. She has found it easy to bring Descriptive Inquiry into her courses and has found colleagues and administrators consistently intrigued by the work. That said, without leadership authority, she has found it hard to gain momentum for the work outside her own teaching. Given the importance of leadership, this chapter zooms in on leaders and aspects of the work they do in a focused way.

BUILDING SCHOOL CULTURE

A culture, too, is a work of imagination, or a failure of it.

—Christian Wiman (2018, p. 15)

School leadership is a position in which there is vested authority. In hierarchical systems, principals are seen, within boundaries, as the ones in charge, the ones responsible for taking the authoritative ideas of the system and seeing that they are implemented in their schools. This is authority with a downward direction. The principals who speak in this book seek to use their authority differently, more democratically. Their vision is one that recognizes the voice of teachers, of families, and of students, that seeks to share decision making as much as possible and make space for the authority of the question. Descriptive Inquiry has proven to be a richly constructive and dependable structure for enacting this vision.

Helping create and shape a school's culture is one of the important aspects of the role of its leadership. The culture provides the context for much that happens in the school, for example: (a) how teachers relate to and work with children and their families, (b) how teachers work with one another and with the school leader, (c) what ideas and questions are viewed as important, and (d) how time is allocated. All school cultures reflect the values of the society and the system in which the school exists and the people who have worked and who are working in the school. For example, for Rachel's teachers to grow together, they needed to establish a collaborative culture. Jane described a culture in which the person was placed at the forefront and in which people came together to help one another to see students from a more generous and holistic lens. Further, as Rachel and Jane have described in Chapters 4 and 6, respectively, cultures can be modified over time if leadership and teachers can find an agreed-upon process for undertaking the work involved.

Before I share how the principals we interviewed described how they work to shape their schools' cultures, I ask you, the reader, to reflect a bit about your own school culture. Begin by thinking about an anecdote that reveals an aspect of your school's culture. Think of a story that comes quickly to mind when asked to consider your school. Ideally, do this with a colleague so that you can share. In what ways might this story provide insights into your school culture? Is this story a positive one for you, providing details that make you pleased to be where you are? Is it one that highlights concerns? Have efforts been made to change the culture? What resulted from those efforts? What themes emerge from the story or stories? Are there any metaphors that emerge as you consider themes?

The school leaders we interviewed for this book have much to say about their work to shape their schools' cultures. To begin, I share the metaphor each principal said captured the role Descriptive Inquiry had in her school. Jane's metaphor for Descriptive Inquiry as it worked for her and the school is "home for thinking." Alison's is that of weaving, with Descriptive Inquiry as the thread holding the creation together. Judith sees schools as a dynamic organism, a living thing, and in Descriptive Inquiry she found a means of developing the school's lifeblood, that is, understanding of children. Michelle's vision of school is based on the values of respect for children, families, and teachers and the honoring of diversity. For her, Descriptive Inquiry became a way to develop a school that worked to live up to those values. All these visions are about culture and cultural values. As they elaborated on the meanings of these metaphors, several strands about how Descriptive Inquiry helped these principals shape the cultures of their schools emerged: the development of a schoolwide ethic; school as a place for thinking and ongoing learning; the role of the structure and discipline of description; and the need to work against the isolation of teachers from one another, of the leader from teachers and of families from the school. To discuss the ways Descriptive Inquiry helped school leaders do this work, I will pull forward the ideas I hear in the interviews. I invite the reader to do the same as I am sure there is more in each story that I did not hear or understand.

The Development of a Schoolwide Ethic

> Ethical thought consists of the systematic examination of the relations of human beings to each other, the conceptions, interests and ideals from which human ways of treating one another spring, and the systems of value on which such ends of life are based. These beliefs about how life should be lived, what men and women should be and do, are objects of moral inquiry; and when applied to groups and nations, and, indeed, mankind as a whole, are called political philosophy, which is but ethics applied to society.
>
> —Isaiah Berlin (1991, pp. 1–2)

The practice of Descriptive Inquiry supports and deepens an ethic that is grounded in a core belief in the value of the person and the importance of human capacity and defines how people speak and work together. This ethic became a core of the cultures of these schools. You will read in the sections below the ethic that guided the schools and the ways in which this ethic was cultivated by Descriptive Inquiry. As you read, consider what ethic might underlie your own school. Do you find this ethic corresponds with the values that brought you to teaching? Are there elements you'd like to reinforce or change?

Knowing children well became an expectation in all the principals' schools. Jane described two aspects of this part of their work: language and seeing from different vantage points. Describing observations to others helps develop language.

> What really began to change was the way we talked about children. If somebody is saying that a kid is lazy and then someone being able to say, well, what do you mean by that? What does that word mean? Short of doing a Reflection on the Word, which we may have if it was a word that was coming up a lot, we certainly help the person give examples and describe what he or she was witnessing or experiencing. . . . So people began to do that, not all people, but many people began to take more responsibility for questioning people about the language they were using. That certainly happened in the formal meetings, but it was happening more and more in the casual conversations that people had.

Given Judith's defining metaphor for school "as a dynamic organism, a living breathing thing that supports children . . ." she goes on to say that this view of a school requires that

> all of your work has to be about the children, and understanding the children and what they're doing so that you can build curriculum to support the children and you can write authentic narrative pieces about the children, and talk to the children with their parents, and really get to know them more deeply. . . . You have to support [this stance] by professional development and becoming used to really thinking about the children. The descriptive work is a vehicle for really knowing and understanding children and understanding practice, too. Examining things in an organized way and not just—that kid or those teachers. Really setting a framework for sitting down and conducting your research and your looking and your thinking. So it provides a context.

At the Earth School under Alison's leadership, teachers recognized an ethical imperative of "knowing children well"—what to do when a child was struggling but the teacher was not certain about how to support the child in the classroom and their understandings of the child led the teacher to believe that recommending an IEP was not the right immediate direction.

The Support Team is probably the best example of how Descriptive Inquiry was woven in, as this was a regular school-based structure based on knowing children well for their strengths and using that knowledge to design a specific support, whether it be a small-group puppetry project, gardening on the roof, math interventions, a co-teaching opportunity for a teacher who wanted support . . . the list goes on as this was an in-house authentic team not mandated by the outside (there was no funding to cover this). Through a collaborative, diverse team of educators we were able to look closely at a child and her work, plan specific supports and in 6–8 weeks follow up to see what progress looked like. The rounds of support, rethinking, tweaking, trying again . . . is Descriptive Inquiry at its best.

A power of Descriptive Inquiry is that the process allowed the principals to make tangible changes to practice that reinforced the more abstract ethics they strove for. For example, the ethic of "knowing children well" through description led to the development of language that supported expansive thinking and careful speaking about children. Colleagues learned to see and talk with one another differently and to work with children more particularly. Michelle describes an extension of this aspect of school culture: children becoming more interesting to their teachers.

And obviously when we were doing Descriptive Reviews of Children's Work, this in-depth looking at what a child does and all of the facets, from handwriting to the gesture, to how much they were writing or what they were writing about or how they were drawing. It gave teachers an opportunity to see children in a much deeper way, and the children became much more interesting to them, you know. They certainly became more interesting to me. So from that it also nurtured their ability—it gave them a lot more to work with in terms of making decisions about what the next steps for these children were or what they could do to move that child on to the next phase. So, that in terms of practice was good.

Building ways to implement a collaborative spirit among colleagues and to become known to one another is a related aspect of the ethic created. Michelle describes this as something she came to rely on:

It also opened up the field so that everyone could bring in what it was they're good at because one of the things about Descriptive Review is that you do uncover what people are good at, what children are good at, what teachers are good at, and I think that it made it possible for them or easier for them to collaborate, and to accept ideas from others, you know, up to a certain point. You know, this isn't panacea, but it definitely does create lots more openings in terms of conversations, and it creates lots more openings in terms of having teachers be okay about collaborating and having people coming in and out of their classroom, working with them, etc., that kind of thing. I think it's incredible for teacher practice to have that happen, you know, for their own practice, but also their attitude or the spirit with which they enter into the work of the classroom and curriculum.

Not that work with colleagues was always smooth. As Jane describes, the threads of work—using description to know children well and building a community of teachers comfortable with developing their practice through their creation of knowledge about children and using disciplined inquiry processes to help them reflect on their teaching—came together unevenly in the school when the question was about the quality of work being done by peers. When describing the influence of Descriptive Inquiry on teachers' practices, Jane said, "it influenced them tremendously. That doesn't mean that we didn't have venting sessions. Screaming out 'I can't do this anymore!' and 'I am going crazy!' It was most challenging in the area of peer judgment. That was where it was hardest for people to be descriptive." Judgment of peers was an area about which Jane as leader wrestled with her teachers. In the interviews, Jane tells multiple stories in which she grapples with how to balance her own strong ethics with what the teachers were doing.

While still a teacher in the art room, Jane was asked to mentor a teacher new to the school. Not wanting to do this alone, she suggested that a group form, the members of which the teacher selected. She continued this practice when she became school director. There to support the teachers, the purpose of this advisory group was to work with the teachers on issues they brought for consideration.

One of the reasons why we had the advisory group was to be able to talk to very sensitive issues, not as a whole staff. At one point there was interest in the peer review that was going on in another school. I had no problem with peer review, but I didn't feel that what I saw from that school was a safe way of doing peer review. And I felt that doing a Review of Practice would be a safer way of—and probably a more informative way of—knowing somebody else's work. . . . I was actually voted down one year on peer review. They wanted to review a particular teacher, an experienced teacher who came to us that year, and he was not in the classroom. He was a support person, special ed. He wasn't doing well. I met with him a lot. . . . He was not averse to meeting with me, but he was uncomfortable. So they wanted to have this review in March. I said, "You can do it, but I am not participating. I'll sit here, but I am not going to participate because I am concerned about this." Well, oh boy, was I right. It was horrible. And I said at the next meeting that I could not be the head of a school in which teachers conducted themselves in the way that they did. He left the school at the end of the year. And this happened with a couple of other people as well—either from the whole group doing it or people who were appointed by the whole group. I said until we can figure this out, I am using my executive authority that we are not going to do it or get a new director. Because what I found was that people did not speak generously about the person, did not ask questions. They didn't have the same curiosity about the person as they had about children.

Cecelia did a review of two teachers and a paraprofessional about how they work together to help her work be more visible because the para was very contentious. I think that Review was very helpful for people to see that balance of how we could address interpersonal and interprofessional relationships. But I must say I had to be at the helm or Cecelia had to be at the helm for those. There was no one who could separate their particular feelings from the situation in a way they could with a child. We did get a lot better at talking to one another about our questions in a respectful and many times, descriptive way. And, I think we got better about talking to each other privately about other people. Sara Hanhan had a list of reflective questions for her student-teachers that we worked on at the Summer Institute. What we decided to do as a staff was take one question that we all addressed, and individuals chose two. We shared those and that was a way of people talking about their vulnerabilities. I remember Katya saying, "Oh, finally I can talk about what I really do in the classroom and not hide." She felt safe enough in that form to do it. So when there was a framing question, it was a lot easier than when there was a "let's get this person." When the person "got gotten," who was held responsible? Me! . . . But I think peer work is far more sensitive than anything I ever did around children and parents. And I guess that's because you see each other every day and the nature of the teacher wanting to be the best and feeling they're the worst.

Given the themes across these stories, Jane's ethos of honoring the individual came up against teachers' difficulty in seeing the capacity of a peer. Jane felt that some teachers had difficulty applying the respect they held for children to a colleague. These are thorny and sensitive challenges. Descriptive Inquiry was a means for Jane to get things back on track ethically when her connection with the teachers slipped a bit.

School as a Place for Thinking and Ongoing Learning

Of course school is a place for thinking and learning—for students. A key precept of progressive education is that, for children to think and learn, adults need to be doing the same. However, schools do not always encourage this possibility for the adults who live and work there. A basic way Descriptive Inquiry supports this aim is through helping teachers and the leader take an inquiry stance to their work with children and with one another, acknowledge the authority of a question, and become what Jane calls "a home for thinking." Alison named the basics of this aspect of the work: "the stance among teachers [was] that they didn't have all the answers and that the questions were as important." Jane described her teachers over time developing comfort with describing and a vision of what engaging in inquiry could do for them in their work. As this comfort increased, they began to ask questions that emerged from their work and interests and to share their questions and work with colleagues.

> After 9/11, one teacher decided that we needed to sing a lot more patriotic songs, so he said that to me and . . . I said, how about this? I'll ask the staff if we can push a Monday agenda to another week, you introduce songs to us, and we will talk about them. We'll do a Reflection on patriotism, and we will talk about what songs really fit what we believe in this school and what songs we really don't want here. And that's how we did it. When a classroom was completely falling apart with a new teacher and it was a total mess, we met in there and asked ourselves how the physical environment supports a way of being in the classroom. When we had a special ed child who had cerebral palsy, she had trouble maneuvering her way around the room. We went into the room and set it up so that she had something to hold on to no matter where she had to go.
>
> Because I met with everybody once a week, I knew what they were thinking about. Carol and Nancy were interested in dramatic play; they asked if we could describe a video of dramatic play, and they initiated that. And then, one of the children in that video was someone who eluded Nancy about [how to support his] writing so we then looked at his writing and related to how we saw him developing story in dramatic play. That very much came from the teachers. Sally, a major LEGO fan, said to me, "I don't know what to tell the parents about why LEGOs are important." So we did a description of a piece of LEGO work and we took language from that [for talking with parents]. It just really, really lived in the school.

A second way the principals described their schools becoming places of ongoing learning for their teachers was helping them think beyond the superficial, beyond their assumptions. For Judith, Descriptive Inquiry is the vehicle for developing the kind of understanding of children necessary for a "living, breathing" school, the means of building the school and the individual teachers' practice in that school. She says that Descriptive

Inquiry does this by helping teachers think about their language, work with colleagues around teachers' questions, build curriculum around children's interests, and get beyond the surface in their thinking and work with children.

> I have found that teachers can spin, making assumptions about who children are or what they do. . . . Linda did a Descriptive Review about a little girl—we were looking at children who were learning English as another language—that's another thing Descriptive Inquiry lets you do. It lets you look at a group of children and helps you understand them better, and you can put into place what they need. So this little girl was very compliant. They were doing a study on the body, and she was really interested in it, and was doing it, and doing all the stuff around it, and going to project time. But then she said something about the brain was blah blah blah, so at a deeper level, she really wasn't getting what was going on at all. So if you looked at her in a superficial way, or if you looked at just her output, it was all fine. But if you really looked at her, it was just superficial. So that's kind of a more benign version of spinning. Like you could easily think she was okay. But I'm teaching and they're not getting it. That's the spinning. Like there's something wrong with the kids, or you know, this one is lazy or—not that anyone said anything like that. But it was also a way to look at yourself without passing judgment on yourself. It's not, "Oh, I did a really bad job at that," but "What do I have to do next so that they'll get it more?" So it's not cut and dried like a test or even a practical test where you're asking the kids whether they can do something or not do something, not that they got it or didn't get it, but where are they in the getting of it and how can I feed this particular child?

Finally and basically, these school leaders wanted to value their teachers' intelligence. Again, Judith speaks of how Descriptive Inquiry helps teachers to create knowledge through reflection on their practice with children.

> I think it also values teachers' intelligence. I think too often teachers are batted down and trashed, and I think this work honors them in a good way and lets them be decision makers and have agency, and be grown-ups.

The Role of the Structure and Discipline of Description

A third facet of Descriptive Inquiry's role in helping leaders shape the culture of their schools in ways that supported their vision is the disciplined nature of the process. These principals were taking care of themselves and making their schools places that enabled teachers' care of self by using Descriptive Inquiry to help them enact their philosophies. Based on the discipline of description and requiring collaboration as a way of working, Descriptive Inquiry provides a way of working that the school community can use for a variety of purposes. First of all, Descriptive Inquiry provides a transportable structure: the careful framing of issues and questions to guide the work; the use of a go-round, which asks members of the group to wait their turn and encourages each person to speak; and the use of description as the core mode of speaking, holding interpretation to the final rounds of the process. Jane sees being vigilant about the use of description and following the structure of the inquiry process as providing discipline for a group and some safety for people expressing their thoughts.

As noted earlier in this chapter, Michelle's emphasis was on unifying values and how Descriptive Inquiry helped build a culture around them. Because of the "rules" of the process, she sees Descriptive Inquiry as one of the ways she was able to build a community in which members trust and respect one another, honor diversity and the strengths that children and adults bring, and allow for growth.

> So the practice, basically the way of talking about children, there are rules in Descriptive Review, and one of the most important rules has got to do with not allowing for any labeling and not allowing for any mixing up what you see with making judgments about it. . . . The observational part slows them down, and not being able to make judgments about it for a while also slows them down because once you make a judgment there's closure, and you just don't want that to happen, so the slowing down of that process was interesting.

The democratic nature of the Descriptive Inquiry structure comes through in Alison's description. As with the other principles, this lives in the inclusion of voices.

> Because we used Descriptive Inquiry, our formal professional development and other kinds of meetings with parents, committees, and such were always grounded in processes that allowed and expected everyone to share and listen to one another. Parents, over time, realized that a meeting at the school about their child generally included various staff members and took up to an hour. Most parents came with their own questions and also understood that we weren't going to push anything on them. We were going to collaborate to figure out how best to support their child, and then we were going to meet again and again if necessary.

The Need to Work Against the Isolation

This fourth thread of culture building and shaping cuts across the ethos of teachers believing that the safest things for them to do is close their doors and do their own thing in that protected space. In contrast, the principals we interviewed described Descriptive Inquiry creating a public and shared space in which teachers could be known and know others.

Judith names helping teachers break down the barriers that often enforce a kind of isolation in a school and develop the knowledge that they are part of a team as an important aspect of school leadership. Striking in Judith's testimony is the degree of inclusivity; administrators, teachers, paraprofessionals, and families are all brought into the conversation. That these groups are talking with one another is itself somewhat unusual. That the conversation is democratic is incredibly rare.

> Linda told me that this year or last year they looked at some old work that we had done, and they were like, "Oh, this is really amazing that you had talked about that; it was important work." And that's something else, that whether or not people are moaning about preparing, they always consider it important work. And it also helps people see themselves as part of the team that's working with the child. It's not only the classroom child and the specialists who are over there doing their own thing disconnected, but when people were doing a review, the teacher the year before might say something, the phys ed teacher, the librarian, the Spanish teacher, all would have a little piece of it too, a chance to say something. I think that's an important thing because usually those people are out in left field and the paraprofessionals often would say something. It also elevated the paraprofessionals, I think. We would do some work at the beginning of the year before school started, or election day, and some of the parents did come to the after-school meetings too. And they were also at an equal level; they had a point of view; they had experiences. One that stands out to me is when we talked about when we were children in school, when did we feel known, when did we feel misunderstood or not liked, and when did school align with our particular interests. Questions like that. And it was very powerful what came out of it for people and people felt kind of released to be able to talk about that, and then what does that mean in terms of building our school.
>
> There should be more time built into the school day to look at kids' work, talk about kids and observe kids, be with colleagues. Oh, I think one of the important things about descriptive work, too, is if you look at teachers as being very isolated, this has teachers being not isolated. And it breaks down those barriers, and it also lets teachers be

comfortable in front of each other, and be open and honest, and not have to hide.

Coming out of hiding. Breaking down barriers. These actions point to a kind of vulnerability different from that which is at the root of the need to hide or create barriers. It is a vulnerability that opens the teacher to a new kind of learning. Michelle describes this:

> Isolation does breed vulnerability, and the more isolated you are the more vulnerable you are when in contact with somebody else. I think the slowness and the nonjudgmental but deep observations of what one sees allows you to find the language to say things that you need to say without being hurtful. It does help build trust, you know, and trust is essential in schools among teachers, among people who are working together. We did create [it]. We did have a community that could talk to each other and could disagree.

Building on the trusting community culture Alison found at the Earth School, teachers were able to develop individual learning projects. They worked with colleagues on their own inquiry projects and, with peers, explored an area of teaching important to them.

> Teachers also had an area of focus or an essential question that was on their minds—we would discuss this together in connection to observations and feedback sessions not only with me, but through Peer Mentorship. We did this for several years—teachers were matched/self-selected with others who they could observe and spend time together debriefing without me around, and these areas of focus/questions of practice were also explored through grade team work and whole staff PD.

Judith described the multiple ways she saw Descriptive Inquiry deepening the community of her school. She found it helped teachers work better with families; helped teachers feel part of a team, breaking the isolation often experienced by teachers; and helped the school staff as a whole work on difficult issues.

As noted but deserving of its own discussion, alongside the isolation adults can feel inside the school, families can feel separated from their children's school too. All these principals name their desire to bring families into the conversations of the school as an important part of the school culture they desired. Again, though this desire is frequently named by teachers and administrators, it is more often stated than achieved. Judith notes that working with families successfully starts with knowing their child well. She comments,

I've also said some hard things to parents that they have accepted, and teachers have said hard things and they say, "Well, you know my child. You really know that child, so I'm hearing what you say."

Judith went on to say that the teachers and parents together worked on social and curricular issues:

We worked with a consultant around diversity and understanding each other. And I don't think we would have gotten to that place or been able to really work in that honest and raw way if we didn't have the experience, teachers and parents together looking at questions. Parents said the work that we did on Saturdays or after school was so important—that work was so important to them. . . . We did some curriculum work; we did some Reviews of individual children; we looked at children's work; that coming together in a really equal and honest way and a nonjudgmental way—and about the kids. Not about power issues around kids. . . . It was really coming together around children and for children that was important for the school. And it allowed us to do work with the families, which might have been difficult.

Michelle takes this a step further in her description of her school's efforts to bring families into their conversations in order to engage them in a dialogue about and deepen their understanding of the ways the school was educating their child:

We also did a lot [with families]. Teachers wrote long reports about children every year, at least twice a year, and it really helped them with the language, doing that, helping them to describe the progress, where the children were, the progress they were making in nonjudgmental ways, and that really also has a lot to do with how the school communicated with parents. It was interesting because parents are often used to, "Okay, so is my child at the top of the class? My child got a B. How come I'm looking at this paper? It's got a lot of scribbles on it." Parents have a way of looking at school often, which would reflect a lot of the education they had when they were young kids, which was very quantifiable and very based on grades and stratification of where you are in the chain of achievement, where you are compared to everybody else. And I think that the [descriptive narrative] reports that they would get sometimes would puzzle parents a whole lot, which would bring them into a conversation with teachers, and if they weren't happy they would have a conversation with me about it. But it would also help them see; it would help them understand what it was that their child was doing in school in a way that most parents don't really have access to. So often, and I can't say always, but often it did. I think that's one of the reasons why parents love this school, because they felt that first of all they were being spoken to with respect. I think Descriptive Review really helps. First of all Descriptive Review is extremely respectful, and having teachers speak respectfully about children is something that sometimes surprises parents, especially when they felt like there might be reasons not to.

Families also deepened the school's understanding of who they, the families were, and their concerns and ideas about education and issues of equity. Trying to genuinely hear families and their stories was an important part of Michelle's vision for her school. She explains:

Well, basically the diversity and inclusion issues were ones that were really huge and they were important issues. They were issues that were then brought to the whole community, and parents participated in those discussions, and we would have meetings with parents or we'd have parent evenings at least two or three times a year when some of these issues were addressed, and where parents were able to come and often open up and talk about their own story in ways that allowed for everyone else to become much more aware of who these people were, where they came from, and how they thought. You know, these evenings weren't necessarily easy. They were not easy in approaching them, but the greeting after those meetings was much more expansive. It meant that people who hadn't greeted each other before in the hallways did greet each other in the hallways, and you know, more connections were made. So I think that is an example of how the Descriptive Processes informed work with families.

Additional Thoughts on the Development of School Culture

Several ideas stand out about Descriptive Inquiry that make it an enabler of the work these principals describe for shaping their school's culture: the structures of the process, the discipline of description, and an ethic of respect and trust that permeates relationships and the ways work is done in these schools. Together, this allows Descriptive Inquiry to create a "holding environment" in the sense used by Ellie Drago-Severson (2004), in which individuals are developmentally supported and challenged so that they can develop. The teachers and their leaders feel safe enough to let themselves be vulnerable to colleagues, to ask questions that matter to them, and to find the language needed to discuss complex and difficult ideas and points of view.

The people within these schools' cultures are "held" in ways that enable meaningful and lasting change. They shift their thinking, language, and practice on their own volition, not because they are compelled to do so. This is what makes it possible, I think, for teachers and leaders to take an inquiry stance, to be willing to know children well enough to challenge their own practice, and to lower barriers between them and colleagues and between them and families.

NEGOTIATING COMPETING VALUES

One of the things school leaders in collaborative communities need to do is work in the space that tensions among different value commitments and institutional structures create. This is especially true when schools attempt to live out progressive values within a culture and educational bureaucracy whose values tend to centralization, standardization, and directives. For me, Berlin's (1991) ideas about the impossibility of finding a definitive solution because of the important reality of competing values have been a touchstone in thinking about this difficult aspect of the work of school leadership. Berlin writes,

> If the old perennial belief in the possibility of realizing ultimate harmony is a fallacy, and the positions of the thinkers I have appealed to—Machiavelli, Vico, Herder, Herzen—are valid, then, if we allow that Great Goods can collide, that some of them cannot live together, even though others can—in short, that one cannot have everything, in principle as well as in practice—and if human creativity may depend upon a variety of mutually exclusive choice: then, as Chernyshevsky and Lenin once asked, 'What is to be done?' How do we choose between possibilities? What and how much must we sacrifice to what? There is, it seems to me, no clear reply. But the collisions, even if they cannot be avoided, can be softened. Claims can be balanced, compromises can be reached: in concrete situations not every claim is of equal force—so much liberty and so much equality; so much for sharp moral condemnation, and so much for understanding a given human situation; so much for the full force of the law, and so much for the prerogative of mercy; for feeding the hungry, clothing the naked, healing the sick, sheltering the homeless. Priorities, never final and absolute, must be established. (p. 17)

It is important for leaders to know that conflicts can result from competing good things. It is also important for leaders to have ways to work through the conflicts, to find the balances and compromises that can work currently. And, it is important for all participants in a school community to know that priorities are "never final and absolute."

Working as a leader of a school and of schools of education and working with leaders of progressive schools in a large urban setting, I found Descriptive Inquiry helped negotiate many sets of tensions and find priorities among the possibilities: among the ideas and commitments of teachers; between what is valued and practiced inside the school and what is valued and expected from the system (to which schools belong but can feel outside of). The needed negotiation of competing values raises interesting issues about where authority lies. My work with the leaders of City-as-School, as documented in a story written by Rachel, provides one example of how value tensions play out in a school. Rachel describes our first bit of work together as we discussed the possibility of introducing Descriptive Inquiry to the teacher leaders of the school. The story picks up in the midst of our first conversation about the possibility of leading a retreat with the teacher leaders at the start of the school year. Rachel writes,

> Toward the end of our conversation, I shared with Cecelia that a central challenge in previous years had been coming together around an instructional focus. Each school in the Department of Education is required to have this yearly instructional focus toward which the whole school is working. I explained to Cecelia that, historically, the principal, Alan, and I had chosen our school's instructional focus during the summer, submitted it to our superintendent, and then introduced it to the faculty. I shared that this practice had created tension; teacher leaders had struggled to translate the instructional focus to their teams, and some faculty members had felt resentful because the instructional focus had been imposed on them. As a result, our efforts to work on a single area of focus as a whole school often depended on Alan and me consistently reinforcing the instructional focus in Friday morning faculty meetings and other venues like classroom observations.
>
> I also shared with Cecelia that a related tension had emerged between our instructional focus and the social-emotional aspects of our work. Since the very first time we were asked to have an instructional focus in my second year at City-as, faculty members argued that we should have a social-emotional focus too. The push for more attention to social-emotional development as opposed to academics had surfaced repeatedly in our professional development committee meetings the previous year, with a few members in particular advocating for a focus that would support students who are in crisis and experiencing trauma. As a committee, we had struggled to work with the tension productively and had essentially agreed to disagree. This had interfered with our ability to do schoolwide work in our Friday meetings the previous year, and we had compromised by holding faculty-to-faculty workshops on topics as varied as layered curriculum and mindfulness training and then allowing people to choose.
>
> When I shared this with Cecelia, she quickly noted that the tension between the instructional and social-emotional parts of our work was

artificial and reflected the district's narrow definition of instructional. I felt relieved when Cecelia said this and, for the first time, believed that we, as a school, could negotiate this tension productively.

I also shared with Cecelia that in July prior to the retreat (not long before she and I met) our superintendent had encouraged the schools in our network to work on "cognitive engagement" by facilitating a workshop on the topic. I had attended and was excited to see this more holistic approach to learning emphasized. While the workshop spoke to me, I expressed concern to Cecelia that the term *cognitive engagement* might seem removed from the local language of the school and that, therefore, faculty members might reject it. Cecelia echoed my concern. She suggested replacing *cognitive engagement* with *meaningful work*, noting that people "use their minds well" and are "cognitively engaged" while doing, making, or creating meaningful work. The idea of *meaningful work* resonated with me and Alan. Additionally, Cecelia provided language for connecting "meaningful work" to "cognitive engagement," which Alan and I needed in speaking with our colleagues and our superintendent. She suggested that we create the opportunity for the teacher leaders to think about points of connection and divergence between the two. I agreed. Our focus question for our retreat with the teacher leaders, therefore, was: How can we create meaningful work with our students and each other? How can Descriptive Inquiry help us with this?

Finally, I expressed concern to Cecelia that faculty members might reject Descriptive Inquiry because Alan and I made a unilateral decision to bring it to the school. Specifically, they might reject the decision because they had not been involved in making it. To this Cecelia said, "You are making a leadership decision to bring Descriptive Inquiry to the school. You are doing this because you believe that Descriptive Inquiry is a process that will help the school more fully live its values. You have to explain this to people." She helped me to create talking points for explaining the leadership decision to bring Descriptive Inquiry to the school. Her response allowed me to feel comfortable making a leadership decision around process that was grounded in the values of the school. I carry this guiding principle for making leadership decisions with me to this day. It has become part of my stance regarding school leadership.

I knew that it was still possible that the teacher leaders could reject Descriptive Inquiry. If they had a terrible experience during the retreat or if Cecelia had a terrible experience working with us, the work would likely not continue (or would take a very different form). A lot hinged on the retreat.

Rachel's story illustrates descriptive knowledge-making in the moment. Asking her to be as descriptive as possible, listening closely, and working to understand her ideas about and interpretations of her situation, I said back to her what I heard and offered another way to think about her questions and purposes. In the spirit of making my meaning-making process transparent, I put alongside Rachel's description some of the thinking I was doing during our conversation. I invite the reader to put their interpretations of Rachel's story alongside mine and explore what you might have said to Rachel if you had been talking with her.

In this first conversation with Rachel, who came to me after attending the 5-day Summer Institute on Descriptive Process run by the Institute on Descriptive Inquiry, I was intrigued by the possibilities she saw for her school in the integration of Descriptive Inquiry into their ongoing work, among them creating a better tone in the relationships among the teachers and having a more democratic process for decision making. Given Rachel's interest in democratic decision making, I was alert to what sounded like a top-down process when it came to defining the school's instructional focus. Hearing that teachers felt their school leaders were ignoring an important aspect of the school's work with students, I interpreted the leaders of the school as using a process that was parallel to that used by the district—that is, the leader decides, the school follows the directive. The value commitments embedded in the Descriptive Inquiry process shaped the suggestions I made. First, separating the academic from the social-emotional is the result of seeing human beings as a collection of parts rather than integrated wholes. Imposing one understanding over the other, as the district was doing, creates a tension for teachers who have a different conception. The frame of meaningful work brings the two aspects of learning together into a whole. And, second, it was important to recognize that an instructional focus was imposed on the principals from the outside and, in turn, the principals were imposing it on the school, and the teachers were left powerless by not having any say in what the instructional focus was to be.

Rachel's concern about imposing Descriptive Inquiry on the teachers was also of note, but I saw this a bit differently. Rachel was inside the school; she saw possibilities for how Descriptive Inquiry could help the school deepen its work around its core values, possibilities she wanted to explore. In other words, as principal, she had access to information that the faculty didn't have about what was needed and how it might be implemented. As part of her positional authority as principal, she was acting on this knowledge to support her staff. All this was fodder for the planning we did for the retreat.

WORKING ON DIFFICULT ISSUES

Leadership work in schools ideally means dealing with and not ignoring issues and ideas that are difficult to discuss because they create discomfort and feel divisive. Earlier in this chapter, Jane described the way assessing peers became a conflict in her school and how she tried to work this through with her teachers. I share here a story about another kind of issue that can set up conflict: how a school seriously acknowledges and works on issues of race. Critical to the life and work of a school and to the education of children, my experience has taught me that race is a topic easily set aside as toxic. Each principal touched on issues of racial difference in her interview, and it was particularly salient in Michelle's. Picking up on this theme and interest for the Earth School, in the story below, Abbe, the principal of the Earth School at the time we wrote this book, describes a conflict she was confronted with in her work with parents. In terms of descriptive knowledge-making, this story tells how a principal recognized an issue that was emerging in her school and how she used Descriptive Inquiry to work on that issue and move it out of the status quo.

> The Earth School has always valued diversity and inclusion. In recent years, the staff has focused on increasing critical consciousness about race during professional development. All staff members began basic racial equity training through an organization called Border Crossers. This group leads workshops in schools across the city and was contracted to help teachers critique various aspects of the school's practice with a racial equity lens. The staff extended this work through individual inquiry projects. As the school leader, I increased my efforts to raise racial equity issues with the parent body. I did this in a number of ways: through my newsletters, on a bulletin board, at School Leadership Team and Parent Association meetings, at our annual parent-teacher collaborative study day, and at the Annual Town Meeting. For example, at the Town Meeting, I presented a keynote on historical school segregation and desegregation efforts to contextualize our participation in the Chancellor's Diversity Pilot. I was surprised when a small group of White, usually supportive parents pushed back at my efforts at the end of the school year. They largely articulated a "color-blind" perspective, by which they meant that we should look beyond race with the idea that we can simply see people. I recognized this perspective immediately because in all honesty it resonated with earlier iterations of my own point of view. From this standpoint and citing this line from the Mission, "We work to be a place where children and adults from diverse backgrounds come together to celebrate our differences, to appreciate our common humanity, and to contribute to our community," they viewed the focus on race when

talking about diversity as inherently divisive and particularly unsuitable for children. My initiatives to focus attention on race were thus viewed as a contradiction to the school's mission statement.

After my initial reaction of horror, I brought my story to the Institute on Descriptive Inquiry: sharing my newsletters, survey comments, my bulletin board, and, of course, my Recollections. Through the feedback that I received and many subsequent conversations, I have worked to have a constructive response, to see the concerned parents as "canaries in the mine" (Shalaby, 2017, p. xv), revealing a toxic climate around race and even more so, my own intolerance with what I perceive as White denial and ignorance. I began to see that my surprise at the pushback was indicative of my own naiveté. As I was working against my own racial blindness, I thought these parents had the same intentions. Through the process, it became clear that I needed to remain open to this important "feedback" so as to address it more proactively while mustering greater fortitude and persistence.

Cecelia and I have a long history of working together using Descriptive Inquiry with staff and, many years ago, ran a "Parent-Teacher Inquiry Group" to collaborate with parents around issues of standards and accountability. After the Summer Institute session, she suggested that she and I do a group with parents around issues of diversity and racial equity. Trusting both Cecelia and the processes, I unhesitatingly took her up on the offer, and we began planning the group. I knew from experience that this group would not attract the full range of our parent body. I anticipated that it would attract some of the "pushback" group as well as others interested in discussing the topic.

Our first task was coming up with wording about the group that would be attractive and nonthreatening, with the goal of enticing more parents to join. We decided to call the group The Diversity and Difference Study Group, and we advertised the group on fliers, at parent meetings, and in the newsletter:

> Join Abbe Futterman and Cecelia E. Traugh for an open exploration into issues of diversity and difference. Explore the importance of diversity for the education of children. Consider the challenges and rewards of being a parent in a diverse community. The Diversity and Difference Study Group is an opportunity for dialogue with other parents and Abbe on this important topic. We are pleased to welcome Cecelia E. Traugh from Bank Street College as facilitator.

We originally scheduled three fall dates and later added three winter/spring dates. Meeting in the morning, we had from 8 to 15 participants with fairly steady attendance. Twelve of the parents attended at least four of the six meetings. There was a great span of cultural and language diversity, including recent immigrants from Germany, Japan, Nepal, Colombia, and Mexico. About half of the participants identified as White. The group was college educated (except one) and economically secure. As the group seeking a "color-blind" approach were largely White and college educated, I felt the flier had successfully attracted those I needed to work with on this particular issue.[1]

How did Descriptive Inquiry figure into this struggle to find a way forward? Because Abbe trusts the inquiry process, she saw it as a vehicle for good conversation. She could imagine its possibilities. As many of the principals noted at the beginning of this chapter, Descriptive Inquiry provided us with a structure we found allowed hard things to be said and heard. It also provided a structure that let her, as school leader, be part of a democratic community instead of an authority. This, we felt, would mitigate the ways in which Abbe's clear and passionate beliefs on the topic might be alienating and silencing others.

Preparation emerges as key. Through the year, together Abbe and I planned the group's work. We shared Recollections of times when we first became aware of our difference or another person's being different. We reflected on the ideas of marginalization, privilege, and absorption. We read "Zora" from *Troublemakers*, by Carla Shalaby (2017); "The Early Years: Is My Skin Brown Because I Drink Chocolate Milk?" from *Why Are All the Black Kids Sitting Together in the Cafeteria?*, by Beverly Tatum (2017); and "Disarming the Nuclear Family" by Willow McCormick (2013). Through all these activities, each one emerging from the ones prior, we connected the conversation to group members' experiences, what they saw happening with their children, and the school and what it offers. For the final session, we read a passage from James Baldwin (1963) [quoted at length in Chapter 11] calling for an education that promotes challenging the status quo and asking questions. We discussed at length the connections of his ideas to the work of the group (and the implications of his ideas for the school's mission, which we also read).

The group's responses were uniformly positive. They wanted to continue this work. What is important to Abbe and me is that we found a way to work with parents on what had been seen as an untouchable topic. The parents could share their stories, which grew more personal through the year, and their interpretations of events and ideas, and they could listen to one another carefully. It does take courage on the school leader's part to do this kind of work, but not doing it may be a shirking of responsibility. Instead, Abbe bravely used her leadership to bring in the processes, and then she stepped back into the position of community member during conversations. The processes served as a structure that enabled conversation across difference. In letting the processes do the work, Abbe could create a space for meaningful conversation. Finally, Abbe's story showcases some of the nuances of the Descriptive Process. Though Abbe as principal is an authority, having another person serve as chair allows for her to engage more democratically as well. Just as a president also has a vote, Abbe, in stepping into the confines of the space that Descriptive Inquiry creates, could add her voice into the multitude.

INTEGRATIVE RESTATEMENT

As we explained in Chapter 3, at the close of Descriptive Inquiry sessions, the person chairing the group provides an integrative restatement—that is, shares with the group the threads and themes they think run through the descriptive conversation and suggestions of other ideas that might sit alongside those generated by the group. Again, I invite the reader to think about how you might summarize the thinking of this chapter and what theories or schools of thought you see complementing or contrasting with the ideas described here.

Reading a draft of this chapter, Abbe said that it gave her, a longtime practitioner of the inquiry process, new insights into Descriptive Inquiry. Alison too commented that the chapter gave her insights into current tensions in her school. For me, setting these principals' stories alongside each other proves to be about building schools as ethical, knowledge-making, humane institutions intent on doing their work in values-based ways that support the growth of children and adults.

Many theoretical stances could be placed alongside the ideas about leadership named in this chapter; for example, various theories of institutional change. For my purpose here, I choose to look at how the stories illustrate how some of the philosophical ideas that are important to this book apply to leadership.

Schwartz and Sharpe (2010) highlight that an often significant element of practical wisdom is finding a way of framing a question that allows for growth. This was powerfully showcased in Rachel's story, in which she found herself initially confused by the tension between her administrative bosses and her school colleagues. Yet, neither the teachers nor the administrators saw social-emotional development as divorced from more traditional academic learning, but pushed to see these areas of development as competing camps, they had found themselves at odds. Significantly, what I saw was confusion created by external dichotomies. Helping Rachel recognize this by reframing this conundrum as an externally imposed binary, I gave Rachel an entry point to redirect the work to how to best enact the school's values.

Throughout this chapter, many of the principals provided similar examples of the ways that Descriptive Inquiry helped teachers find language to express their values as well as come to methods in alignment with their own guiding principles.

Sometimes, though, values were themselves at stake. What was needed was not new frames but the ability to talk across difference. Jane's poignant story about tensions among teachers showcases an example of when she had to work through strong differences in values between herself and her staff. Abbe, too, sought a way to work with deep differences of value. After engaging in a Descriptive Review at the Summer Institute with people disconnected from the school, she saw that Descriptive Inquiry could allow her an entry into an especially challenging conversation in which different values were at stake. Abbe's story highlights the nuances and pain involved in a struggle in deep-rooted values and the power of the Descriptive Processes to support this.

Another thread I find in some of the principals' stories is self-care. These principals used Descriptive Inquiry to help their teachers conduct themselves well, to develop their ethical selves and in turn a culture that intended to support ethical action. They used the structures of Descriptive Inquiry to help the community do the practicing necessary for developing the disciplined habits of taking time to describe rather than quickly interpret or judge. The stories bring to my mind Foucault (1997) when he writes that just as a wrestler repeatedly "practices the few moves that he needs to triumph over his opponents," one must practice exercises that "will enable us to bear up against events that occur" (p. 99).

Finally, the role of the collaborative outside person who engages with the leader and brings their perspective and distance is a thread worth noting. There is power in having a trusted reflective partner with whom a leader can talk through issues and questions. This type of collegial work with someone outside of the school helps leaders make decisions and take risks.

NOTE

1. It is important to note that Abbe later formed additional parent groups that resonated with a wider diversity of parents.

CHAPTER 11

A Reflection on the Idea of the Practically Wise School

Cecelia E. Traugh and Cara E. Furman

We opened this book with a call to teach for "human dignity" (Carini & Himley, 2010, p. 9). We began with questions about what it means to be a teacher and to support teacher growth within this framework. We have argued throughout that doing so requires democratic institutions that help teachers develop practical wisdom in the service of this goal. We close now with the question: What is a school?

Schools are made things. As institutions, they are founded. They are human works. These ways of conceiving their origins help us know that they can be made again and founded anew. They can be rethought and reimagined. And, just as the definition of the teacher is value-laden and philosophically advised, so is that of the school.

This book has been about a process that helps us reimagine and remake. We have described how Descriptive Inquiry can move us as persons to

- remake our perceptions of people and our working relationships,
- see possibilities and disrupt the status quo, and
- enact our values and put ourselves on the life path of care of oneself à la Foucault.

We maintain that Descriptive Inquiry can be a vehicle for the teacher to become practically wise.

This book has also been an argument that Descriptive Inquiry can be a process that remakes schools into practically wise and democratic institutions, places that support and even require their human occupants to continually rethink themselves and their actions. We argue that schools have the potential to be places that support the kind of care of self that results in relationships and practices that enact human dignity.

Schools that commit to using Descriptive Inquiry commit to remaking themselves through learning how to enact some core values. Through inquiry, they commit to becoming the following:

- A "public space," a polity where children, educators, and families are known through their words, deeds, and selves. Arendt (1998) argues that a key part of the human condition is to be known as a thinker and an actor. To be seen is therefore an essential part of being human and, as we have argued throughout, it is through the polis, the public democratic spaces, that we are seen.
- Places that base their work on the strengths and capacities that each person brings and so serves children and families equitably by enacting an antiracist, social justice stance.

> As subjects of regimes of knowledge, students enter a world of statements wherein they find their identity and place of "belonging" (a contradictory desire, as it is also a site of exclusion), other subjects who occupy their same predicament, and the meanings that govern their possibilities for moving among social spaces. (Broderick & Leonardo, 2016, p. 63)

- This passage underlines the importance of children being part of a school society that works to see and know them as they are and uses a language of strength and possibility.
- Places for meaning and meaning-making over knowledge transmission or reproduction. As do Gunilla Dahlberg, Peter Moss, and Alan Pence (2013), we "distinguish dialogue between human beings, which expresses and constitutes a relationship to a concrete Other, from monologue, which seeks to transmit a body of knowledge and through so doing make the Other into the same" (p. 64).

A key part of practical wisdom is that what is right is determined by values and context. In highlighting four different schools, seven principals, and numerous children and teachers, we seek to highlight the degree to which context is both the environment in which one works and the people operating in this environment. Just as we build on the strengths of a particular child and teacher, in each school Cecelia built on what was in place: focusing on the strengths of the people in the institution and its structural strengths while also raising hard questions.

We close this reflection with the passage from Baldwin that Abbe and Cecelia discussed with parents at the Earth School:

> The purpose of education, finally, is to create in a person the ability to look at the world for himself, to make his own decisions, to say to himself this is black or this is white, to decide for himself whether there is a God in heaven or not. To ask questions of the universe, and then learn to live with those questions, is the way he achieves his own identity. But no society is really anxious to have that kind of person around. What societies really, ideally, want is a citizenry which will simply obey the rules of society. If a society succeeds in this, that society is

about to perish. The obligation of anyone who thinks of himself as responsible is to examine society and try to change it and to fight it—at no matter what risk. This is the only hope society has. This is the only way societies change. (1963)

How can we disrupt calcified systems that oppress children? Baldwin writes, "no society is really anxious to have that kind of person around" who "thinks of himself as responsible" and, in doing so, "examine[s] society and tr[ies] to change it and to fight it." Just as "no society is really anxious for such a person," we would argue that neither are most schools. Even schools that position themselves as on the forefront of change tend to replicate and reinforce the world as is. We hope that this book serves as a call for schools to remake themselves, to be animated and animating places where children and staff are deeply known. Our children and educators deserve nothing less.

References

Abu El-Haj, T. R. (2003). Practicing for equity from the standpoint of the particular: Exploring the work of one urban teacher network. *Teachers College Record, 105*(5), 817–845.

Anderson, M. (2015). *The first six weeks of school* (2nd ed.). Center for Responsive Schools Inc.

Arendt, H. (1998). *The human condition* (2nd ed.). University of Chicago Press.

Aristotle. (1999). *Nicomachean ethics* (T. Irwin, Trans.; 2nd ed). Hackett Pub. Co.

Baldwin, J. (1963, December 21). *A talk to teachers.* Saturday Review. https://www.spps.org/cms/lib010/MN01910242/Centricity/Domain/125/baldwin_atalktoteachers_1_2.pdf

Baltuck, N. (1995). *Apples from heaven: Multicultural folktales about stories and storytellers.* Apple Boat Press.

Ben-Peretz, M. (1995). *Learning from experience: Memory and the teacher's account of teaching.* State University of New York Press.

Bensman, D. (2000). *Central Park East and its graduates: "Learning by heart."* Teachers College Press.

Berger, R. (2003). *An ethic of excellence: Building a culture of craftsmanship with students.* Heinemann.

Berlin, I. (1991). *The crooked timber of humanity: Chapters in the history of ideas.* Alfred A. Knopf.

Broderick, A., & Leonardo, Z. (2016). The deployment and distribution of "goodness" as ideological property in schools. In D. J. Connor, B. A. Ferri, & S. A. Annamma (Eds.), *DisCrit: Disability studies and critical race theory in education* (pp. 55–67). Teachers College Press.

Calkins, L. (Ed.). (2003). *Units of study for primary writing.* FirstHand.

Carini, P. F. (1975). *Observation and description: An alternative methodology for the investigation of human phenomena.* North Dakota Study Group on Evaluation.

Carini, P. F. (1979). *The art of seeing and the visibility of the person.* University of North Dakota.

Carini, P. F. (2001). *Starting strong: A different look at children, schools, and standards.* Teachers College Press.

Carini, P. F., & Himley, M. (2010). *Jenny's story: Taking the long view of the child: Prospect's philosophy in action.* Teachers College Press.

Clandinin, D. J. (1985). Personal practical knowledge: A study of teachers' classroom images. *Curriculum Inquiry, 15*(4), 361–385.

Cochran-Smith, M., & Lytle, S. L. (Eds.). (1993). *Inside/outside: Teacher research and knowledge.* Teachers College Press.

Cole, A. L. (1997). Impediments to reflective practice: Toward a new agenda for research on teaching. *Teachers and Teaching: Theory and Practice, 3*(1), 7–27.

Council of Chief State School Officers. (2011). *InTASC Model Core teaching standards and learning progressions for teachers 1.0*. Interstate Teacher Assessment and Support Consortium (InTASC).

Dahlberg, G., Moss, P., & Pence, A. R. (2013). *Beyond quality in early childhood education and care: Languages of evaluation* (3rd ed.). Routledge, Taylor & Francis Group.

De Marzio, D. M. (2007a). Teaching as asceticism: Transforming the self through the practice. *Philosophy of Education, 2007, 349–355*.

De Marzio, D. M. (2007b). The care of the self: Alcibiades I, Socratic teaching and ethics education. *Journal of Education, 187*(3), 103–127.

Delpit, L. D. (2006). *Other people's children: Cultural conflict in the classroom*. New Press.

Dewey, J. (1944). *Democracy and education: An introduction to the philosophy of education*. Free Press. (Original work published 1916)

Dewey, J. (1975). *Moral principles in education*. Southern Illinois University Press.

Dewey, J. (1997). *How we think*. Dover Publications. (Original work published 1910)

Dewey, J. (2007). *Human nature and conduct: An introduction to social psychology*. Cosimo.

Dewey, J., Sharpe, A., Sleeper, R. W., & Boydston, J. A. (1991). *The later works, 1925–1953. Vol. 14: 1939–1941: [essays, reviews, and miscellany]*. Southern Illinois University Press. (Original work published 1939)

Drago-Severson, E. (2004). *Helping teachers learn: Principal leadership for adult growth and development*. Corwin Press.

Edwards, C. P., Gandini, L., & Forman, G. E. (Eds.). (1993). *The hundred languages of children: The Reggio Emilia approach to early childhood education*. Ablex Publishing.

Elbaz, F. (1983). *Teacher thinking: A study of practical knowledge*. Croom Helm Curriculum Policy and Research Series. Nichols Publishing Company.

Fenton, E. (1967). *The new social studies*. Holt, Rinehart and Winston.

Florio-Ruane, S. (1991). Conversation and narrative in collaborative research: An ethnography of the written literacy forum. In C. Witherell & N. Noddings (Eds.), *Stories lives tell: Narrative and dialogue in education* (pp. 234–256). Teachers College Press.

Florio-Ruane, S. (2001). *Teacher education and cultural imagination: Autobiography, conversation, and narrative*. Lawrence Erlbaum Associates.

Foucault, M. (1997). *The essential works of Michel Foucault, 1954–1984* (P. Rabinow & J. D. Faubion, Trans.). New Press.

Foucault, M. (2001). *Fearless speech* (J. Pearson, Trans.). Semiotext(e).

Foucault, M. (2012). *The courage of truth (The government of self and others II): Lectures at the Collège de France, 1983–1984*. Picador.

Freire, P., & Macedo, D. P. (1996). *Letters to Cristina: Reflections on my life and work*. Routledge.

Fullan, M., & Hargreaves, A. (1996). *What's worth fighting for in your school?* Teachers College Press.

Furman, C. (2014). Reflective teacher narratives: The merging of practical wisdom, narrative, and teaching (Doctoral dissertation). Teachers College, Columbia University.

Furman, C. (2016a). Growing in community: Collaboration between teachers and academics in education. *Teacher Education and Practice, 29*(3), 512–530.

Furman, C. (2016b). Learning to teach: Developing practical wisdom with reflective teacher narratives. *Philosophy of Education, 2015*, 139–148.

Furman, C. (2017). Ways of knowing: Implications of writing curriculum in an early childhood classroom. *Curriculum Inquiry, 47*(3), 246–262.

Furman, C. (2018). Descriptive inquiry: Cultivating practical wisdom with teachers. *Teachers and Teaching: Theory and Practice, 24*(5), 559–570.

Furman, C. (2019a). Responding to the writer in student writing. *Schools: Studies in Education, 16*(2), 175–195.

Furman, C. (2019b). Hospitality: Welcoming the unknown student. *International Journal of Inclusive Education*, 1–15. https://doi.org/10.1080/13603116.201 9.1707298

Furman, C. E., & Larsen, S. M. (2019). Interruptions: Reflecting-in-action in pre-service math methods courses. *The New Educator, 15*(2), 101–115.

Furman, C. E., & Larsen, S. M. (2020). Interruptions: Thinking-in-action in teacher education. *Teachers College Record, 122*(4), 1–26.

Gallas, K. (1998). *"Sometimes I can be anything": Power, gender, and identity in a primary classroom.* Teachers College Press.

Gasoi, E., Hare, A., Malloney, N., & Stevens-Morin, H. (2016). Professional development of, by, and for the practitioners of the Washington teachers inquiry group. *Schools: Studies in Education, 12*(2), 273–293.

Geertz, C. (1973). *The interpretation of cultures: Selected essays.* Basic Books.

Green, E. (2015). *Building a better teacher: How teaching works (and how to teach it to everyone).* Norton.

Hadot, P. (1995). *Philosophy as a way of life: Spiritual exercises from Socrates to Foucault* (A. I. Davidson, Trans.). Blackwell.

Halverson, R. (2004). Accessing, documenting, and communicating practical wisdom: The phronesis of school leadership practice. *American Journal of Education, 111*(1), 90–121.

Hansen, D. T. (1995). *The call to teach.* Teachers College Press.

Hansen, D. T. (2001). *Exploring the moral heart of teaching: Toward a teacher's creed.* Teachers College Press.

Hansen, D. T. (2011). *The teacher and the world: A study of cosmopolitanism as education* (1st ed.). Routledge.

Himley, M., & Carini, P. F. (Eds.). (2000). *From another angle: Children's strengths and school standards: The Prospect Center's descriptive review of the child.* Teachers College Press.

Himley, M., Strieb, L. Y., Carini, P. F., Kanevsky, R., & Wice, B. (Eds.). (2002). *Prospect's descriptive processes: The child, the art of teaching and the classroom and school* (Rev. ed). The Prospect Center.

Jackson, P. W., Boostrom, R. E., & Hansen, D. T. (1993). *The moral life of schools* (1st ed). Jossey-Bass.

Kelley, R. D. G. (2002). Beyond the "real world" or why Black radicals need to wake up and start dreaming. *Souls, 4*(2), 51–64.

Knoester, M. (2008). Learning to describe: Describing to understand. *Schools: Studies in Education, 5*(1/2), 146–155.

Korthagen, F. A. J. (2001). *Linking practice and theory: The pedagogy of realistic teacher education.* L. Erlbaum Associates.

Kroll, L. R., & Meier, D. R. (Eds.). (2018). *Documentation and inquiry in the early childhood classroom: Research stories from urban centers and schools.* Routledge.

Lawrence-Lightfoot, S. L. (1983). *The good high school: Portraits of character and culture.* Basic Books.

Leafgren, S. (2009). *Reuben's fall: A rhizomatic analysis of disobedience in kindergarten* (International Institute for Qualitative Methodology Series). Left Coast Press.

Lemov, D. (2010). *Teach like a champion: 49 techniques that put students on the path to college.* Jossey-Bass.

Levinson, M. (2015). Moral injury and the ethics of educational injustice. *Harvard Educational Review, 85*(2), 203–228.

Levinson, M., & Fay, J. (Eds.). (2016). *Dilemmas of educational ethics: Cases and commentaries.* Harvard Education Press.

Little, T., & Ellison, K. (2015). *Loving learning: How progressive education can save America's schools.* Norton.

Love, B. L. (2019). *We want to do more than survive: Abolitionist teaching and the pursuit of educational freedom.* Beacon Press.

Lyons, N. (1990). Dilemmas of knowing: Ethical and epistemological dimensions of teachers' work and development. *Harvard Educational Review, 60*(2), 159–180.

McCormick, W. (2013, Summer). *Disarming the nuclear family.* Rethinking Schools. https://rethinkingschools.org/articles/disarming-the-nuclear-family/

McDonald, J. P. (Ed.). (2003). *The power of protocols: An educator's guide to better practice.* Teachers College Press.

Meier, D. (2002). *In schools we trust: Creating communities of learning in an era of testing and standardization.* Beacon Press.

Meier, D. (Ed.). (2015). *Teaching in themes: An approach to schoolwide learning, creating community, and differentiating instruction.* Teachers College Press.

Meier, D., & Henderson, B. (2007). *Learning from young children in the classroom: The art and science of teacher research.* Teachers College Press.

Noddings, N. (2003). *Caring: A feminine approach to ethics and moral education* (2nd ed.). University of California Press.

Nussbaum, M. C. (1992). *Love's knowledge: Essays on philosophy and literature.* Oxford University Press.

Oyler, C. (1996). *Making room for students: Sharing teacher authority in room 104.* Teachers College Press.

Phelan, A. M. (2005). A fall from (someone else's) certainty: Recovering practical wisdom in teacher education. *Canadian Journal of Education, 28*(3), 339–358.

Polakow, V. (1994). *Lives on the edge: Single mothers and their children in the other America.* University of Chicago Press.

Ravitch, D. (2016). *The death and life of the great American school system: How testing and choice are undermining education* (Rev. and expanded ed.). Basic Books.

Ray, K. W., & Cleveland, L. B. (2004). *About the authors: Writing workshop with our youngest writers.* Heinemann.

Ray, K. W., & Glover, M. (2008). *Already ready: Nurturing writers in preschool and kindergarten.* Heinemann.

Rilke, R. M. (1987). *Letters to a young poet* (F. X. Kappus & S. Mitchell, Trans.). Vintage Books.

Rodgers, C. R. (2011a). A case of learning to teach social studies at the Prospect School Teacher Education Program. *The New Educator, 7*(3), 215–238.

Rodgers, C. R. (2011b). From the guest editor—Learning to see: The Prospect School's Teacher Education Program's beginnings. *The New Educator, 7*(3), 200–214.

Ruitenberg, C. (2016). *Unlocking the world: Education in an ethic of hospitality.* Routledge, Taylor & Francis Group.

Rukeyser, M. (1996). *The life of poetry.* Paris Press.

Santoro, D. A. (2018). *Demoralized: Why teachers leave the profession they love and how they can stay.* Harvard Education Press.

Schwartz, B., & Sharpe, K. (2010). *Practical wisdom: The right way to do the right thing.* Riverhead Books.

Scott, J. C. (2008). *Seeing like a state: How certain schemes to improve the human condition have failed.* Yale University Press.

Shagoury, R., & Power, B. M. (2003). *The art of classroom inquiry: A handbook for teacher-researchers* (Rev. ed). Heinemann.

Shalaby, C. (2017). *Troublemakers: Lessons in freedom from young children at school.* New Press.

Sherman, S. C. (2013). *Teacher preparation as an inspirational practice: Building capacities for responsiveness.* Routledge.

Smith, R. (1999). Paths of judgment: The revival of practical wisdom. *Educational Philosophy and Theory, 31*(3), 327–340.

Smith, T. J. (2007). *Teaching the children we fear: Stories from the front.* Hampton Press.

Tatum, B. D. (2017). *"Why are all the black kids sitting together in the cafeteria?": And other conversations about race* (3rd trade paperback ed.). Basic Books.

TERC (Firm). (2008). Pearson Education, Inc.: Scott Foresman.

Traugh, C. (2005). Trusting the possibilities: Giving voice to Vito's ideas. *Teaching & Learning: The Journal of Natural Inquiry and Reflective Practice, 20*(1), 55–72.

Traugh, C. (2009). *A way of thinking about teaching and becoming a teacher.* Unpublished manuscript.

Traugh, C., Seletsky, A., Kanevsky, R., Woolf, K., Martin, A., & Strieb, L. (1986). *Speaking out: Teachers on teaching.* North Dakota Study Group on Evaluation.

Van Manen, M. (1991). *The tact of teaching: The meaning of pedagogical thoughtfulness.* Althouse Press.

Wiman, C. (2018, January 15). Obituary written by Christian Wiman on The Poet of Light, Richard Wilber. https://wissai.wordpress.com/2018/01/15/obituary-the -poet-of-light

Wood, C., & Wrenn, P. (1999). *Time to teach, time to learn: Changing the pace of school.* Northeast Foundation for Children.

Index

About the Authors

Cara E. Furman, Ph.D., is an assistant professor of literacy education at the University of Maine at Farmington. Prior to this, she was an urban public elementary school teacher. Published in journals such as *Curriculum Inquiry, Education and Culture, Educational Theory, International Journal of Inclusive Education, Studies in Philosophy and Education,* and *Teachers College Record,* her research focuses on teacher development as it intersects with Descriptive Inquiry, inquiry, culturally sustaining inclusive teaching, and progressive literacy practices. Having studied both philosophy and education, she integrates qualitative research on classroom practice, teacher research, and philosophy. She is the co-director of the Summer Institute on Descriptive Inquiry and co-leads inquiry groups for local teachers. She can be reached at cara.furman@maine.edu.

Cecelia E. Traugh is dean of the Graduate School of Education at Bank Street College. Prior to coming to Bank Street, September 2015, Dr. Traugh was dean of the School of Education at Long Island University, Brooklyn, and the director of its Center for Urban Educators (CUE). Throughout her career, she has combined her roles as a teacher, administrator, and researcher in pursuit of the kind of education that grows out of a valuing of the capacities of children, parents, and teachers. She has worked collaboratively with parents, teachers, and administrators to make classrooms and schools more supportive of children's and teachers' growth, thinking, and learning. Some of Traugh's areas of concentration are descriptive school-based inquiry; curriculum development and evaluation, including qualitative evaluation; and the preparation of teachers for urban schools. Her current work in schools includes schoolwide inquiry groups in small schools across Manhattan and Brooklyn. These inquiry groups use the Descriptive Processes developed at the Prospect Center in North Bennington, Vermont to investigate issues important to the inclusive education of all children and to the ongoing development of the schools themselves. She can be contacted at ctraugh@bankstreet.edu.

Jane Andrias has been an educator for over 50 years. She was a New York City public school classroom teacher and art teacher and was the third School Director/Principal of Central Park East 1 in East Harlem. Since her retirement in 2003, she was an adjunct professor of Descriptive Inquiry and Teacher Research at Long Island University Graduate School (LIU), co-creator of the LIU Elementary Teacher Center, and a workshop leader and classroom advisor for NYC public school teachers through the elementary Teacher Network in the Center of Literacy Studies at Lehman College. She has continued to be an independent educational consultant for principals, teachers, and parents in several progressive elementary and secondary schools. She has been a board member and student of PerDev Perceptual Development Resources and the Institute on Descriptive Inquiry. Both of these institutions have informed and shaped her as an educator, artist, parent, and citizen.

Laurie Engle is a retired public school teacher. Born and raised in NYC, she received her master's degree in early childhood education from City College. She was a founding member of two progressive public schools in the East Village, where she taught pre-K and K for 27 years. Since retirement she has worked as a staff developer with early childhood teachers in public and independent schools. She has also worked with groups providing legal aid for undocumented immigrants in Brooklyn where she lives with her family.

Abbe Futterman is on the faculty in the Leadership Department at Bank Street College of Education. She is co-founder and former principal of the Earth School (PS364M), a public elementary school in New York City. Abbe has worked extensively with Descriptive Inquiry Processes and protocols for school development through collaborative inquiry, and frequently leads study groups for parents, principals, and teachers. Abbe lives in Brooklyn with her two daughters.

Alison Hazut is a school leader with over 25 years of educational experience. She has worked in NYC schools as a teacher and leader for most of her career. Many of those years were spent at the Earth School, a progressive public school where diversity and inclusivity were at the heart of its mission. She is a seasoned staff developer and specialist in curriculum development, assessment, and progressive pedagogy. Alison currently leads a small public school on Long Island.

Rachel Seher serves as the principal of City-as-School, a public experiential learning school located in the West Village and serving youth ages 17–21 from across New York City. Rachel has worked in progressive public education for over 15 years, and this is her 9th year at City-as-School. She is active in the Consortium for Performance-Based Assessment and a member of the board of the Progressive Education Network of New York. She spends much of her time at City-as-School and also enjoys family time, reading fiction, cooking, and riding her bicycle in Prospect Park in Brooklyn.